QUILTING
TOGETHER

To: Lottie
From: family & friends
Date: June 28, 1983
Please be advised
that we whose lives
you have touched
love you.

ERIC

AMY

PAULA

JOCELYN

RUTH

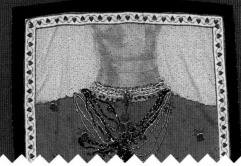

QUILTING TOGETHER

How to Organize, Design, and Make
Group Quilts

Paula Nadelstern · LynNell Hancock

CROWN PUBLISHERS, INC.　　　NEW YORK

Designed by Nancy Kenmore
Copyright © 1988 by Paula Nadelstern and LynNell Hancock

◆

Published by Crown Publishers, Inc., 225 Park Avenue South, New York,
New York, 10003 and represented in Canada by the Canadian MANDA Group.

CROWN is a trademark of Crown Publishers, Inc.

Manufactured in Japan
◆
Library of Congress Cataloging-in-Publication Data
Nadelstern, Paula.
Quilting together.

Bibliography: p.
Includes index.
1. Quilting. 2. Group work in art. I. Hancock, LynNell. II. Title.
TT835.N33   1988   746.9'7   88-7081
ISBN 0-517-56894-2

10   9   8   7   6   5   4   3   2   1
First Edition

*T*o
our mothers,
Clara Lyman
and
Marna
Hancock

C·O·N·T·E·N·T·S

"*If I am
not for myself,
who will be for me?
If I am
only for myself,
what am I?*"

Rabbi Hillel

*E*very year, parents in my local Bronx cooperative nursery school are expected to raise thousands of dollars by bake sales or by bazaars. When it was my turn to be a nursery parent, I suggested a route never traveled before: the raffle quilt. Blank stares greeted me when I tacked up the first sign-up sheet. These were hard-core New York urban apartment dwellers I was dealing with—the only needle most of them knew about was the obelisk in Central Park. Hesitant parents trickled into the first meeting. Techniques were explained, themes, fabrics, designs, and schedules were decided, and, most remarkably, inhibitions were gradually relaxed.

Ideas for the individual quilt blocks were batted about at the second meeting, which was held in an apartment filled with the hubbub of infants and toddlers. Parents looted through button collections for snowman eyes, through fabric scraps for Mother Goose's shawl, through ribbons and lace for gingerbread house trim. With the kitchen table lost under pinking shears, embroidery thread, marking pencils, coffee, and baby bottles, there was no turning back.

Six weeks later, on a nasty winter morning, the newborn quilt enthusiasts held their collective breath and laid out the twenty-four appliquéd squares that everyone had diligently created in stolen time. Each block was pretty remarkable, but would they all work together? Carefully, the giant puzzle pieces were moved around until everyone was satisfied. Then, with two sewing machines racing, three irons sputtering, and a pocket calculator calculating, the patchwork borders

were pieced together, the quilt top connected. After the top was batted and backed, the entire quilt was attached to a portable quilting frame custom-made by a nursery school father.

The next few weeks were consumed by quilting bees—sessions filled with coffee, conversation, and the tedious but satisfying business of making tiny consistent stitches to accent the design and to hold the three layers in place. When the parents finally looked up from the project, spring had come, their children were five months older, and they had somehow molded themselves into a cohesive collection of quilters that had created a rather remarkable piece of art.

The first *Scenes of Childhood* quilt (page 89) amazed everyone, especially its creators. Not only did all the pieces fit, but the quilt was visually stunning; *and* it raised more than a thousand dollars for the school. It now hangs muse-like on the nursery wall, inspiring future fund-raising projects. Four more quilts have been spawned since this first adventure, two of them without my direction. It's an official nursery tradition now, with a life all its own.

I've gone on to coordinate a dozen projects with a variety of other groups, while trying to build my own reputation as a professional quiltmaker. One group quilt represents the work of a first grade class to raise money for the children of Ethiopia. Another is a wedding friendship quilt for a childhood friend. My most recent project, stitched by employees of my publisher, produced a cloth-bound library gift for their chairman of the board. Each quilt is as varied and unique as the personalities who worked on it. Each is pictured in these pages. And each one balances the ingredients essential for an inspired quilt—control and spontaneity.

Shared labor went out with the mechanical age, but it still has its place in homes and church basements where people gather to sew. And it's still a viable tradition in our Bronx neighborhood. LynNell and I are neighbors in the Amalgamated Housing Cooperative —the oldest co-op in the nation. These dozen apartment buildings are peopled by self-called "cooperators," instead of tenants. Everything from the credit union to the concert hall to the baby play group is run by collections of people.

I asked LynNell to help me with this book project when I saw her writing in the Amalgamated Nursery School Newsletter. We're actually a rather peculiar pair to the world of the quilt. She is a millionth-generation American with vague ties to Daniel Boone, dropped into the New York neighborhood from the alien planet of Iowa. Her apartment walls are filled with the quilts made by her midwestern great-grandmothers. I am a first-generation American, with no tradition of quiltmaking within my family. LynNell claims she can't sew to save her life. I love to sew. In fact, although I started out with a career in occupational therapy, I now consider myself a full-time quilt artist.

This book evolved from my experience with various collections of would-be quilters, and took shape as the slides of women's communal projects trickled into our mailboxes from all parts of this continent (plus one from England). The multitude of projects and the varieties of designs encouraged us to feature not only pictorial appliqués, but also samplers, repeat patterns, and pieced medallions. It became obvious that we were going to have to abandon the classic term *friendship quilt* in our book title when tremendous peace projects and national contest quilts came into our scope. These days, complete strangers are either congregating at the quilt frame, or mailing in their blocks from overseas!

Quilts have an undeniable appeal. Artists are attracted to their infinite design and color possibilities. Traditionalists enjoy their links to ingenuity, hard work, and the American way. Feminists point to quiltmaking's roots in women's lives—its recent revival is a testament to women's ability to look into their past and revive what is theirs. Historians like to uncover political and economic trends between the stitches. And just plain folks can't resist snuggling up in the warmth of a bed cover made by people they love.

Like autograph books, quilts, by their very nature, tell stories about the people who worked on them, about the people who received them. And the stories are always uplifting. They pinpoint the threads that tie humans together, not the seam rippers that divide them. No matter how primitive, or how dazzling, a quilt made by a group is always a treasured reminder of the good things people share.

HOW TO USE THIS BOOK
◆　◆　◆

This book is for anyone who has ever made, or wanted to make, a quilt with a group of people. It points to myriad design possibilities and to excuses for making them: gifts for weddings, retirements, anniversaries, Silver Jubilees, for a town's birthday, for a best friend's going-away, for fund-raising, for fun. It's written with the group coordinators in mind, and it's geared toward the beginner. But any participant, from baster to blockmaker to blue-ribbon quilt artist, will benefit from it.

Browse through the color photographs in Part 1 for inspiration, for color schemes, for manageable design ideas, or just for amusement. If nothing else, these pages display a fascinating collection of group quilt folk art. The history section gives you a feel for the tradition you are about to join. Every kind of project is here, from the primitive to the divinely inspired, from the friendship gift to the project for global peace. Meet these quilts. Read their stories. The tales they tell are often as appealing as the stitches that bind them.

The how-to text focuses on group pictorial appliqué quilts. But the instructions can easily be transferred to almost any kind of design you choose: simple house blocks, ornate medallions, samplers, repeat design quilts. Part 2, "Designing the Quilt," takes you step by step through a quilt's evolution: from conceiving the idea to organizing the group, to designing blocks and layout, choosing fabric, colors, and borders. Part 3, "Sewing the Quilt," gives complete instructions on every facet of quiltmaking—appliquéing, embroidering, assembling the quilt top, batting, backing, and quilting the sandwich. We tried to be thorough so that you will never get stuck in the middle— say, come binding time—and have to call up Great Aunt Marna to get you out of a tight spot. Part 4, "Working with the Group," gives organizing ideas for guilds, fund-raisers, This Is Your Life quilts, pen-pal quilts, and children's projects.

Whether the ages of your participants are three or ninety-three, whether the goal is for a fund-raising project or a private collection, whether you choose a block design or a blockbuster design, *Quilting Together* will provide decisions and suggest techniques.

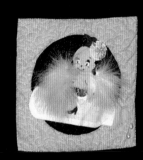

1

AN ALBUM OF GROUP QUILTS

Background
·
THE CROWN QUILT
·

A Short History of Group Quilts

*Q*uilts are warm and cozy documents of human history—dignified, precious, as useful as the beds they cover and the walls they adorn. The story of the quilt is woven warp and weft into the story of America. The tales these fabric heirlooms tell are not about hair-raising battles or about political squabbles in Independence Hall. They provide intimate sketches about the women who felt duty bound to make them. They paint their hardships and humor, their families and friends. Quilts also exhibit some bottom-line pioneer instincts: the ability to enlist neighbors in the process of recycling old clothes into bedclothes, and an aesthetic need to create patches of beauty out of a sea of scraps.

Before the days of mass-produced comforters by Montgomery Ward, folks had to sleep under something, and that something was without exception a quilt by Mom. Quiltmaking to our preindustrial foremothers was as necessary as dodging Indian arrows. It was also the only accepted canvas of self-expression available to women who could barely write. Quilts announced women's political views, their whims, friendships, and objects of admiration in useful, beautiful bed covers. Beth Gutcheon in *The Perfect Patchwork Primer* calls them "the blues of the American woman." Just as "the blues" makes harmony out of hopeless despair, quilts make artful statements about the early settler's ache for colorful coherence.

There are virtually no examples of the very first quilts. Most were nearly worn out before they were sewn together. The first

settlers, woefully unprepared for the New England winter wind chill factor, ripped up fabric already thin with use to make the first American covers—then stuffed them with paper, leaves, dried corn husks, or whatever was handy. Women waited until their linsey-woolsey (linen warp, wool weft) petticoats were frayed to a frazzle before shredding them into pieces for covers. New fabric was a luxury that was hard to come by—Great Britain made sure of that. Sensing a real threat to its booming textile industry, the king of England wonked the colonists with outrageous laws, surcharges, and fines, designed to keep them buying British.

With all these economic spit wads flying in the background, womenfolk were still expected to keep their families warm at night. The "make-do" principle of American living was set in motion. They made do with what they had, and what they had was generally a pile of worn-out scraps. Hence, the single patch was born: an American innovation designed to save space (no quilting frame was needed) and to save materials. The first blocks were crazy-style, pieced and quilted in the lap, then sewn together at the end. When these domestic wizards could afford to give up some seam allowance, they began cutting shapes out of the scraps—rectangles at first—and pieced them together like bricks in a block. "Bricks" was the name they gave to the pattern. No nonsense. The blend of fabrics in a controlled pattern lent a touch of sanity to their otherwise rough-and-tumble daily existence.

After Britain was bayoneted out of the picture, economic hardships eased. Fabric and leisure time became more plentiful, and women began to take their quilting skills into the masterpiece arena. From the late eighteenth to the late nineteenth century, elaborate quilts for special occasions were designed—for weddings, for a man's coming of age, for the new neighbors, for a friend moving west, for a community figure who needed honoring, for a fund-raiser. More often than not, a group of women was recruited to work on these projects of love, and the first American communal quilts were born.

It was the same impulse that inspired neighbors to pitch in and rebuild barns after the inevitable fires, to exchange baling techniques and apple-paring skills. Quilts are big projects. One woman hunched over a giant quilt frame counting ten stitches to the inch is a very lonely woman. Our pre-TV predecessors found it a lot more efficient and a lot more fun to quilt and chat, simultaneously.

Quilting parties (or "bees," as they're often called, in honor of the efficient insect community) were an important social event. They provided a grand excuse to be creative, to show off skills, to make friends, and exchange news and political ideas. Carrie Hall tells us in *The Romance of the Patchwork Quilt in America* that famous feminist Susan B. Anthony delivered her first talk on equal rights for women at a quilting bee.

Women would piece tops of their own design during the winter months, saving the tedious quilting stitches for a gathering of friends when the weather cleared up. Neighbors didn't dare miss a bee for fear of getting their good names stung unmercifully. There was plenty of incentive around to improve one's needle skills. Only good quilters were rewarded with coveted invitations. Beginners were usually given KP duty, missing out on all the good gossip.

Bed covers were big dowry items for our ancestors. A girl was required to bring a baker's dozen of them (both functional and beautiful) to her first home.

> At your quilting, maids don't dally
> Quilt quick if you would marry
> A maid who is quiltless at 21
> Never shall greet her bridal sun!

This was no sentimental ditty. Quilts were needed to use in place of doors and windows, as extra insulation, as mats for infants, as bandages, as fund-raisers for the local churches. A girl who couldn't quilt was as useless as a boy who couldn't split logs.

Twelve quilt tops were carefully planned when a girl was born, each design becoming more complex as her yet unseen needlework skills developed. The thirteenth *pièce de résistance* was designed by the girl herself, hopefully inspired by the man of her dreams. Because the biggest expense to the quiltmaker was the back and the batting, the thirteen tops weren't quilted until a flesh-and-blood male had officially proposed.

The most exquisite *Bride's Quilt* top was reserved for the grand engagement quilting party (yesterday's wedding shower), a major social occasion. Marriage was, after all, a girl's only option in life. A frame was set up in the warmest room, meals were served, children were paid a penny a day to keep the needles threaded, and men joined the gathering after supper for what Ruth Finley, in *Old Patchwork Quilts and the Women Who Made Them,* calls the "grand frolic."

Stephen Foster (of "Swanee River" fame) told of such courting goings-on in the 1856 song, "The Quilting Party":

> In the sky the bright stars glittered,
> On the banks the pale moon shone,
> And 'twas from Aunt Dinah's quilting party
> —I was seeing Nellie home.

Heart quilting patterns were reserved for wedding tops, and only die-hard enemies stitched broken vine patterns (omens of short, disastrous lives). After the quilt was finished, the stitchers would place a cat in the middle and fling it like Mickey Mouse on a trampoline. Folklore dictated that whomever the cat landed nearest would be the next to marry—the bridal bouquet theory reenacted on the bed cover. See Smithsonian *Bride's Quilt,* page 7.

Freedom Quilts for a man were just as momentous items as bridal quilts for a woman. They were given, along with a "freedom suit," on a boy's twenty-first birthday—an important event because it meant the end of his apprenticeship to his work and his family. The custom went out of fashion around 1825. (It's noteworthy that the term *freedom* never applies to the female counterpart quilts.) Unlike with bride's quilts, the boy was not usually involved in the group creative process. Appliqué blocks made by admirers were brought to a family-sponsored party, then pieced and quilted for his hope chest. See Smithsonian *Groom's Quilt,* page 8.

Lenice Ingram Bacon tells of an amusing example in her book *American Patchwork Quilts.* The recipient, Henry Thompson Leighton, must have been *the* hot ticket in Blackstrap, Maine (unless he happened to be the only man). His coming-of-age quilt, made in the mid-1800s, consists of forty pink and lacy appliquéd squares all made by former girlfriends. His mother diplomatically embroidered the word "Friendship" in the center panel, and the quilt was used on his wedding bed. One can only imagine what his wife thought of sleeping under a giant pink valentine to her husband from forty female admirers. Maybe she swallowed her pride and counted herself one lucky gal just to nab him. Or maybe she had a blue quilt just like it, somewhere in the closet.

Album quilts became all the rage in the mid-1800s. Each quilter would bring her premade square to a piecing and quilting party. Like books, albums are composed of something like pages—a series of appliqué blocks, each different from the next, and each signed and sometimes inscribed with original poetry by the maker. Baltimore women went wild with the concept, and created, in a two-decade span between 1820 and 1840, America's classics—elaborate designs depicting symbols of honor, densely appliquéd in reds and greens. Baltimore Albums are lush, stately, highly accomplished group quilts, each block more talent-ridden than the next. The final products were generally presented to persons of honor in the community—brides, ministers, political figures. See *Album Quilt,* page 9.

Wreaths, flowers, baskets, fruit, and laurel leaves—all symbols of affection and enduring strength—appear in profusion on the albums. The techniques used to achieve realistic results are mostly appliqué, piecing, trapunto, and embroidery.

Often pious, always sentimental, album stitchers couldn't help sewing sound advice in the ditches. Cousin Walker Washington from Virginia was given an album quilt as a going-to-college gift in the mid-1800s. One square warned against using his learning for greedy purposes:

> Ask Heaven for Virtue, Health,
> But never let your prayer be Wealth.

The album fad, with its competitive edge ("My fruit basket is really going to floor Bernice!"), petered out by the end of the nineteenth century. Its twin sister, the *Friendship Quilt,* took over. The distinction between friendships and albums is a little more blurry today, but a friendship quilt was originally a more homey version of the album. Often using scraps of a friend's clothing, blocks of a uniform design were executed by one or several persons, then passed around for signatures and inscriptions before piecing them together. Certain patterns, like the snowflake, became popular because their center patches begged for signatures. The chimney sweep pattern was so common in New York State that it became known as the "Friendship Block." Signatures and little poems were executed in India ink, stencils, or embroidery.

The Friendship Medley Party, an antique version of the surprise shower, and a "sprightly and genteel mode of entertainment," if Ruth Finley does say so herself, evolved from this happy tradition. Medley quilts, like samplers, consist of blocks in a variety of patterns, each signed by the maker. Partygoers would execute impromptu blocks at a friend's house, and then piece them together in raucous revelry—much to the surprise of the hostess. See *Autograph Album Quilt,* page 10.

In some areas, ludicrous errors were sewn onto albums and friendships—like an upside-down person—so God wouldn't assume the quiltmaker was competing with his own patent on perfection. Then again, God's paranoia can be a pretty good all-purpose excuse when you discover a big blooper on your finished quilt.

When a special gift was needed for special people in the community, quilts were very often the answer, then as now. Ministers were the number one recipients of group quilts. Erica Wilson in *Quilts of America* tells the story of a devoted parishioner who, in 1890, wanted to give a horseback-traveling Methodist preacher a special friendship quilt made by his many congregations. The only conceivable way to organize it in pre-reliable postal service days was to have the Pastor Williams himself carry the blocks in his saddlebags from parish to parish. The end of the line was Mrs. Wilcox and friends, who pieced them all into a special gift.

"We only had time to quilt for cover in those days settlin' in . . ." Mrs. Wilcox writes, "but in this quilt we outdid ourselves appliquéing each one of us a block. Pastor Williams said he never seen anything so pretty. It was a treasure."

Fund-raisers were another major reason to pour stitchery talents onto a quilt top. Again, church-related groups benefited the most. There were many ways to approach a fund-raiser. The group could design and make a quilt, then raffle it off. Separate groups could make blocks and pay for the privilege of incorporating them into a quilt. Or a repeating pattern quilt, such as embroidered compass-fan or small-triangle piecework, would be made; then space would be sold to people to have their signatures permanently embroidered onto the quilt. The idea was the smallest space for the most money. Often the total raised would be embossed on the final product.

The 1882 crazy patchwork beauty pictured on page 10 embodies the former idea. Different Kentucky Baptist churches and individual members paid a minimum of $18 for the privilege of piecing blocks with their special insignia in satin, velvet, embroidery, and oil painting on silk. The project raised $5,000 for a faltering children's home—an astronomical amount for those days—and it hangs in the orphanage's board room to this day. Inspired by its success ninety-three years before, the same home organized a similar fund-raising quilt in 1976. The space cost was inflated to $500 per square, raising more than $40,000 for a new child-care program. See *Fund-Raising Slumber Throw,* page 12.

Quiltmaking took a nosedive into obscurity at the turn of the century. Mass-produced coverlets made it obsolete. Delicate, decorative, highly fashionable Victorian crazies turned the former practical quilt into an unusable study in lugubrious detail. Ruth Finley, no fan of Queen Victoria, notes that the quilt "vanished in the general night, as it were, of hideousness, following a Victorian era of bad taste."

◆　　◆　　◆

Group quilts have been experiencing a tremendous revival ever since the 1976 Bicentennial. "Handwork" now implies quality, not poverty. More than seven hundred guilds have sprouted up worldwide in the last decade. Many of our nation's poorest women are benefiting the most. Quilt cooperatives for whites in Appalachia, blacks in Alabama, and Oglala Sioux Indians in South Dakota are creating communal works for profit.

Different impulses drive contemporary women to stitch ensemble, but the goals are the same as they were for our ancestors: fund-raisers, special gifts, community events, new babies, sick friends.

Not all of today's quilters are just demonstrating their affection for antique quilts by copying them. Thanks to the efforts of contemporary artists around the country, the quilt has made its official leap from bed to wall, from craft to art, allowing textiles and designs to run to the avant-garde. Beautiful repeating pieced butterfly or basket patterns are still being executed with exquisite results. But you'll also find soft-sculpture, stained glass, liquid crayons, fur, and leather on quilts where once only fabric dared to tread.

Some projects are witty, like *Ms. Sue: Alive and Liberated*—a spoof on the cute, be-bonneted, chubby little girl pattern that's very popular in gift "shoppes." Other quilts embody extremely serious global goals, like *The Joint Soviet-American Peace Quilt,* designed as a friendship exchange between Americans and Russians.

Some quilts are spectacular, like the *Newton Commemorative,* a bicentennial cameo of the Massachusetts town. Others are plain and deceptively simple, brimming with delicious detail, like the *Apple Box Labels,* a fund-raiser for the Yakima Valley Museum in Washington. Some are very closely tied to their ancestors, in design and impulses. A newly formed group of Baltimorians pays homage to the stately quilts of their ancestors by reviving the famous albums in nine miniatures.

But you can hardly imagine a group of Delaware ladies, schooled in *Godey's Lady's Book* of the virtues of housework, getting together to work on a *Spike the Rat* pillow quilt, or the literary *Crown Quilt,* which sports "101 Uses for a Dead Cat."

While no one has the nerve anymore to ask the neighbors to help build their house, communal quilts are being made all across America—in New York apartments, rural farmhouses, corporate offices, synagogues, churches, public schools. These new projects are not just sentimental forays into our past, but vibrant, contemporary works of art that express the modern need for friendship.

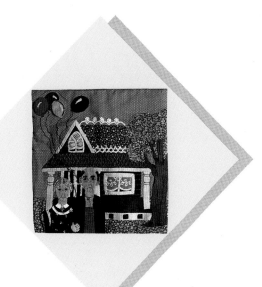

An Album of Group Quilts

BRIDE'S QUILT

◆

Caroll County, Maryland. 1851. 92 inches square.

Elizabeth Jane Baile composed this appliqué gift of love for her husband, Levi Manahan, for their wedding, October 30, 1851. Bouquets, wreaths, flowers, fruit (some outlined with button-hole stitches), and a scroll with a hand-penned poem commemorate the occasion. The entire red-and-green-on-white cotton masterpiece is bordered first in a sawtooth pattern, and then with lyrical padded strawberries. An ink inscription on the quilt says: "Commenced June 1850/Finished October 30, 1851." Just in time to make it to the altar! (Collection of the Smithsonian Institution. Photo number: 73-7657)

GROOM'S QUILT

◆

Pawling, New York. 1850. 103 inches square. Appliquéd and pieced album made by friends and relatives of Mr. Benoni Pierce as an engagement gift.

The eighty-one squares, each with a different design—some traditional patchwork, some appliqué pictures, some incredibly contemporary looking—are all signed by their makers. Among the typical birds, trees, and flowers is a square that depicts a little girl in lace pantaloons skipping rope. Another reads "Lois Marcy Green" in appliqué—presumably Benoni's bride. A green gridlike sashing defines and separates each sampler block. The entire collage is then bordered in an exquisite design of pieced triangles broken up in even intervals by appliquéd vines. (Collection of Smithsonian Institution. Photo number: 73-5119)

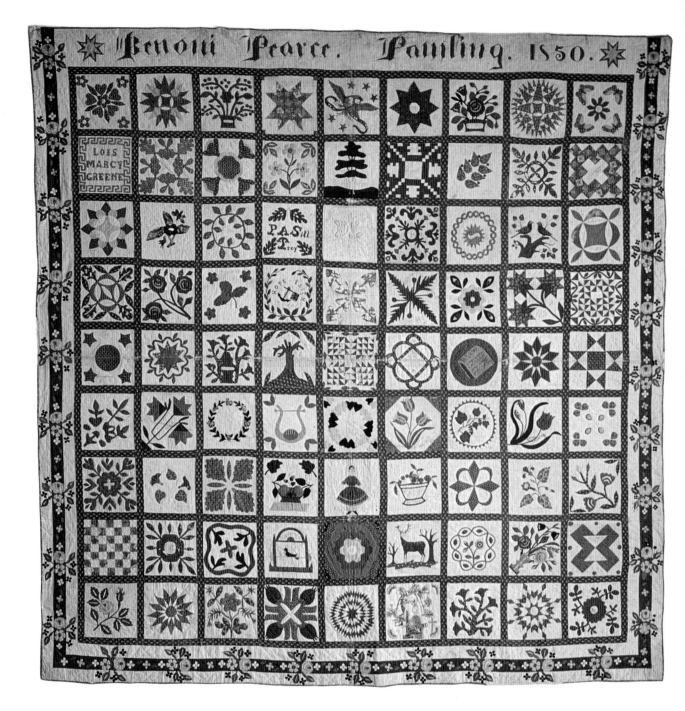

ALBUM QUILT
•

Probably Baltimore, Maryland. Mid-nineteenth century. 91 × 92 inches.

The flag, the central eagle, and the profusion of fruit and flower-filled cornucopias indicate that this highly accomplished album was probably made for a political figure. The appliqué—in predominantly reds and greens on white cotton, with some silk—is so refined it almost looks painted. A delicate, simple, and perfect red binding defines this masterpiece. (Collection of the Smithsonian Institution. Photo number: 73-4263)

AUTOGRAPH ALBUM QUILT

◆

Probably Morristown, New Jersey. 1842–1844. 85 × 75 inches. Gift to Mary H. Taylor of New Jersey, possibly a birthday present from her sister. Unquilted.

Lest you think all antique quilts are totally intimidating works of art, we present this charming cotton friendship medley, with its rather willy-nilly design. Personality, rather than perfection, rules this quilt. All but two of the sixty-eight blocks are signed by both men and women; many are stamped with patterns and poems. The large center square is inscribed with "Hester Willard to her sister, Mary. Morristown, April 12, 1842." It's fun to pick out old traditional patterns, like the album star and the chimney block, that are still being stitched today. (Collection of the Smithsonian Institution. Photo number: 78-9641)

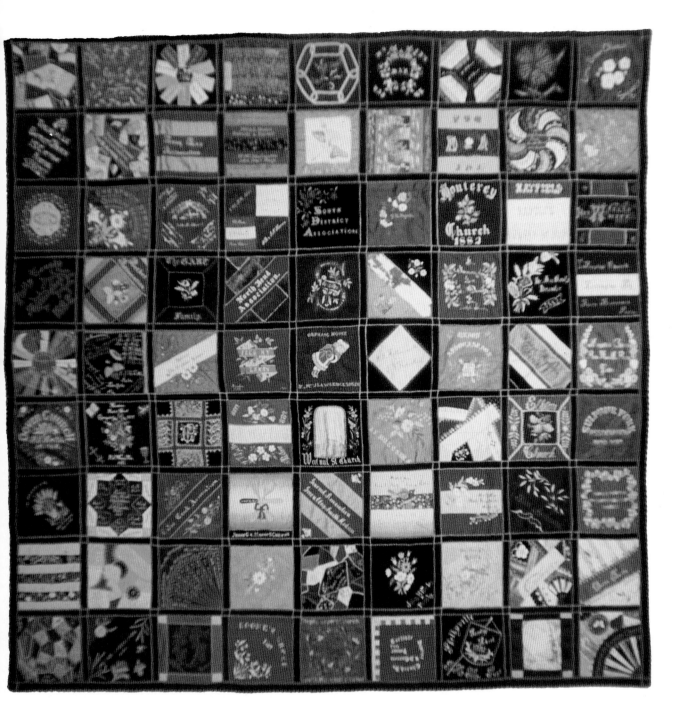

KENTUCKY BAPTIST HOME FUND-RAISING QUILT

◆

Middletown, Kentucky. 1882. 96 inches square. Made as a fund-raiser for the Kentucky Baptist Home for Children.

This 1882 crazy patchwork beauty consists of eighty-one squares, each made by an individual or a group to raise money for orphans. Different Kentucky Baptist churches and individual members paid a minimum of $18 for the privilege of piecing blocks with their special insignia in satin, velvet, embroidery, and oil painting on silk. The project raised $5,000—an astronomical amount for those days—for the Kentucky Baptist Home for Children. The quilt now hangs in the orphanage's boardroom. Inspired by its success ninety-three years before, the same home organized a similar fund-raising quilt in 1976. The space cost was inflated to $500 per square, raising more than $40,000 for a new child-care program. (Collection of the Kentucky Baptist Home for Children.)

FUND-RAISING SLUMBER THROW

◆

Findley, Ohio. 1890. 69 inches square. Made by members of the Trinity Lutheran Church to raise money for a new church. Appliquéd, pieced, painted, and embroidered on silk.

This Victorian block medley was assembled by ladies of the Trinity Lutheran Church. When the fund-raiser was over, they presented the top to Reverend Stuckenburg, in 1893. Thirty years later, his wife finally attached the batting and back, and bordered it in black satin. (Collection of the Smithsonian Institution. Photo number: 76-2678)

VARIABLE STAR SCRAP QUILT

Newington, Connecticut. 1986. 94 × 106 inches. Twelve-inch blocks pieced by 56 members of the Newington Schoolhouse Quilters. Two-inch sashing, 5-inch border. Designed by Ann Marie Wosczyna. Quilt-as-you-go. Won in a guild drawing by Marianne Amo.

A group of Connecticut quilters exhibits its mastery of the scrap pile in this antique-looking pieced project designed for the 1986 Vermont Quilt Festival's "star" theme. A core group of five put together kits of muslin for background, a floral print in many muted colors for the star's center, and four chocolate strips for sashing. Participants, ranging from true beginners to seasoned sewers, rummaged through their private stashes for shades of brown, beige, blue, gold, or rust to use both for the stars' points and for the sawtooth border. The eye tends to dart around this seemingly subdued work, first catching dark blue stars, then pink ones, then the reds—rendering a startling, twinkling effect. Can such a well-orchestrated quilt contain the stamp of individuality? Look closely at the quilting patterns in each of the block's corners. (Photograph by Ann Marie Wosczyna.)

FRIENDSHIP CACTUS BASKETS

•

Santa Monica, California. 1986. 73 inches square. 1¼-inch sashing strips, 2¼-inch nine-patch intersections, 1¾-inch border. Thirteen 12-inch squares machine-pieced and signed by members of the Scrappy Quilters of Santa Monica for member. Designed and hand-quilted by Barbara Gillette.

At each of the Scrappy Quilters' monthly meetings, one member is chosen at random to coordinate her friendship quilt, using a pattern of her own choice. When it was Barbara's turn, she distributed kits to willing fabric fanciers, which included a photocopy of her favorite pattern, ecology cloth for background, and fabric for the baskets. Word traveled through the Scrappy grapevine that the twelve-inch blocks might look unwieldy, but when the final layout was unrolled, the dissenters were pleasantly surprised. Barbara had managed to "float" the big baskets on point, dividing them with intricate three-strip lattice and nine-patch intersections. (Photograph by Robert Perin.)

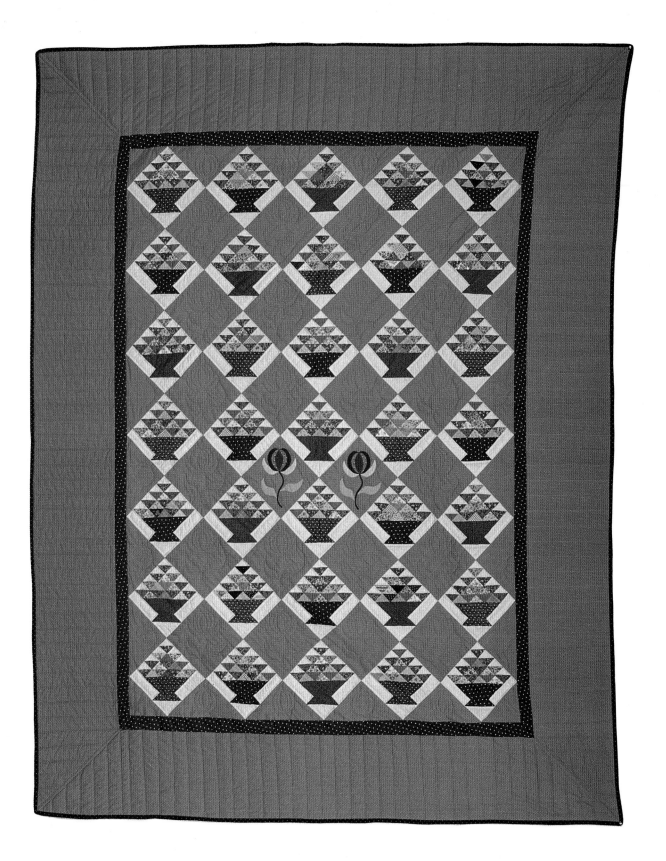

BEYOND FRIENDSHIP

◆

Newton, Massachusetts. 1985. 86 × 108 inches. Thirty-five pieced and twenty-four solid 8-inch blocks, machine-pieced and appliquéd by Eight Hands Around quilting group for member Rowena Fisher. Two-inch brown border, 12-inch outside border. Assembled by Louise Horgan. Hand-quilted by Rowena Fisher.

With their spectacular Newton Commemorative Quilt *(page 58)* safely behind glass, a small band of eight fabric fanatics who worked on it agreed to continue their quilting connection. One of their first secret endeavors resulted in this classic friendship quilt for Rowena, the Newton project's chief designer and coordinator. The pattern and colors were gleaned from Rowena's remembered musings. The variety of prints in three browns, pinks, butterscotch, muted blue, and lavender on unbleached muslin gives this soft, textured quilt an antique look. The two appliquéd love apples (his and hers) in the center blocks gave Rowena the idea to quilt the same motif into the remaining solid squares. Taking cues from meticulous quilters of days gone by, Rowena stitched a pocket to the back of this gift, bearing the quilt's story, signatures of all who contributed, and extra basket patches for future repairs. Quilts of this quality are inevitable heirlooms. (Photographs by David Caras.)

BASKET OF FLOWERS

Rapid City, South Dakota. 1982. 81 × 95 inches. Thirty 13-inch blocks, appliquéd by the Black Hills Quilters Guild for member Mari Etta Fowler. Designed and hand-quilted by Mari Etta Fowler.

Spirited flowers dance inside serene blue baskets in this highly contrasting quilt designed by Mari Etta Fowler. She chose the pattern from a quilt book, and provided the Black Hills Quilters with the background, basket, and leaf fabric. Contributors appliquéd flower colors of their own choosing. Two-inch black sashing and two-and-one-half-inch borders make the enclosed colors of the blocks seem visually rich and clear in tone. (Photograph by Paul Jones.)

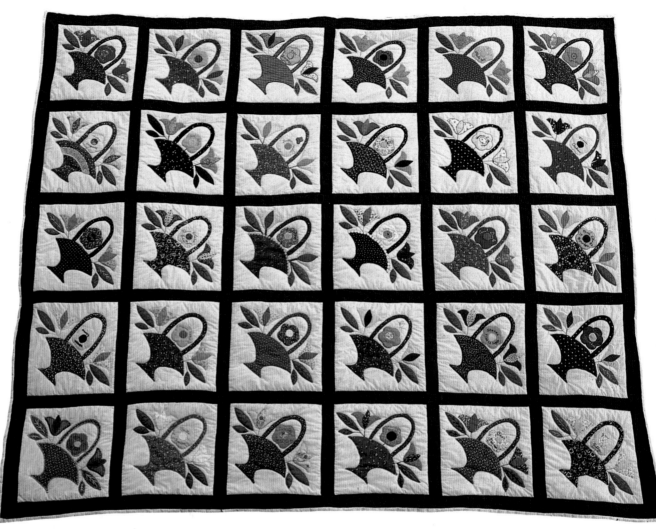

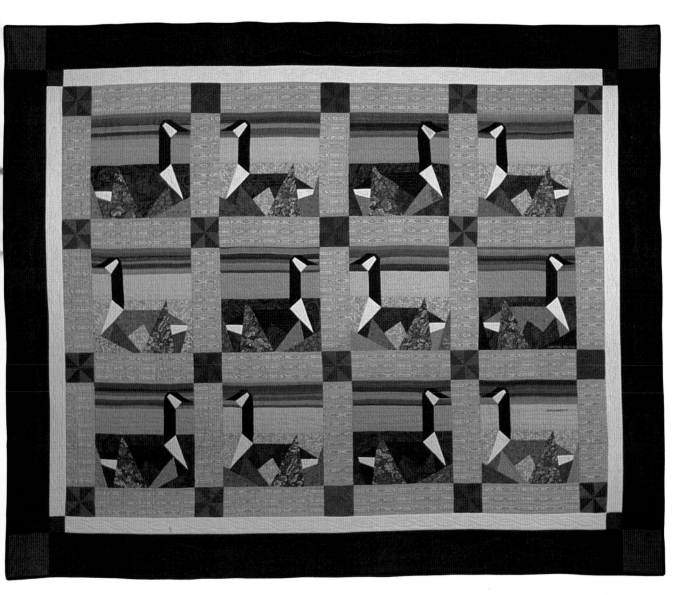

CANADA GOOSE
IN THE MEADOW
AT SUNSET

•

*Sudbury, Ontario, Canada. 1984–
1986. 64 × 78 inches. Twelve
signed 12-inch blocks hand and
machine-pieced, 1983. A pen-pal
quilt, designed and assembled by
Nyla Gorham. Hand-quilted by
Carol Prusila.*

*Inspired by an idyllic week at
the Mackinac Quilter's Vacation,
Nyla Gorham agreed to join
eleven other vacationers in a
friendship quilt exchange. Each
sent instructions for their own
quilt to participants through the
mail. Many quilters asked for
"any star pattern," or "any basket," but the fabric choices were
always pre-planned by the origi-
nator. Nyla designed a contemporary pieced block depicting a
goose resting in a meadow after
a long hard day. Her kit of fabric
included black, white, gray, an
Indian madras stripe, and two
blues, all beautifully reflecting
the serenity and muted colors of
dusk on a Canadian lake. "All
geese facing left were supposed
to be brown, and all facing right
were supposed to be a very dark
green, which I called black-green.
Four people understood that to
mean brown, black, or green. By
the time the fourth bright green
goose arrived in the mail I was
reconciled, and now am pleased
at the added interest they have
created." (Photograph by Nyla
Gorham.)*

MOTH QUILT

◆

Albany, California. 1981. 71 × 88 inches. Twenty hand-appliquéd 14-inch blocks with 3-inch sashing. Designed, machine-pieced, and hand-quilted by an adult education class taught by Roberta Horton.

Every student left Roberta Horton's ten-week intermediate adult education class with added expertise on the quilting frame, lasting memories of an enriched sharing experience, and one lucky person even walked out with the class-made quilt. For each of her group projects conducted between 1973–1981, Roberta helped decide the single motivating theme (hex signs, exotic birds, Egyptian symbols), and the colors and fabrics. Students came to the second session with line drawings from the library to be enlarged to twelve inches, and then translated into fabric and onto the fourteen-inch neutral blocks, using Roberta's no-math method (page 173). Photographs of moths were used for this fluttering quilt in order to re-create the insects' colors. Her standard fourteen-inch block provided elbowroom around the quilting frame, and gave each student adequate space to play with design. Simple, bold-colored, highly contrasting lattice is Roberta's trademark. (Photograph courtesy of Roberta Horton.)

BUTTERFLIES

•

Rapid City, South Dakota. 80 inches square. Twenty-five 14-inch blocks, appliquéd, embroidered, and signed by the Black Hills Quilters' Guild for member Sharon Flueckinger. Assembled and hand-quilted by Sharon Flueckinger.

Four appliquéd butterflies convene around the blockmaker's signature in each of these friendship squares made by Black Hills Quilters. Sharon distributed the pattern and muslin squares to guild members, instructing each to choose her own colors. "I've learned if I was to do it again, I'd coordinate my colors, by either furnishing a main color, or asking people to use spring or fall colors," Sharon says. But the effect of the "spreading" hues of these multicolored insects, grouped in clusters of darks and lights with an occasional bright red or hot pink, produces a fluttery, cheerful effect. The compatible light ending is created by the five-inch beige border. A darker border might have imprisoned the vibrating quality of these calico butterflies. (Photograph by Paul Jones.)

MONKEY WRENCH
•

*Berkeley, California. 1986. 89 ×
108 inches. Eighty 9-inch blocks,
1½-inch sashing, 1½-inch sawtooth border. Machine- and
hand-pieced by 80 employees of
the Berkeley Public Library as a
retirement gift for maintenance
worker Don Dias. Hand-quilted
by Lieu Chien of the Laotian
Handicraft Center.*

*This signature surprise gift
demonstrates how a traditional
repeat quilt can be personalized
by a clever bunch of folks. Berkeley Library workers chose the
Monkey Wrench pattern, not only
for its obvious connection to the
quilt's intended—a custodian—
but also because it's very "forgiving" to beginners. Starr La-
Tronica and Phyllis Partridge
conducted makeshift quilting
workshops for their colleagues.
"It's amazing how many librar-
ians don't like to read directions," noted Starr. Muslin
background was provided by the
core group, but the often ingenious fabric selection was left up
to the blockmaker. One print
sports a cowboy motif, because
Don grew up on a ranch; another
has kitchen utensils, because
Don jokes about hating to cook.
A green mini-paisley print sets
each tribute apart, and the whole
work is bordered by a sawtooth
pattern. The quilt was completed
the afternoon of the retirement
dinner. Don plans to take up
quilting in his retirement. (Photograph by John A. Bottomley.)*

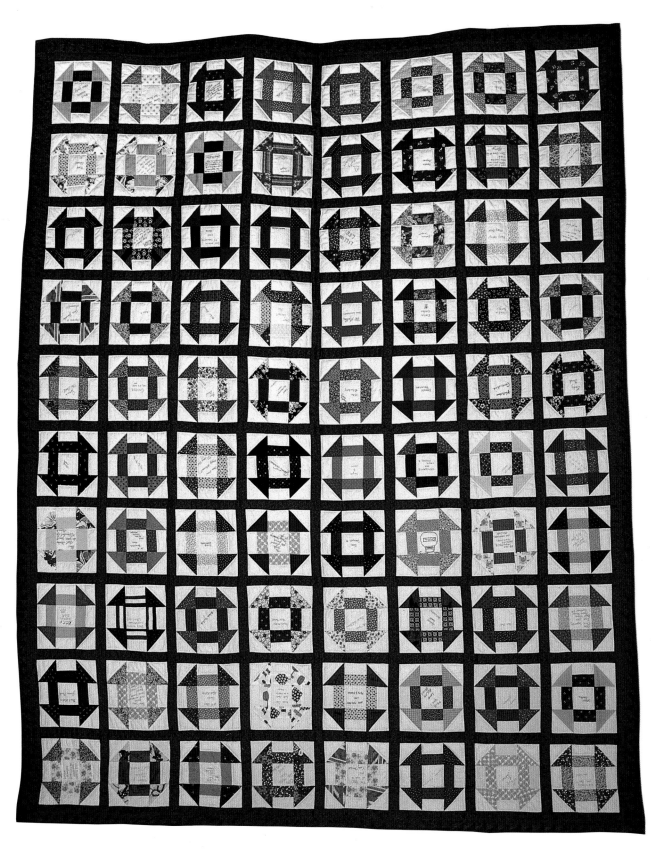

GRANDMOTHER'S FAN

•

*Berkeley, California. 1986. 60
inches square. Four 24-inch
blocks. Machine-pieced and hand-
quilted by Pat Bell, Claudia Berger, Starr LaTronica, Mitzi Yatabe, and Phyllis Partridge,
employees of the Berkeley Public
Library, as a retirement gift for
Kimie Kurahara.*

*Illustrating how West can meet
East in a very inventive and
tasteful way, employees of Berkeley Public Library transformed a
traditional American pattern—
"Grandmother's Fan"—into a
personal tribute to a Japanese
woman. Japanese prints and Ikat
fabric are the primary materials
in this bold red and black work.
Using the Sashiko quilting
method, Kimi's family crest is
quilted in scarlet in the outer triangles. Since the family crest for
women follows the female line,
the quilters used the "mon" for
Kimie's maiden name, Nomura.
She was completely surprised
when the quilt was presented at
a retirement party for both herself and custodian Don Dias.
Kimie had shared in the secret
labor of Don's quilt, but had no
idea that her coworkers were
simultaneously preparing her an
equally splendid send-off. (Photograph by John A. Bottomley.)*

LAUREL CROSS

•

*Pullman, Washington. 1986. 90 ×
108 inches. Forty-two various
blocks designed, hand-pieced,
appliquéd, and hand-quilted by
the Patchin' People as a fund-
raiser.*

*Even though the raffle money
from this meticulous medallion
went toward a good cause—
Pullman's local hospital—the
Patchin' People admit that it was
not an easy project to part with.
Design inspiration for this blue
and white abstract came from
the "Arrowroot" pattern that ap-
peared in* Quilter's Newsletter
Magazine. *A committee of five designed the quilt, using four center
blocks to create the medallion
motif, and the similarly patterned outside squares set on
point. The white-on-white prints
provided large areas for the
group's old-fashioned plume and
crosshatched quilting skills. The
border consists of three strips: a
one-inch light blue strip sand-
wiched by two 1½-inch navy
blue strips. Although the Patchin'
People enjoyed many compli-
ments for* Laurel Cross, *their favorite was from a college student
who gazed at it for a long time
and said: "I would pay a dollar
just to look at that quilt!" (Photograph by Jim and Lucy Kittrick.)*

STAR OF THE PALOUSE
·

*Pullman, Washington, 1987. 90 ×
104 inches. Designed, pieced, and
hand-quilted by the Patchin' People as a fund-raiser.*

*This red, white, and blue-print
pattern gave the Patchin' People
a second opportunity to exhibit
their meticulous piecing and
quilting skills. Like the* Laurel
Cross, *the* Star of the Palouse
*looks like the work of a single
skilled stitcher, not of a diverse
committee. The simple design—
a variation of the* Royal Star of
Pennsylvania *taken from* Quilt
World *magazine—is pieced in
colors and repeated in the white
background using quilting
stitches. This bold and elegant
fund-raiser earned $1,200 for the
local hospital guild. Many of the
Patchin' People are also members
of the guild that made* Palouse
Hills *(page 28). Moscow, Idaho,
is only eight miles over the Washington border from Pullman.*
(Photograph by Lucy Kittrick.)

THE SILVER JUBILEE QUILT

Norfolk, England. 1977. 90 × 100 inches. Traditional patchwork and "English Method" over papers. Not quilted. Designed and coordinated by The Quiltery, Talcolneston Hall.

The idea to make a commemorative gift for the Queen's Silver Jubilee comes from the nineteenth-century tradition. This royal gift incorporates three old crown patterns. "King David's Crown," the central motif, is a grand, sixteen-pointed affair in three tones of gray, surrounded by a border of squares divided diagonally into fours. Gray trumpeters herald their own appearance in two areas of the square. One organizer writes: "It was quite difficult cutting out the fabric with the trumpeters, as some faced to the right, and some to the left, and I wanted them to pair." "King's Crowns" lie diagonally across each square and join, creating a zigzag effect. The proportion of the quilt is elongated by "Queen Charlotte's Crown" at the head and foot. Thirty-two traditional "album star" blocks surround the middle section. The center of each star bears the embroidered signature of each person who helped piece the quilt, some of whom had never sewn a stitch before. Obviously, they are fast learners— they were given only a week to complete their block. (Photograph courtesy of The Quiltery.)

24

THE GILBERT HOUSE
•

Yakima, Washington. 1987. 80 × 95 inches. Hand-pieced, appliquéd, embroidered, and quilted by the Yakima Valley Museum Quilters Guild.

The theme of the Yakima Valley Museum Quilters Guild's annual fund-raising quilt is inspired by the community's historical and cultural past (see Apple Box Label Quilt, *page 80). This breathtaking creation, which raised $5,000, is a faithfully accurate reproduction of the H. M. Gilbert Homeplace, a local turn-of-the-century farmhouse on the National Historical Register. The quilt's grand plan was inaugurated and overseen by a design committee which distributed meticulous kits with detailed instructions. The only bad planning on this talented guild's part was to order too few raffle tickets—although the drawing was held in December, the tickets sold out by September. (Photograph by Bobby Hanson)*

MONADNOCK SAMPLER QUILT
•

Peterborough, New Hampshire. 1984. 80 × 100 inches. Appliquéd, pieced, and hand-quilted by the Monadnock Quilters Guild as a fund-raiser for the New England Quilter's Guild Museum Fund. Eighteen 12-inch blocks surround a 36 × 48-inch center medallion. Three-inch sashing on the medallion's top and bottom; 2 inches everywhere else.

Regional touches unique to the Monadnock region of New Hampshire provide the theme for this stunning medallion that raised $1,000. The view of Mount Monadnock in the center panel includes the state tree of New Hampshire—the white birch. Between sampler blocks in traditional patterns are ten original designs, including the state bird (the purple finch) and the state flower (the lilac). The four corner blocks are adapted from the traditional "Moon Over the Mountain" pattern—rechristened "Moon Over Monadnock." The assembled project was installed on a quilt frame at their local quilt shop, where members could drop in and stitch anytime. Besides being ingenious raffle sellers, this group with mixed experience was quick! The layout was decided in half an hour, and the whole quilt took three months to complete. (Photograph by Richard C. Johnson.)

SOUTHWESTERN MEDALLION

♦

Tucson, Arizona. 1986. 72 × 96 inches. Designed by Laurie Sivers. Twenty 12-inch blocks plus medallion, hand-appliquéd, embroidered, hand-pieced, and hand-quilted by members of the Tucson Quilters Guild for its annual show.

Just as New Hampshire quilters feel comfortable working with blues and greens for mountain landscapes, Arizona quilters lean naturally toward browns, oranges, and sand colors for desert scenes. This stark, sunny medallion is bordered by a beautiful earth-tone pieced pattern, which is repeated around the center scene. In between the ten cactus flowers (the guild's logo) in the surrounding sampler squares are birds, owls, frogs, cactus, and even an oasis. The Tucson quilters have group quilt production down to a science. A "mother" and her hand-picked assistants cut templates, purchase fabrics, and provide bags of fabric shapes and directions for the group at large. After a gestation period of exactly nine months, the final product is born, displayed, and raffled at their annual guild show. (Owned by Eleanor Johnston. Photograph by Bob Waller.)

PALOUSE HILLS QUILT
•

Moscow, Idaho, 1985. 72 × 96 inches. Designed by Shirley Nilsson, Monica MacFarland, and Vicki Purviance. Six vertical strips of fields, hand-appliquéd onto muslin, machine-embroidered, and hand-quilted by members of the Palouse Patchers guild. Hand-appliquéd vine border.

Idaho's forested mountains and rolling crops of wheat and peas appear in lush earth tones in this sensational pictorial. Sophisticated touches, such as the receding fence, and the use of cool colors on the bottom that gradually blend into warm colors at the top, help provide perspective that is relatively rare in pictorial quilts. The flowing pea-vine border, sprouting with flower buds and little leaves, gives an unusual classical touch to the otherwise abstract scenery. By placing a pair of wheat tufts on either side, the designers give us the impression that their border vine is symmetrical all over, without having gone to the painstaking trouble of making it equal. The vine's stem is made from thirty yards of continuous bias stitched in half lengthwise; its raw edges were pressed under. Palouse Patchers, who contributed more than seven hundred hours of work to the project, know a masterpiece when they see one. When the finished quilt rolled off the frame, beauty overcame profit, and no one could bear to raffle it away. (Photograph by Mark Lamoreaux.)

28

AMISH
FRIENDSHIP QUILT

•

*St. Paul, Minnesota. 1985. 86 ×
94 inches. Signed sampler blocks,
12 inches square. Setting strips,
3 inches; borders, 4 inches.
Designed, machine-pieced, and
hand-quilted by Sue Stein.*

*In her quilted-art series of
sampler quilts, Sue breaks up the
traditional set of even rows of
blocks. Taking a whirl with pin-
wheels and flying geese patterns,
she creates colorful movement
that carries the eye around the
whole surface of the sampler
quilt. This magnificent example,
adapted from an old Amish quilt,
is a variation on the old-fashioned signature quilt. Piecing
was done with scraps and with
intentional "mistakes" in fabric
placement in order to imitate an
old look. The solid color quilt
blocks were signed by friends,
family, and members of Minnesota Quilters before being assembled into an overall pattern. In
this remarkably rich and well-
balanced medley, every block and
pieced panel gives us new patterns, new motifs, with slight but
definite variations. Black sashing
and the repeating triangle shapes
unify this lively pieced collage.
Sue recommends a specific pen
for signing quilts: Pigma Ball–03,
Sakura, Japan. It is very fine and
survives many washings. (Photograph by C. Emmett Shogren.)*

JULIA'S FRIENDSHIP QUILT

◆

Sunnyvale, California. 1983. 50 × 62 inches. Eighteen blocks of various sizes, machine-pieced and appliquéd by Julia Borne and members of the Peninsula Stitchery Guild-Fiber Fanciers. Designed, sun-printed, machine-pieced, and hand-quilted by Julia Borne.

There is a method to the disparate communal fiber creations of the following three quilts made by this talented guild as an elaborate Christmas gift exchange. Each member designed a single block, and re-created it nine times in the color preferences of the other eight stitchers. For some it was a strain to work the patterns in colors the designer could live without, but everyone was pleased with the final results. Julia chose an asymmetrical layout, juxtaposing her blue and green gift blocks with eleven of her own design (including nine sun-printed patterns). The variety of irregular borders merges all the blocks into an energetic, flowing whole. (Photograph by Lou Borne.)

NANCY'S FRIENDSHIP QUILT

•

Sunnyvale, California. 1984. 54 × 71 inches. Ten 12-inch blocks, machine-pieced and sun-printed in brown, blue, and rust by the Peninsula Stitchery Guild-Fiber Fanciers. Designed, appliquéd, and machine-channel quilted by Nancy Ellen Armstrong.

Nancy's harmonious fusion of nine different blocks on a subtle brown paisley stripe is deceptively simple. There is a lot going on in this quilt. The one-and-one-half-inch solid beige fabric frames around each design dilute the contrast between the blocks and background. Nancy gracefully combines two different orientations for the sampler blocks, which are appliquéd onto the background, making them look as if they are melting calmly into the relatively busy ground fabric. Without the neutral frame, the designs would compete with the striped wallpaper fabric. The choice of a low-contrast stripe in vague, muted colors for the large "negative" areas of background suggests texture, space, and stability. This quilt, with its inherent charm and clarity, manages to convey a mood both animated and soothing. (Photograph by Lou Borne.)

WILLIE'S
FRIENDSHIP QUILT

◆

Sunnyvale, California. 1986. 61 inches square. Nine 12-inch blocks, machine-appliquéd and pieced by the Peninsula Stitchery Guild-Fiber Fanciers. Designed, machine-pieced, and hand-quilted by Wilma Wool.

Rich fall colors are the consistent design element in Wilma's friendship sampler. The nine various blocks are cast in compatible values of blue, gold, rust, and brown. Since the blocks did not all measure twelve inches square, the widths of the rust, gold, and black block frames vary from three-quarters to one and one-eighth inches. True brown sashing, two and one-half inches wide, discreetly organizes visual attention. By duplicating many of the internal colors in the four-inch pieced triangle border, Wilma accents and unifies the overall separate but equal design. (Photograph by Lou Borne.)

CONSENSUS: WITH A LITTLE HELP FROM MY FRIENDS

◆

Aloha, Oregon. 1985. 31 × 66 inches. Created from nine twelve-inch blocks made by the Peninsula Stitchery Guild-Fiber Fanciers for member Judy Kellar Fox. Designed, machine-pieced, and hand-quilted by Judy Kellar Fox.

Judy began this striking contemporary composition with nine different friendship blocks, all in shades of blue-green, and all, originally, intact. For over a year, the big square blocks hung pinned to her sewing room drapes while she struggled to find a layout that pleased her. Then the idea hit: she would slice them up along the diagonal, and reassemble them into a graphic collage. "After photocopying all the squares intact, doing a mock-up with photocopies, and working through the emotional impact of the cutting up, I came up with a piece I like. So do my friends who made the original squares. Only a real friend would encourage you after you cut up something she had spent hours creating!" Judy integrated the quilting lines into the overall design to control and collect attention. The compatible coupling of excellent technique with a vibrant design lends balance and special beauty to this unorthodox sampler quilt. (Photograph by Judy Kellar Fox.)

THE ROSE QUILT

◆

West Bend, Wisconsin. 87 × 101 inches. Forty-two 12-inch hand-appliquéd, embroidered, counted, and cross-stitched blocks made by the Kettle Moraine Quilt Club to honor original member Rose Berchem. Machine-pieced by Barb Hinz. Hand-quilted by the St. Francis Cabrini Quilters.

Rose's garden grows in shades of moss green, burgundy, and pale pink. (Kathy Doman, who conceived and organized the gift, was specific about color choices on the instructions. Comments like icky! yuk! *and* ugh! *were attached to the forbidden hues of kelly, turquoise, chartreuse, and bright red.) Along with the block of ground fabric, and five rose patterns drawn to scale, each contributor received good-humored but realistic reminders: finish within the month since no one had time to "come collecting," and "Keep it a secret!" Each unique rose, signed in embroidery, is framed by one-half-inch burgundy print, one-and-one-half-inch muslin, one-half-inch burgundy print, with two-and-one-half-inch muslin squares in each corner. Carol Butzke cross-stitched a poem entitled "Warm Thoughts," which Rose once shared with each member at one of the earliest meetings. Rose says that "memories of the members float up from the quilt each time I look at it!" (Photograph by Don Berchem.)*

LOURETTE QUILT

◆

Rochester, New York. 1986. 85 × 100 inches. Forty-two 12-inch blocks, hand-appliquéd and pieced, assembled and hand-quilted by members of the Genesee Valley Quilt Guild. Three-inch border.

A tour along the rows of this well-balanced cloth document takes us through two decades of American needlework history. The blocks were made between 1947 and 1967 for Florence Lourette, one of the guild's original members. Most of the appliqué blocks were made by women who joined the club in the thirties and forties, when appliqué was more popular than piecework. Florence was never able to assemble them, so returned the stack to the guild shortly before her death. Four members (Hutch Frederick, Helen Shepard, Mildred Daley, and Dora Ryan) arranged them within a two-inch antique-looking green sashing, and marked the quilting patterns that Helen Shepard designed. After basting, the club quilted during shows and demonstrations, finishing it at long last in 1986, just in time for their Fiftieth Anniversary Show. (Photograph by Karen LaDuca.)

BALTIMORE FRIENDSHIP ALBUM

Baltimore, Maryland. 1984–1986. 37 inches square. Nine 9-inch blocks, appliquéd and signed by the Baltimore Album Quilters for member Mimi Dietrich. Assembled and hand-quilted by Mimi Dietrich.

Two years ago, nine Baltimorians, inspired by the famous stitchery of their nineteenth-century ancestors, decided to re-create miniature Baltimore Albums, using the same wreath and basket patterns, the same lush red, green, and gold colors, the same regal borders, as the classics of old. Each needleworker chose one pattern from antique examples, and duplicated it exactly nine times on their muslin squares. Quilters returned home from monthly meetings one block richer, until, after nine months, everyone had enough pieces for her own quilt. Mimi's miniature, the first to be finished, is richly quilted, and bordered in a five-inch festive festoon pattern. The narrow red border is three-eighths inch. The borders and quilting on all nine will differ according to the tastes of each quilter, but one layout scheme was agreed upon early: "We hope that 100 years from now, someone will try to find these nine quilts. Isn't it fun to dream!" This quilt won a blue ribbon at the Maryland State Fair. (Photograph by Dorothy Hunt.)

CHRISTMAS FRIENDSHIP

•

Rockland County, New York. 1984. 88 × 74 inches. Thirty blocks, hand-pieced and appliquéd by members and good friends of the Heritage Quilters of the Hudson Palisades for Claire Kammer. Two-inch red sashing, and 2½-inch borders. Assembled and hand-quilted by Claire Kammer.

Members of the Heritage Quilters of the Hudson Palisades were so certain that their friend Claire Kammer would regain her eyesight after brain surgery that they made friendship blocks for her during her hospital stay. Four days before she entered the hospital, Claire distributed pieces of green, red, and gold fabric for appliqué on white background squares and asked members to design their own Christmas sampler block. "I happened to cut some of the background blocks a bit larger than twelve inches because I could only see with one eye at the time, and blurry at that," Claire recalls. "The colors looked so bright and cheerful to me. The next year, I spent many wonderful hours quilting this special quilt while I recuperated, grateful to be able to see again." The quilt was displayed at the fifteenth annual Christmas Festival in the Bear Mountain Inn Gallery, 1985. (Photograph by Joyce Murrin.)

PEARL'S QUILT

•

*Holton, Kansas. 1979–1980. 88 ×
108 inches. Thirty-five 12-inch
blocks, hand-pieced by friends,
family, and colleagues of Jackson
Heights School's second grade
teacher, Pearl Lear, as a retirement gift. Assembled by Shirlene
Wedd. Hand-quilted.*

Pearl Lear began her college
education at the age of fifty, and
her teaching career at age fifty-
six. Eleven years later, as her first
second-grade class was graduat-
ing from high school, Miss Lear
retired. This quilted thank-you
for a teaching job well done was
created by twenty-six mostly nov-
ice quilters: her friends, family,
and colleagues, ranging from the
principal to teacher aides to the
school custodian. Each traditional square done in bold school
colors—green and gold—is jam-
packed with memories and
meaning. A block appropriately
named "Jackson" (for the
school) stabilizes the four corners. The never-ending "Wild
Goose Chase" pattern was chosen for the first four-inch border
"because they say teachers spend
their days chasing children
around the room." The next one-
inch green strip is embroidered
with the names of the students
from her first class. The entire
quilt, which took a year to quilt
in hoops, is framed in a three-
inch diamond pattern "because
that is how precious we feel Miss
Lear is." (Photograph by Joyce
Shupe.)

SAMPLER BABY QUILT

•

Santa Monica, California. January 1986. 45 × 60 inches. Twelve 12-inch blocks machine and hand-pieced, machine- and hand-appliquéd, and machine-quilted by the Scrappy Quilters of Santa Monica, for member Rosanna Blumenberg. Quilt top designed by Linda Graham and Danita Rafalovich-Smith.

Timing is important for a baby quilt. Twelve members of the Scrappy Quilters gave themselves two months to complete bright blocks of their own design choice for one of their newest members, who was pregnant with her second child. Everybody made the deadline, and the entire cheery creation was machine-pieced and machine-quilted in just two days. Teddy bears, hearts, patchwork, and pussycats spell b-a-b-y quilt. The multicolored lattice and borders add festive flavor to the pastel pastiche. Two-inch color strips were pieced for the lattice. Four-inch strips were pieced for the border. (Collection of Rosanna Blumenberg and Family. Photograph by Danita Rafalovich-Smith.)

SPIKE THE RAT PILLOW QUILT

•

Sacramento, California. March 1984. 48 × 36 inches. Twelve 12-inch blocks made for baby Emily Page by a group of her mommy's relatives and high school/college friends, under the direction of Jill Russell and Bonnie Allen. Satin, cotton, chintz, felt, plastic, eyelet lace, metallic fabric, vinyl. Quilt-as-you-go.

Here's a cuddly idea for a group of good friends: pillow quilts for mothers-to-be. Each square is a quilt-as-you-go pil-low. Jill and Bonnie secretly ask husbands for addresses of their wife's family and sewing friends. Willing participants are sent kits that include four border strips, a thirteen-inch ground fabric, and a square of batting. Stitchers are given four to six weeks to return finished pillows. Emily Page was born in the Year of the Rat, hence fat Spike in the upper left corner. Some designs are wordplays on Emily's last name: the buggy under Spike says, "Baby News: Buck Makes First Page" (Buck is her mom's maiden name). A chocolate kiss in metallic fabric recalls the stitcher's favorite food item. The bee represents the logo of the Sacramento Bee, where Claudia is a reporter, and the baseball player refers to Paul's favorite team: the Dodgers. All the pillow squares were hand-pieced by Jill Russell in time for the various baby showers. (Col-lection of Claudia and Paul Page. Photograph by Julian Veovich.)

PEZ PILLOW QUILT

•

Alameda, California. January 1983. 48 inches square. Made for Molly Russell by her mommy's family and high school/college friends, under the direction of Bonnie Allen. Chintz, velvet, plastic, cotton, satin, aida cloth, felt. Appliqué, patchwork, cross-stitch, needlepoint, embroidery. Quilt-as-you-go.

Molly's mom, Jill Russell, must have had a thing for candy as a kid. Four of these sixteen twelve-inch squares depict some kind of goody or another: the upper left square represents the Russell couple's extensive Pez head collection (125 plus!) that once made the local papers; a box of Whoppers is appliquéd next door. Two more ice cream cones complete the sugar high you get just looking at these scrumptious plum-bordered pillow squares. (Collection of Jill and Ned Russell. Photograph by Julian Veovich.)

ARGYLE AND AMISH SCHOOLDAYS

◆

Santa Monica, California. 1986. 70 × 80 inches. Fifteen 8-inch-square schoolhouse blocks, machine-pieced by the Scrappy Quilters. Two-inch sashing. Designed, machine-pieced, and machine-quilted by Linda Graham.

For the past six years, the Scrappy Quilters have picked one member at their monthly meeting to coordinate a friendship quilt, using a pattern of her own choice. When Linda Graham's name was chosen, she knew that she wanted a traditional schoolhouse quilt in Amish colors. Linda supplied muslin for the common ground fabric and solid shades of pink, purple, blue, and gray for the pieced houses. She came up with a clever layout scheme, alternating the friendship houses with her own fifteen eight-inch square "cornerstone" blocks. The combination of the two blocks side by side creates the illusion of an elaborate diagonal sashing with the schoolhouse blocks set "on point." Linda personalized her own house by machine-appliquéing two little kittens lounging in the windows. The simple two-and-one-quarter-inch border of four-inch four-patches set on point reminded Linda of argyle socks when it was finished—hence the quilt's title. (Photograph by Danita Rafalovich-Smith.)

MORNING, NOON, AND NIGHT

•

Allegheny County, Maryland. 1982. 81 × 106 inches. Forty-eight 10-inch blocks, machine-pieced and hand-quilted by the Schoolhouse Quilters Guild for founder and friend Jane Patterson. Two-inch pieced sashing; two-inch corner blocks. Designed by Dorothy Stone and Jane Patterson.

This gifted guild met regularly in a restored little red schoolhouse—the same one-room structure in which Jane spent her grammar school years. The unusual color gradations represent the school throughout a typical day—serene and quiet at dawn, exploding with activity during the school hours, and lamplit for evening meetings. The cotton fabrics were donated from scrapbags; some pieces were toned and mellowed by tea-dying. A narrow black border separates the blocks from the pieced border of rectangles, which repeats all the block fabrics. Each block was constructed by many hands, in assembly-line style. Around the same time that Jane and her family decided to sell their farm and move to Georgia, the members asked her to help design a special quilt to be used as the guild's logo. Jane, stunned when the finished quilt was presented to her as a going-away memento, wondered how so many women could keep such a secret so long. (Photograph by Charles L. Patterson.)

PATCHWORK ACRES

Long Island, New York. 1985. 82 × 102 inches. Twenty 15-inch blocks pieced, appliquéd, and lap-quilted by the Long Island Quilter's Society. Coordinated and assembled by Margot Cohen.

Margot Cohen chose patchwork houses for the theme of her cooperative guild venture, and appointed herself "Burghermeister" of the plots of fabric. Each "architect" received a simple house pattern with instructions to "Fix up your home," with any colors, fabrics, and embellishments. Sixty stitchers returned their developed squares—enough for three quilted villages. All three quilts are sashed in a different way. In the white lattice joints of "Patchwork Acres" pictured here, Margot stenciled two-story red buildings. In a second quilt, called "Quilttown," she pieced red and green blocks at the intersections of navy cotton sashing to represent traffic lights. Margot's hard-sell real estate pitches are the main reason so many quilters responded. One day, when trying to solicit a certain block, Margot dialed the wrong number and managed to convince the total stranger who answered that quilting would be perfect therapy for her surgery recuperation. Although the woman had not sewn in many years, she ended up contributing a beautiful block to this unique housing project. (Photograph by Thomas Cohen.)

TARBELL HOUSE

◆

*Cincinnati, Ohio. 1981. 60 × 73
inches. Twenty 11-inch blocks
made by the Pendleton Neighborhood Quilting Group as a house-
warming gift for member Brenda
Tarbell. Embroidery, traditional
and reverse appliqué. Machine-
pieced and hand-quilted.*

*This cozy quilt is filled with
rich city scenes: apartments,
streets, schools, laundry lines, all
compiled from a common scrap
basket. The Pendleton group is
bound by its pledge to restore an
inner-city neighborhood, "not an
easy place to live," Brenda
writes. "Many of us are raising
very small children and rebuild-
ing nineteenth-century homes at
the same time. We really count
on each other's support." The
squares reflect the friendships
that blossomed in the cloistered,
cherished hours devoted to com-
mitting their household scenes to
fabric. One woman proudly depicts the chair she reupholstered,
another strings her wash from
building to building, a third
shows her sister standing in the
courtyard catching the keys to
her apartment. Each scene has a
one-inch frame in the stitcher's
choice of fabric. The whole composition is bordered in a one-
inch maroon print, and again in
a five-inch toasty floral brown.
(Photograph by Jay Bashmen.)*

A HOUSE FOR ALL SEASONS

◆

Bronx, New York. 1985. 59 × 84 inches. Sixteen 10-inch hand-appliquéd and machine-pieced blocks by the parents, grandparents, staff, and friends of the Amalgamated Nursery School. Two-inch sashing and borders. Machine-pieced houses by Lynn Silver and Dee Gomez; 46 × 10-inch top and bottom panels machine-pieced by Paula Nadelstern. Machine-quilted by Esther Sas.

To every patchwork house there is a season on this third annual nursery school fundraiser. Parents were asked to embellish prefab homes according to a predetermined time of year. The first column has shades of gray yards for winter, the next two have bright florals for spring and summer, the fourth has earth tones for autumn. The squares are as diverse as the skills and personalities of their creators. A majestic, snow-laden tree in the upper left corner—a composition of perfect simplicity—is achieved by an innovative layering of a white cotton trim reminiscent of feathers. The use of only four fabrics in the pieced houses, plus the same pin-dot sky blue background, insures visual cohesion. Note that the houses consistently face in alternate directions. (Owned by Ray and Sara Freedman. Photographs by Allen Feigenberg.)

H·O·U·S·E
Q·U·I·L·T·S

DETAILS
•
"Winter Scene," Nancy Mann.
•
"Trick-or-Treaters,"
Lorraine Butler.
•
"American Gothic,"
Paula Nadelstern.
•
"Autumn," Minia Sas.

OUR NURSERY NEIGHBORHOOD

◆

Bronx, New York. 1987. 10-inch blocks, hand-appliquéd by parents, staff, and friends of the Amalgamated Nursery School. A fund-raiser designed by Paula Nadelstern, coordinated and pieced by Dee Gomez and Teri Cohen Meskin. Tied by two fifth graders and former nursery students, Luba Feigenberg and Caryn Solomon. Top panel designed and pieced by Paula Nadelstern. Additional machine-quilting by Teri Cohen Meskin.

After exploring a wide range of fantasy themes in four previous fund-raisers, nursery parents decided to return to their urban roots for this project, stitching a group quilt from the fabric of the community. The quilt is in the shape of one of the Amalgamated cooperative's oldest apartment buildings, with its Tudor-style spires in the top panel, and its archway flanked by velvety stones in the lower center block. Each window block, sashed with "bricks and mortar," contains a typical neighborhood scene— jogging, acting, playing, parking, and depositing money in the local credit union. (Photographs by Bobby Hansson.)

DETAILS

◆

"Feeding the Pigeons,"
Ariya Blitz.

This remarkable square, made by a first-time quilter, shows a smiling senior citizen couple sitting by a lamppost in Van Cortlandt Park, reading an embroidered newspaper and feeding beads to Ultrasuede pigeons.

◆

"Volkswagen,"
Sandy Gold-Medina.

In a less bucolic quilt square, an illegally parked Volkswagen displays button headlights, rick-rack bumpers, and the requisite "Please Do Not Block" sign.

HOUSE ON THE HILL

•

Staten Island, New York. 1983. 90 × 105 inches. Fund-raising quilt designed by Susan Frye, and hand-pieced by eleven members of the Staten Island Civic Association. Cotton, chintz, rayon, polyester.

The hilly St. George neighborhood in Staten Island, once graced with elegant Victorian homes, was, until very recently, a slum. "People slowly began to renovate the long-empty structures," Susan Frye says, "and the local civic association decided to hold house tours to celebrate." This opulent quilt, which commits to fabric eight actual neighborhood structures, was raffled off at the first festival in 1983. A group united not by their quilting experience, but by their community spirit, met every Tuesday for four months until their tribute was complete. Stitchers were given free color rein with the twelve-inch traditional pieced houses in the borders. Their only instructions: make them "cheerful." Brighton Heights Reformed Church, a landmark on the island, was pieced with an amazing twenty-six stitches to the inch. By contrasting the reds and blues in the houses with black print sashing and border, these fabricated buildings finally receive the attention they deserve. (Collection of Marion Fisher. Photograph by Bobby Hansson.)

SAILORS' SNUG HARBOR

◆

Staten Island, N.Y. 1984. 72 × 90 inches. Designed by Susan Frye, machine- and hand-pieced by five members of the Staten Island Civic Association to commemorate the borough's Cultural Center. Machine-quilted by Susan Frye.

The Tuesday night Staten Island neighborhood quilters had such a good time with the House on the Hill *fund-raising project (page 50), they decided to create another tribute to their neighborhood, just for fun. This time they focused their needles on Sailor's Snug Harbor, formerly a seaman's estate, and now Staten Island's Cultural Center. The artists, most of whom work at the center, recreated the harbor's art school, gardens, and galleries. Look carefully at the lower left hand corner. A "phantom" building—a chapel that was torn down—is quilted into the empty space. The connecting structures between the buildings are called "hyphens." The eight-and-one-half-inch floral border print, in antique-looking browns, gives the scene a Victorian flavor, reflecting the area's architectural design. The rose, brown, and white buildings unite as each interacts with the dark green background fabric. (Collection of Susan Frye. Photograph by Bobby Hansson.)*

CARBONDALE COMMUNITY HISTORICAL QUILT

◆

1852–1969. Carbondale, Illinois. 1982–83. 102 × 78 inches. Twenty-four 14-inch blocks made by 27 women and men to commemorate the history of Carbondale, Illinois. 1¾-inch sashing, 3¾-inch border. Coordinated by Millie Dunkel. Appliqué, embroidery, cross-stitch, crewel, petit point, mirror embroidery, silk screen, photo printing, strip-pieced, and painted. Quilt-as-you-go.

Inspiration for this pumpkin-framed storybook quilt came when Millie Dunkel took a walking tour of her home town and realized how little she knew about it. Before collecting ideas and a stitching labor force, she found a home for the wall hanging—Carbondale's new public library. The workmanship in many of the blocks is exceptional. The whorling crewel-embroidered clouds above the Methodist Church look postively Van Gogh-esque. The petit point Old Train Station brings to mind watercolor by number. The painted postage-stamp quality of the town founder block is achieved with batik fabric and a gold leaf frame. Fire, squirrels, and a Halloween scene add animation to the stately buildings. (Collection of the Carbondale Community Quilters. Photographs by Bernie Wiethorn.)

DETAILS

◆

"Methodist Church,"
Libby Moore.

◆

"Daniel Brush," Marilyn Boysen.

SUTTON
BICENTENNIAL QUILT

◆

Sutton, New Hampshire. 1984. 72 × 100 inches. Thirty-two 12-inch blocks, one 36 × 12-inch panel, hand-appliquéd by citizens of Sutton to commemorate the town's bicentennial. Embroidery, trapunto, trimmings, fabric folding. Machine-pieced. Designed by Audrey Snitko. Hand-quilted by Betty Whittemore, Wendy Wadman, and Audrey Snitko.

This cloth document represents two hundred years in Sutton, New Hampshire's history, and seven months of weekly meetings in the lives of its needleworkers. Participants chose themes from a prepared list of places and events unique to their village. Indigenous activities such as sugaring, snow rollering, and logging are depicted amid recreations of historical buildings, primeval pines, and American Indians. The block illustrating the country doctor making house calls via horse-drawn carriage was created by Dr. Anne Wasson. The simple two-inch sashing works well to separate and integrate the scrapbag blocks. The final quilt, presented with due ceremony in March 1984, now hangs behind glass at Sutton Town Hall. (Photograph by Susan L. Cochran.)

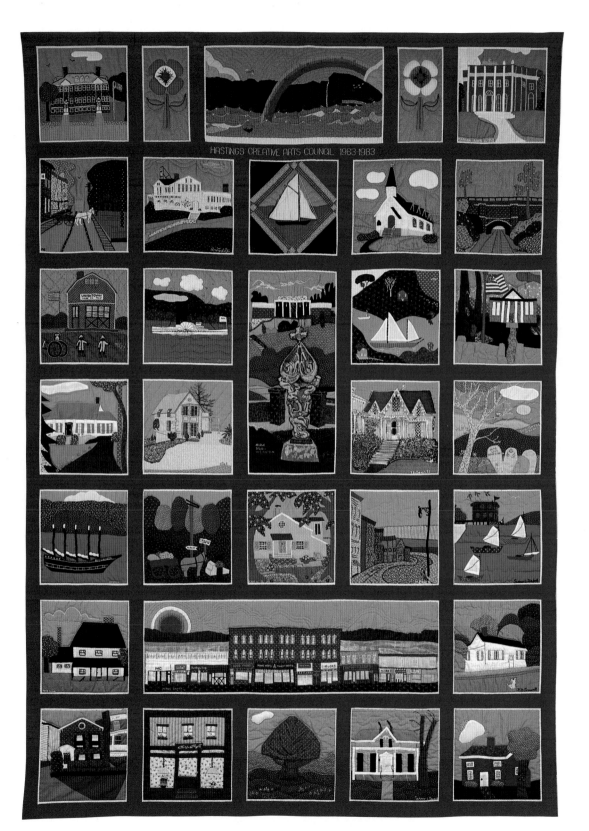

HASTINGS
PAST AND PRESENT

Hastings-on-Hudson, New York. June 1983. 72 × 100 inches. One-quarter-inch muslin frame, 2-inch sashing and border. Thirty-two varied blocks made by 27 men and women in celebration of the twentieth anniversary of the Hastings Creative Arts Council. Five-inch red border frame. Designed and coordinated by Debbie Gaynes. Quilt-as-you-go.

Horse-drawn buggies, a spooky cemetery, and a mid-nineteenth-century Krack House (with a K) are tastefully combined with modern-day sculptures and quaint cafés. Warburton Avenue is pictured twice—once in 1930 (left, second row), and again in 1982 (long panel in the sixth row). Sloops, schooners, yachts, and a be-rainbowed view of the Palisades show how important the Hudson River is to this community. Muslin ground fabric shows up in clouds, windows, and sails. Blue for sky travels through every block. The narrow muslin frames, separating each scene from the rich red sashing, create a very dignified look. Even though organizer Debbie Gaynes remembers having to "call, nag, threaten, and cajole everyone in town" to help on the project, the final result, which hangs in the Hastings Library, was worth it. (Collection of the Hastings Creative Arts Council. Photograph by Martin Merchant.)

HERITAGE WALL QUILT

•

Beaumont, Texas. 1984. 70 × 60 inches. Twelve 12½-inch blocks, pieced and appliquéd by members of the Tuesday Quilters as a gift for the Beaumont Junior Forum Activity Center for Older Adults. One-inch burgundy block frames; 3-inch green sashing; 6-inch border. Coordinated by Anita Murphy.

When Beaumont's senior citizens center announced its intentions to expand, the guild that meets there decided to stitch its own contribution in burgundy and green taffeta to match the new conference room's drapes. Amid the farmlands, oil wells, and rice fields are an old gazebo with Choreboy pot cleaner for a roof and the impressive Port of Beaumont, "the fifth largest in the U.S." The youngest of the Tuesday Quilters who participated (excluding organizer, Anita Murphy) was seventy-three years old. Anita usually never likes to touch a group quilt she coordinates, but with this project she broke all her rules. The night before it was due, she replaced a mysteriously lost block with one of her own, then assembled and finished the quilt herself just two hours before it was presented at a ribbon-cutting ceremony. (Photograph by Anita Murphy.)

DETAIL

•

*"Port of Beaumont,"
Anita Murphy.*

THE NEW YORK
LIBRARY CLUB
CENTENNIAL QUILT
•

*New York City. 1985. 80 ×95
inches. Twenty-one varied blocks
made by nineteen members of the
Manhattan Quilters Guild and the
Empire Quilt Club to commemorate the Library Club's one hundredth anniversary. Hand-quilted.*

*In 1885, Melvil Dewey founded
the New York Library Club, a
professional group dedicated to
enrichment through books. One
hundred years later, his likeness
can be found on a quilt—still in
his top hat, still surveying the
stacks that are organized according to his very own decimal system. Mr. Dewey is surrounded by
scenes of New York—both those
with books and those without.
The bustling Brooklyn Bridge sits
center stage beside the Staten Island Ferry and the famous Manhattan skyline. A sheet of
antiphonal music, a manuscript
page, audio visual equipment, a
computer chip, and a telephone
reference librarian represent
things found in libraries, both
modern and timeless. One of the
Forty-Second Street library's smiling lions guards over the blocks
from above. The burgundy-bound
quilt is currently taking a tour of
New York City's libraries. (Photograph courtesy of the New York
Library Club.).*

NEWTON COMMEMORATIVE QUILT

•

Newton, Massachussetts. 1983. 9 × 6 feet. Machine-pieced, hand-quilted. Created under the auspices of Arts in the Parks, Linda R. Plaut, director; Newton Parks and Recreation Department, Russell J. Halloran, commissioner; and underwritten by a grant from Honeywell. Inspired and coordinated by Rowena Fisher. Designed by Robbie O'Rourke. Completed by 50 Newton residents with Louise Horgan as production supervisor. Permanently displayed, under glass, at Newton City Hall.

Why would twenty-five architects, artists, embroiderers, photographers, and quilters leave their warm homes on bitter New England winter evenings and drive over icy roads to a meeting? This spectacular quilted cameo highlighting Newton's historical structures and events is the answer. Rowena Fisher channeled the artistic talents of the town's residents into a work she hopes "will be a visual delight for all of us in the present and an heirloom for those in the future." Husbands helped wives, mothers joined daughters, and friends found friends, as the twenty-seven flawless blocks evolved. The pictures are joined by vines and flowers to symbolize the group's togetherness and to reflect Newton as "The Garden City." (Photographs by Julian Coen.)

DETAILS

◆

"Houses of Worship,"
Robbie O'Rourke.

◆

"Baury House," Nola Colbert.

RABBI ALFRED WOLF'S QUILT

•

Los Angeles, California. 1985. 63 × 77 inches. Twenty 12-inch blocks appliquéd, embroidered, and hand-pieced by members of The Wilshire Boulevard Temple Quilters as a retirement gift for Rabbi Alfred Wolf after thirty-six years of service. Quilt-as-you-go.

Every year, the Wilshire Boulevard Temple Quilters (ages forty to eighty) jointly produce a quilt to be owned and treasured by one member whose name is drawn from a hat. Rabbi Wolf always presides over the hat. At their 1985 dinner, the name on the paper was the rabbi's—over and over again. "There has to be some mistake," he said. "I'm not a quilter." Then they unfolded the quilt. "It was the story of my life. Each square symbolized something very important to me: the dome of our Temple, the menorah at our camp, my family tree, my hiking boots. It was the most beautiful quilt I had ever seen. These twenty wonderful ladies had taken the trouble to find out what was meaningful to me, who I was, what made me tick. Their quilt told me in the world's clearest language that I was important to them and that they loved me." A miniature satin-stuffed jacket celebrates the rabbi's role as director of Camp Hess Kramer, where the quilt now hangs. When the camp broke out in flames in 1985, this treasure was one of the first items rescued. (Photograph by Esther Parkhurst.)

FESTIVAL OF A LIFE

◆

Swannanoa, North Carolina. 1986. 65 × 86 inches. Made by the Friends of Warren Wilson College quilting group as a retirement gift for its president, Ben Holden, under the direction of Matey Rice and Beverly Ohler. Thirty-six 8½-inch squares; six 19 × 8½-inch panels. Quilt-as-you-go.

Winnie the Pooh, Cookie Monster, a trash collector, and a wise man blinded by his own turban all turn up on this fabric festival of retired president Ben Holden's life. He is clearly an administrator who is not above snitching cookies or dressing up like Pooh Bear to celebrate a birthday. Of course, his official capacity is also represented: graduation ceremonies, Rotary banner, college logo, and the school's Appalachian Music Program. More than fifty men and women painted, appliquéd, embroidered, crossstitched, screen printed, and just plain stitched their memories onto muslin squares; all of them signed the lower-right-hand patchwork block. Warren Wilson symbols—the owl and the spade (signifying wisdom and labor) and the initials WWC—were machine-quilted between the squares. Matey Rice writes, "One square says 'Labor of Love' and that it really is." (Collection of Dr. and Mrs. Ben Holden. Photograph by Richardson L. Rice.)

LOTTIE'S QUILT

◆

Southold, New York. 1983. 52 × 76 inches. One-quarter-inch black frame, ¾-inch magenta frame, 2-inch sashing, 5-inch border. Fifteen 8-inch hand-appliquéd blocks by family and friends (ages 5 to 75) of Lottie Barth for her seventieth birthday. Designed, machine-pieced, and co-ordinated by Paula Nadelstern. Hand-quilted by Lynn Della Posta.

This wall quilt is a rich compendium of the complex and dynamic personality of Paula's Aunt Lottie. Many interesting stories about Lottie's life were unveiled as several generations gathered to exchange ideas for this project. One block follows Lottie's voyage at age sixteen from her native Poland to her new home —New York City's Lower East Side. Another is a sewing niche complete with an abundance of trimmings and a project-in-progress on the old Singer. Lottie's penchant for yard sales appears in the form of a pile of junk that reveals a treasure or two (glittering rhinestones). Lottie cried with joy when she ripped apart the gift box containing the quilt, thrilled that it wasn't "yet another bathrobe!" (Photographs by Bobby Hansson.)

DETAIL

◆

"Sewing Niche,"
Paula Nadelstern.

After years of apartment living, Lottie moved to a house on Long Island, where she set up her dream sewing room overlooking the ocean. A container of pencils and sewing paraphernalia, a basket spilling over with ribbons, an ever-present iron with a realistic cord, and the secondhand Singer make up this realistic still life of Aunt Lottie's hobby room.

CHERYL AND DEAN'S WEDDING QUILT

•

*New York, New York. 1986. 90 ×
100 inches. Seventeen 8-inch
blocks appliquéd, embroidered,
and macraméd by friends and
family of Cheryl King and Dean
Hadiks as a wedding gift. Quilt
top and 10-inch border designed
and assembled by Paula Nadelstern. Hand-quilted by Lynn Della
Posta.*

*When Cheryl, one of Paula's
oldest and dearest friends, announced her wedding plans,
Paula didn't think twice about
the gift she wanted to give the
new couple. Even as she pieced
the complicated frame deep into
the night (forty-four pieces per
border unit!), she was consoled
knowing that Cheryl would appreciate every difficult shape,
every matching corner, every perfectly blended color. The picture
blocks made by Dean and Cheryl's friends and family are a pot-
pourri of childhood memories
and best wishes for the future,
integrated into a "hamsa" pattern—a lucky hand from Middle
Eastern folklore. The water tower
represents the place where Cheryl
and the blockmaker would hide
from the summer camp coun-
selors and have "meaning of life"
talks. The wedding ceremony itself did not move the bride to
tears, but when she opened up
the quilt ... (Photographs by
Bobby Hansson.)*

DETAILS

◆

"Moon and Stars,"
Paula Nadelstern.
The motif represents the children to come in Jewish lore. The flow of sequins and stars between the moon and the sun carries the eye back and forth between the celestial objects.

◆

"Bookshelf," Paula Nadelstern.
The shelf of books incorporates eight different ideas, including Dean's native Greek culinary skills, Cheryl's interest in crafts (and her klutziness on roller skates), and their mutual interest in psychology.

WEDDING CHUPAH

◆

*Brooklyn, New York. 1985. 36 ×
62 inches. Two-inch sashing. Six
12-inch and two 6 × 30-inch embroidered and appliquéd blocks
made by the family of Terry Feinstein and Richard Sasanow.
Machine-pieced by Myra Hirshberg. Designed and quilted by
Paula Nadelstern. Coordinated by
Sonia Hirshberg.*

*Paula was approached by the
proud mother of a bride-to-be to
design and help coordinate a
quilted chupah—the canopy
that shelters a couple during the
Jewish wedding ceremony. Family members came up with the
block themes, and Paula translated them into do-able designs
in fabric. Every participant was
then mailed a detailed kit, including the sketch, instructions,
embroidery threads, necessary
trimmings, and precut shapes
glued to the ground fabric. Romantic memories are stitched
into the linked wedding rings and
the Bridge of Sighs. The bridge,
complete here with gargoyles cut
from black lace, is where the
groom proposed. A cello laid on
a true-to-life embroidered sheet
of actual music reflects the couple's mutual musical interests.
The two-inch lattice is bisected
by blocks of a darker blue to suggest stained glass. The Hebrew
wedding words, rendered in Ultrasuede, translate as follows:
"the voice of joy and the voice of
happiness, the voice of the groom
and the voice of the bride."*
(Photographs by Bobby Hansson.)

"Hamsa," Paula Nadelstern.

The hand of God, an ancient Middle Eastern symbol to ward off the evil eye, is often transposed into a bird of peace. Intricate heart beads on each of the hand's fingers suggest little mirrors. The Hebrew letters spell "Mazel Tov!" (good luck).

◆

Back panel, Myra Hirschberg.

Myra cross-stitched the names of the quilt's contributors onto an off-white needlepoint canvas and attached it to the back of the quilt.

TO CELEBRATE THE MARRIAGE OF
TERRI FEINSTEIN AND RICHARD SASANOW
NOVEMBER 24, 1985

DESIGNED BY PAULA NADELSTERN
STITCHED BY SONYA HIRSCHBERG   PEARL SASANOW
ANNE KLEINFELD   CLAIRE DARROW
PHYLLIS HOLLANDER   MARY FEINSTEIN
RORRI FEINSTEIN   TOBY DEUTSCH
MYRA HIRSCHBERG   ALLISON DEUTSCH
ADELE KAMPF   PAULA NADELSTERN

THE FRIESEN
WEDDING QUILT

◆

San Benito, Texas. 68 × 81 inches. Thirty 11¼-inch muslin squares, 2-inch black sashing. Made and signed by friends and relatives of Richard and Ruth Anne Friesen as a wedding gift. Appliqué, cross-stitch, embroidery, machine-pieced, and tied.

This simple wedding quilt is enriched with toads, scripture, pretzels, autographed inscriptions, butterflies, and wildflowers —all things dear to Richard and Ruth Anne Friesen's souls. Richard is a flower expert, Ruth Anne is attracted to butterflies (for their spiritual symbolism), and they both like a good pretzel now and then. One pair of butterflies is done in the Eastern European *igolochkoy* method—a sort of miniature hooked rug technique. The couple met in a small Illinois Christian fellowship group several years ago; its members maintain an intense bond despite the miles, and many of their squares can be seen on this stark black and white work of love. One patchwork block says, "Jesus loves you warts and all." Richard and Ruth Anne moved to the Rio Grande Valley to work with the Overground Railroad, a program that helps Central American refugees obtain Canadian residency. (Photograph by Ruth Powers.)

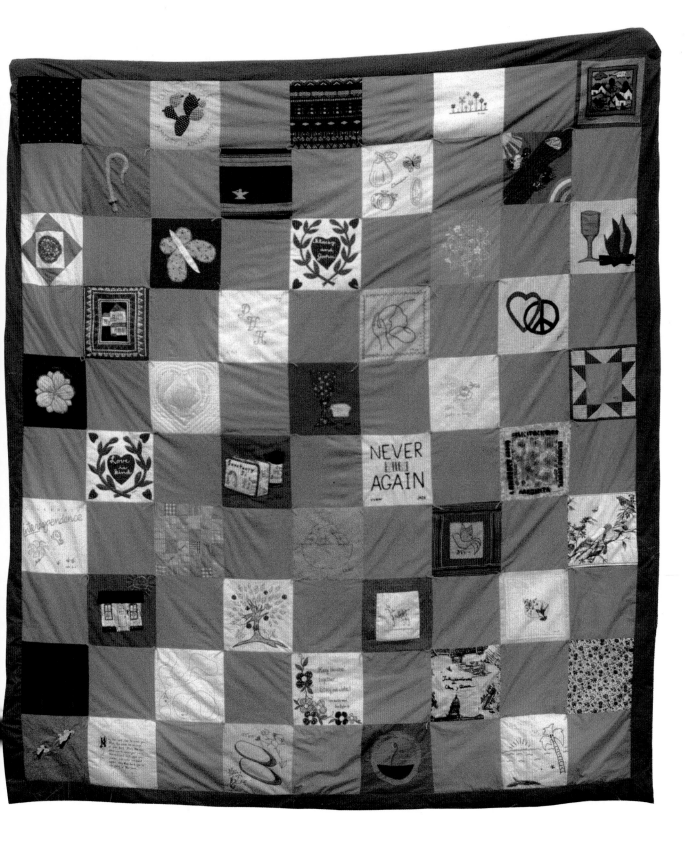

MERKT-BLATZ
WEDDING QUILT

•

Harlingen, Texas. 1986. 86 × 94 inches. Made by friends and relatives of Stacey Merkt and John Blatz as a wedding present. Forty-five 9-inch blocks in appliqué, cross-stitch, painting, and embroidery. Assembled and machine-pieced by Diane Elder. Tied by Stacey and friends.

Stacey Merkt is a sanctuary movement refugee worker in the Rio Grande Valley. Several years ago, around the time her wedding plans were announced, she was arrested and charged with transporting a Central American refugee. The charges were later dropped, but as the trial dragged on, Stacey's cast of friends and family secretly planned this special gift. The tiny images are charged with political ideals, Ecuadoran textiles and in-jokes. Fran Ferrara, a first-grade teacher, depicts in fabric crayons a "Sanctuary, Si!" lunch box and a "Casa Romero" thermos. (Fran is famous for his collection of more than one hundred lunch boxes and Casa Romero is the name of the refugee center where he met the couple.) One block-maker ripped up her favorite shirt for her creation. Another appliquéd little penguins because Stacey is a bird-watcher. (Photographs by Francis Ferrara.)

THE RHODES'S 50TH ANNIVERSARY QUILT

◆

Iowa City, Iowa. 1985. 87 × 109 inches. Fifteen 10½-inch square counted cross-stitch blocks. Machine-pieced and hand-quilted by family and friends.

This was a project of love, designed by Donna Lawler, as a surprise golden anniversary gift for her parents, Emery and Ellen Rhodes. The cross-stitch pictures executed by Donna and friends on off-white cotton squares depict the Rhodes's offspring, their spouses and children, each engaged in a characteristic activity. The grandchildren are shown skiing, piano-playing, and roller skating. The children are shown in their roles as accountant, teacher, secretary, and farmer. The top center square portrays the Methodist church where Emery has served as finance secretary ever since a severe injury prevented him from farming any longer. Emery's eighty-six-year-old sister assembled the blocks, borders, batting, and back and five other friends and relatives quilted the whole. The final quilt, bordered in a floral blue cotton, is displayed in the Rhodes's home on a walnut stand made by a brother-in-law, a woodworker. (Photograph by Kent Studio, Iowa City.)

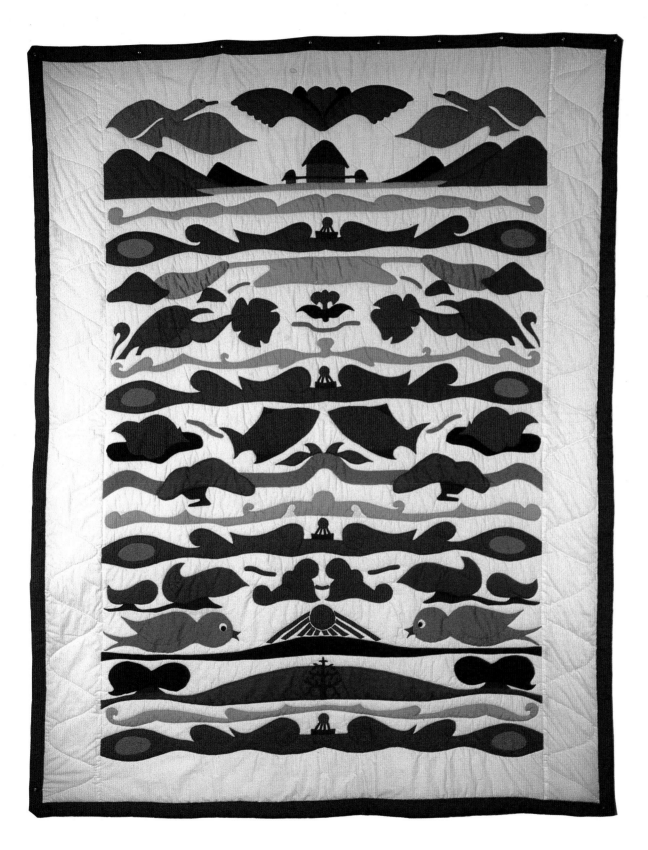

JENNIFER'S QUILT

◆

Philadelphia, Pennsylvania. 1967. An appliquéd birthday gift, made in four pieces by Hazel (mother) and Pamela (sister) Haines for the oldest daughter.

When Jennifer, the oldest of six children, brought home a special high school art project, her mother took one look at it and said, "This looks like a quilt." That was the start of the Haines family tradition—making personalized theme quilts for each child's twenty-first birthday. For their first inspiration, mother and daughters set to work reproducing Jennifer's painting as faithfully as they could into cloth. The work represents an abstract illustration of "The Brook" by Alfred Lord Tennyson. The repeating light and dark blue water motifs conjure up the poem's chorus:

> . . . to join the brimming
> river;
> For men may come and
> men may go,
> But I go on forever.

The original quilt was lost when their house was destroyed by fire in 1971, but a slide of it, though charred, damp, and slightly obscured by someone's head, survived. Pamela Haines and her mother set to work re-creating it from the slide and from memory, guessing, sometimes inaccurately, what was behind that person's head. (Photograph by John Woodin.)

DEBBY'S QUILT

•

Newport, Rhode Island. 1968. Various-sized blocks appliquéd by Hazel, Jennifer, and Pamela Haines for the twenty-first birthday of the second oldest child, Debby.

Debby was deeply involved in the Quaker religion when her twenty-first birthday rolled around—hence the theme of her family quilt. Mom, Jennifer, and Pamela (child number three) worked out the overall scheme, which is a successful religious meeting of emblems and words, characterized by periods of silence. Symbols of light—a central concept in Quakerism—move diagonally across the quilt. A dove peacefully glides by as the lion lies down with the lamb. Radiating lines from a center star move visual attention out toward the male and female Quakers who are surveying the peaceful scene. Love and respect for the quilt's recipient are evident in this subdued grouping of varied size blocks, reminiscent in its earth tones of an aerial landscape. "It was a daring decision to try different-sized squares, since this was just our second quilt," writes Pamela. "We discovered only by accident that the block in the lower left—the traditional signature spot—contained the initials of the quilters, Pamela, Hazel (Mom), Jennifer." (Photographs by Walter Haines.)

DETAILS

•

"Poem," Pamela Haines.

•

"Peaceful Kingdom,"
Jennifer Haines.

TIMOTHY'S QUILT

•

New York, New York. 1984. Twelve triangle blocks appliquéd, embroidered, cross-stitched, and crazy patched by Hazel, Deborah, Pamela, Walter, and Liseli Haines for brother Timothy.

By the time the youngest child's twenty-first birthday rolled around, the Haineses were seasoned quilters, and they were primed for something entirely new. The sisters created a complicated crazy quilt ruled by color and shapes. Even Dad made his sewing debut at age sixty by stitching the map of Manhattan, where Timothy now lives, at the bottom. The clutter of patches is enriched with exquisitely embroidered images representing all aspects—big and small—of Timothy's family life. The exquisite satyr is a replica of a mosaic that Timothy and sister Liseli saw in a Roman villa. The wedding and flute composite illustrates how he played the recorder at all three of his sisters' weddings. The actual musical score by Bach is one that he and Pamela played together. Dinosaurs, cathedrals, and stalled cars on various family trips represent Timothy's evolving passions and inevitable chores. Over the course of eighteen years, the family has made bedspreads for parents and grandparents, weddings and farewells. This set of family quilts offers a continuity that is very rich; we look forward to seeing the next generation's creations. (Photographs by Walter Haines.)

DETAILS

•

"Satyr," Liseli Haines. Liseli managed to re-create an actual Roman mosaic in fabric.

•

"Wedding Portrait with Recorder," cooperative effort.

THE CROWN QUILT

◆

New York, New York. 1986. 90 × 88½ inches. Twenty 8-inch blocks, appliquéd by employees of Crown Publishers, Inc., for Chairman of the Board Nat Wartels's eighty-fifth birthday. Coordinated by Pam Thomas and Erica Marcus. Designed and machine-pieced by ·Paula Nadelstern. Hand-quilted by Sara Miller, an Amish quilter from Kalona, Iowa.

In this regal library stocked with cloth-bound renditions of the publisher's best-sellers, Nat Wartels, Crown's chairman of the board, sits center stage, obscured by a cluttered desk. The titles he surveys range from the whimsical to the divine, from the culinary to the novel. Bette Midler's The Saga of Baby Divine, *swathed in real boa and designer diapers, is perched atop a giant bottle. White spiral embroidery lines recreate the spiritual* Be Here Now *cover, and Judith Krantz's* Princess Daisy *glances over her calico flowers. Twenty Crown employees, from a receptionist to a vice president, contributed their time and talent to this quilted tribute. Medallions, crowns, and beautiful border prints in deep tones provide a subdued, elegant encasement for these animated works of literature. (Photographs by Bobby Hansson.)*

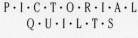
DETAILS

◆

*"The Hitchhiker's Guide
to the Galaxy," Ann Meador.*

By repeating the same button-hole stitch in varied shades of floss, Ann created dimensions and shadows in this graphic block. Glitter is used sparingly to represent the galaxy.

◆

"Nat's Desk," Florence Porrino.

Nat's unique character is expressed in the controlled clutter of this block. (He's the shock of white hair behind the books.) A certain symmetry is created by the variety of lines in the design: the delicate swirly lines of his cigarette smoke and dangling telephone wire are balanced with the straight lines created by the mountains of books.

◆

*"Lee Bailey's Country Weekends,"
Sandra Still.*

Details create texture in this still-life beauty. Using a multitude of fabrics and trimmings, Sandra transformed the original flat photo into a collage in relief.

◆

*"The Rising of the Moon,"
Pam Thomas.*

This block demonstrates how static pictures can be interpreted imaginatively into fabric. An image with depth and distinct temperament is created with swirly silk for the bay water, lace for crashing waves, and shades of brown layers for cliffs.

DETAILS

◆

"The Joy of Sex," Pam Thomas.

Peeking through lace curtains, we see the backs of two heads, two pairs of flesh-colored Ultra-suede knees and toes and the book, The Joy of Sex, opened and ready for reading. Pam left the blue background fabric visible to represent wallpaper.

◆

"The Saga of Baby Divine," Norma Leong.

A bobble earring, real boa, pearls for milk drops, designer diapers, and couched Kewpie doll hair are some of the details and unusual trimmings packed to fascinating advantage into this small, centered design.

◆

"Willie Mosconi on Pocket Billiards," Erica Marcus.

Gaudy trimmings and tacky tweeds are essential elements to the spirit of this book. Erica used big costume jewelry, a glitzy gold band, and a big floral print for the pool-player's shirt. The line of the table edge, combined with the round billiard balls, provides balance.

◆

"Crown," Paula Nadelstern.

The echo quilting pattern in concentric half-circles emphasizes the shape of the crown and creates its own design. Prints and stripes are used to represent the jewels and ornate bands imperative to a proper crown.

DOLLS

◆

Rapid City, South Dakota. 1983. 84 inches square. Twenty-five 13½-inch squares, hand-appliquéd, buttonhole-appliquéd, counted cross-stitched, embroidered, and signed by the Black Hills Quilters Guild for member Marie Andrew. Assembled and hand-quilted by Marie Andrew.

Sunbonnet Sue resides amid dolls of all patterns and nationalities on this friendship project made for Marie Andrew. Marie has an extensive collection of porcelain dolls for which she fashions clothes, so it was only natural that she choose her favorite subject when her name was drawn at a guild meeting. She distributed muslin squares and asked quilters to appliqué any kind of doll they could imagine onto it. (Photograph by Paul Jones.)

APPLE BOX LABELS

◆

Yakima, Washington. 1979. 103 × 110 inches. Fifty 9 × 10-inch blocks, appliquéd, embroidered, hand-quilted by members of the Yakima Valley Museum Quilters Guild, for their second fund-raising project.

One of the reasons this checkerboard quilt looks like old apple crates stacked in a warehouse is because the stitchers were working from the real thing—fifty antique labels within the Yakima Valley Museum's extensive collection. Each block is a mirror in miniature of its old paper antique. The "Hy-Land Kids" are perfect reproductions down to their dimpled chins. Shades of gray embroidery make the bell shimmer on "Independent Yakima Apples." Some of the sixty volunteers are related to the orchard owners whose labels they re-created: Sherry Udell made the "Udell's-Unexcelled," Betty Strand made "Strand-Viking." Each participant was given an original label for color matching, plus a photocopy to cut up for appliqué templates. A second group machine-pieced the squares and hand-quilted apple designs in the white blocks. The powerful picture blocks provide dramatic contrast beside the white open spaces. The entire work raised $4,500 for the museum. (Collection of the Yakima Valley Museum, Yakima, Washington. Photographs by Ken Warren.)

DETELS

◆

"Hy-Land Kids," Jane Hutchins.

◆

*"Independent Yakima Apples,"
Lilli Ann Pollock.*

◆

"Clasen," Lucille Rosenau.

◆

"Congdon," Mildred Rogers.

MS SUE:
ALIVE AND LIBERATED

•

*Long Beach, California. 1986.
71½ × 83½ inches. Forty-two
signed 10-inch blocks designed by
friends and quilting partners of
Odette Teel. A pen-pal quilt, inspired, coordinated, and hand-
quilted by Odette Teel.*

Odette had a dream—to lib-
erate Sunbonnet Sue and her pal
Overall Bill from their usual faceless, prim, and proper poses. Inspired by Barbara Brackman and
Laurie Schwarm's 1979 quilt, Sun
Sets on Sunbonnet Sue *(where
the poor doll was all but done
in), Odette enlisted the talents of
quilters from Hawaii to England
to help take the cute old gal
where she's never dared to go.
Sue can be seen protesting the
plight of Mexican-American
maids, operating a chain saw,
racing a funny car, burning her
bra, and hang gliding. In one
square Sue trades her calico skirt
for a nifty jogging suit (instead
of those "hated blue bloomers
from gym class"). Odette chose
green sashing ("for life and
growth") and black intersections
("for drama"), and asked contributors to incorporate both colors in their twelve-inch muslin
squares. Her only other instructions were "have fun, and make
sure Sue's sunbonnet appears
somewhere in the design "hung
on wall, under her foot, whatever . . .")* (Photographs courtesy
of Odette Goodman Teel.)

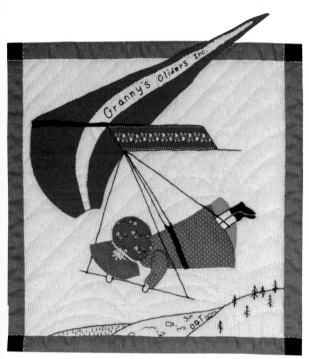

DETAILS

◆

"Hang Glider Sue,"
Odette Teel.

This square embodies Odette's favorite daydreams: to be a grandmother and to hang glide before she dies.

◆

"Hard Hat Sue,"
Nancy Halpern.

Nancy learned to use a chain saw at Haystack, Maine. The initials on the saw mean "Dick Cleveland Fan Club." Dick runs the annual Vermont Quilt Festival, where Nancy often shows her quilts and runs workshops.

◆

"Out of the Closet,"
Jean Ray Laury.

Jean inspired Odette's research into group quilts when she said at a workshop, "Whatever your dream is, begin it."

◆

"Cartoonist Sue,"
Genny Guracar.

Genny is a feminist cartoonist from northern California. Her Sue, looking a little like a fashionable Olive Oyl, is escaping from the top of the famous bonnet to draw for Ms. and Herdles magazines.

VICTORIAN
DOLLHOUSE QUILT

•

Albany, California. 1977. 66 × 88 inches. Two-inch sashing between the blocks, 3-inch border. Fifteen various-sized blocks hand-appliquéd and hand-quilted by students in the Albany adult education class taught by Roberta Horton.

Of all her forty-one group quilts, this is Roberta's favorite. From the cobwebs in the attic to the hams smoking in the cellar, the student-made fabric dollhouse invites all material girls to dive in and play. For this true-to-life class project, Roberta diverged from her usual method of providing neutral base fabric for repeated pattern blocks. Instead, each specific room, which is decorated according to Victorian tastes, is "wallpapered" in a different fabric. Roberta discovered from her vast group quilting experience that if she were instrumental in choosing the colors and fabric, the project worked more smoothly. Roberta's daughter, Cynthia, age sixteen at the time, was given this quilt by the student who won it. Cynthia was told she could have it when she's twenty-one. Meanwhile, it hangs in Roberta's bedroom, the decor of which, oddly enough, matches the sashing perfectly. (Photograph courtesy of Roberta Horton.)

JAPANESE KITES

•

Albany, California. 1979. 71 × 78 inches. Eighteen hand-appliquéd 14-inch blocks with 2-inch sashing. Center panel: 30 × 14 inches. Designed, machine-pieced, and hand-quilted by an Albany adult education class taught by Roberta Horton.

This is the kind of joyous, vibrant quilt that makes you wish you'd been there! The clarity of the images and the symmetry of shapes within corresponding blocks in the layout illustrates the importance of planning that is Roberta's hallmark. Roberta often worked out her group designs in units of four, so that each block would be assured a twin. No one knew exactly where their block would go until the final layout. The four kites in the corners represent one design unit. They could have been paired off anywhere on the quilt, but having them all facing inward from the quilt's outer reaches adds a bold, pure dimension to this brilliant quilt. The delicate black and wheat-colored print fabric, used as common ground fabric, looks textured and in motion. Simple black sashing highlights all the colors and allows each block to display its characteristic sensation independently. (Photograph courtesy of Roberta Horton.)

A Friendship Quilt of Celebrations

New York, New York. 1980. 64 × 86 inches. Made by 18 members of New York's Elder Craftsmen organization to commemorate its twenty-fifth anniversary. Coordinated by Colette Wolff. Fourteen 15-inch squares, 8 partial blocks in the corners. Appliquéd, hand-pieced, hand-quilted, Quilt-as-you-go.

This quilt is a communal expression of joy. A group of senior citizens gathered in midtown Manhattan and decided to set into stitches those special moments in their lives that give them cause to celebrate. Some blockmakers stitched decades of feeling into their work. Ruth Ostrow writes, "I thought back and realized I was happiest as a child when our holidays would come around. I always got new clothes, my mother would cook delicious foods . . . I put all the happy memories of the family and the way we were into my picture."

"My block depicts my arrival in New York City," writes Gertrude Lynn, who barely escaped the Holocaust in 1938. "The New York skyline is greeted by me with outstretched arms—clearly one of the happiest moments of my life."

Colette Wolff writes, "We set out to make a quilt that was more than ornamental. We made a quilt with heart." (Photograph by Jean Deval.)

I LOVE NEW YORK

•

Riverdale, New York. 1983. Twenty-four 8-inch squares, embroidered, appliquéd, and hand-quilted by members of the Hebrew Institute of Riverdale, New York. A fund-raiser, coordinated and machine-pieced by Paula Nadelstern.

From the tenement rooftops to the Twin Towers, from the depths of the underground subway to the tip of the Empire State Building where only King Kong dares to dangle, this fund-raising quilt reflects the textured, multi-ethnic fabric that is modern-day New York City. Hot dog stands, neon lights, the Central Park Carousel, and a Yankee shirt point to some of the city's popular entertainments. The ship-shaped Guggenheim Museum and a Broadway Playbill offer slightly more highbrow culture. The front page of the New York Times, *traced from the real thing, reports the news with rickrack and embroidery floss. Women of Riverdale's Hebrew Institute, all novices, chose the Big Apple theme to augment raffle sales. (Photograph by Bobby Hansson.)*

ME AND MY PIANO
◆

San Francisco, California. 1986. 56 × 63 inches. Nine 16 × 14-inch blocks designed by members of a "round robin" quilting group. Lace, velour, beads. Appliqué, embroidery, cording, padding. A pen-pal quilt, conceived, coordinated, machine-pieced, hand-quilted, tied, and tassled with blue and purple embroidery floss by Susan Schwarting.

Susan Schwarting combined her two passions—quiltmaking and piano playing—in this picture collage. She invited several of her "round robin" quilting contacts to design piano blocks. Her only instructions were that Susan have brown hair, and that her calico cat sit on the bench while she plays. One fabric artist re-created an oriental carpet from a magazine advertisement. A watercolor-looking fabric in the window casts a partly cloudy mood over the room. The musical score in the center square was typed onto the fabric; the black notes are corded, and the white keys are padded for a 3-D effect. Ivory-colored base blocks with dark blue sashing give the quilt an authentic piano flavor. This quilt won a blue ribbon in the Medium Quilts category at the San Francisco Quilter's Guild show, July 1986. (Photographs by Roy King.)

DETAIL
◆
"Me and My Piano,"
Janet M. Miller.

SCENES OF CHILDHOOD

◆

Bronx, New York. 1982. Twenty-four 8-inch blocks, hand-appliquéd, machine-pieced, and hand-quilted by the parents, grandparents, staff, and friends of the Amalgamated Nursery School. A fund-raiser, made under the direction of Paula Nadelstern.

As the parent of a nursery schooler, Paula decided to put her quiltmaking passion to money-making use, and boldly tacked up a raffle quilt sign-up sheet on the school's bulletin board. A handful of eager but skeptical quilt novices gathered in an apartment filled with toddler hubbub, and began looting button collections for their fabric forays back into childhood. Picture books and coloring books were surveyed for full-scale images. With the kitchen table lost under sewing shears, embroidery thread, coffee, and apple juice, there was no turning back. Six weeks later, on a nasty winter morning, the group held its collective breath and laid out the twenty-four appliquéd squares that each had diligently created in stolen time. Half of the fun of this quilt project was watching these confirmed "I'll sew on a button only if a safety pin won't work" needleworkers transformed into confident and proud artisans. (Photograph by Bobby Hansson.)

FANTASIES

◆

*Bronx, New York. 1983. 87 × 64
inches. Twenty-four 8-inch hand-
appliquéd blocks, machine-
pieced and hand-quilted by the
parents, grandparents, staff, and
friends of the Amalgamated Nursery School. Two-inch sashing, 8-
inch border. A fund-raiser, made
under the direction of Paula Nadelstern.*

Based on the success of the
first fund-raising quilt, there was
never a discussion about whether
there would be a second. Fantasy
(of the PG-rated variety) was
chosen as the quilt's theme. One
complete figment of each contributor's imagination is condensed
into each square canvas: streets
are paved with gold, flying car-
pets soar, mythical figures make
their magic. One block was returned with a lone figure on a
deserted island, looking more
like a nightmare than a fantasy.
Organizers took the liberty of
adding some company for him,
as well as a means of escape—a
boat, anchored in the sea of
shaded blue rickrack. Each block
is outlined in a one-inch border
print; one-inch square cornerstones eliminated the need for
ninety-six mitered corners. The
rhythmic folded-ribbon pattern of
the border integrates fabrics from
the sashing, block frames, and
cornerstones. (Collection of Fay
Certilman. Photographs by Bobby
Hansson.)

DETAILS

♦

"Staring at the Stars,"
Annmarie Pitta-LaScala.

Annmarie used the base block fabric in an unusual way—as the slice of Planet Earth. A little bebraided girl is planted on the planet's edge, gazing contemplatively at Saturn's thick gold rings and at a friendly-looking red Martian.

♦

"Treasure Chest,"
Wendy Holtzman.

This is one example where trimming fever triumphs. Pearls, sequins, and other imaginative found objects make up the richly packed treasure in this sunken chest. The common background fabric is used for sky.

♦

"Dragon," Paula Nadelstern.

Inspired from a children's book, this dramatic dragon is dressed in multicolored Ultrasuede scales and a combination of embroidery stitches dotted with gold thread on its tail. Paula merged eight different smoldering shades of needlepoint yarn to "couch" the spirals of smoke that erupt from its menacing throat. The textured yarns twist and wind from the common background, and are eventually smothered in a shadowy black fabric.

♦

"Deserted Island,"
cooperative effort.

Shades of blue rickrack ocean waves lap up to the banks of this isolated island where a half-hidden couple sits serenely.

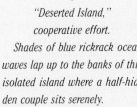

UNDER THE BIG TOP

◆

Bronx, New York. 1986. Twenty-one blocks of varied sizes, hand-appliquéd by the parents, grandparents, staff, and friends of the Amalgamated Nursery School. A fund-raiser, coordinated, designed, machine-pieced, and quilted by Lynn Silver, Dee Gomez, and Johanna Sparks.

A lot of trimmings, sequins, imagination, and a large dose of community spirit can be seen between the stitches on this animated quilt. Episodes of fabric fever are evident in the oversized poodle made from an inside-out sweatsock, and in the fire-leaping lion, boasting a mane of real lamb's wool. The Flying Feigenbergs (affectionately named after the school's director, Beverly Falk Feigenberg) look as if they shop from a Frederick's of Hollywood catalog. Light-dark contrasts are cleverly manipulated by using the same all-over print in a variety of blue values for the tiers of ground fabric, and by shadings of red in the streamers in the side borders. The cool blues recede while the warm reds advance. Conquering this quilt puzzle on graph paper, measuring templates for irregular shapes of varied sizes, and piecing off-grain edges together made this project as difficult to coordinate as it looks. (Photographs by Bobby Hansson.)

DETAILS

◆

"Poodle," Ethel Wickham.

◆

"Clown," Teri Cohen Meskin.
Patches, the calico clown, is
busy spilling festive-looking se-
quin-confetti out of his purple
barrel. Teri secured each sequin
with a bead.

◆

"Hoop-Jumping Lion,"
Dee Gomez.

◆

"Flying Feigenbergs,"
Johanna Sparks.

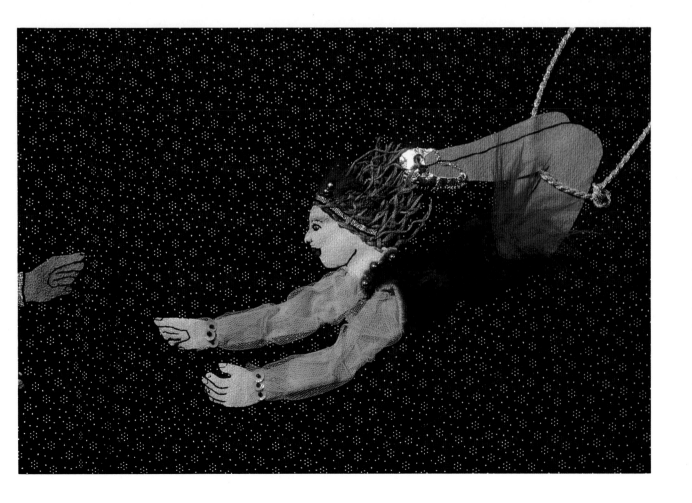

SALUTE TO BROADWAY

◆

New York, New York. 1985. 90 inches square. Sixteen 16-inch blocks hand-appliquéd by thirty members of The Needles End Quilting Group, under the direction of Lupe Miller. Hand- and machine-quilted by Lupe Miller. Commissioned by the Museum of American Folk Art.

The best of Broadway, from Big River *to* 42nd Street, *from* Peter Pan *to* Cats, *is reenacted on this spectacular satiny quilted stage. The soft sculpture* Dancin' *figures in the lower left virtually soft-shoe right off the quilt.* Hello Dolly, *capped in real fuschia plumage, parades down red velvet steps. Real fabrics in creative combinations add class to the costumes: Mr. Higgins from* My Fair Lady *sports a real cashmere coat. Wedding revelers in* Fiddler on the Roof *wear pure silk. Simple black satin sashing dramatically defines each lively scene. Thirty urban stitchers from all walks of life—painters, supervisors, therapists, housewives, restaurateurs—shared fun, moral support, and good wine every Sunday in Lupe's apartment. Some came for breakfast and stayed until dinner; in between they translated* Playbill *covers into beautiful fabric collages. (Permanent Collection of the Museum of American Folk Art.)*

MOTHERING AMERICA

•

Medford, Massachusetts. 1986. 42 × 54 inches. Twenty 12-inch squares made by Tufts University students as a class project.

"Mothering America" is a women's study course at Tufts University, designed to explore the myth and reality of motherhood in America. "Mothering America" is also a quilt—thought up by Professor Elizabeth Ammons as a way to engage her class in the nitty-gritty process of creating women's art. "Quilting is corporate. It is women's art; it is poor people's art; it is functional art," Ammons writes. "But above all it is collectively produced art, and we can learn from that." She challenged male and female students alike to sew a scene, a set of symbols, or a meaningful pattern drawn from course literature (which ranged from Harriet Beecher Stowe to Adrienne Rich) or from personal reflections. Students set to work using appliqué, embroidery, crayons, paint, or hand-piecing techniques on muslin squares. Three scenes are inspired from Alice Walker's novel, The Color Purple. One is an X-ed-out pinup girl, another is an abstract birthing scene (baby's head as globe crowning inside a flower). "We were amazed to see that, in our eyes at least, we had created something beautiful," Ammons writes. This unusual class project is permanently displayed at Tuft's Women's Center. (Photograph by Katie Kemp.)

J.C. PENNEY CELEBRATES AMERICAN STYLE

◆

Eastern Region. 1986. 66 inches square. Sixteen 12-inch hand-appliquéd and machine-pieced blocks. Assembled and hand-quilted by the Martha Washington Quilters Guild, McMurray, Pennsylvania.

From Maine to Hawaii, more than seven thousand customers throughout all of J.C. Penney's fifteen hundred nationwide stores entered original quilt squares in the "J.C. Penney Celebrates American Style" Quilt Contest, sponsored in cooperation with the Museum of American Folk Art, New York City. Each store selected a single best entry and sent it to one of the company's five regional offices, where sixteen top winners were selected and awarded $500 gift certificates. These customer-made blocks display an astonishing array of materials and techniques. Some are original interpretations of traditional patterns, while others are appliquéd with free-form wit and whimsy. In this quilt from the Eastern Region, Miss Liberty's torch illuminates circles of farmland, hand-holding children, a Native American, and eight different versions of Old Glory. The Martha Washington Quilters integrated the predominant red, white, and blue hues of the blocks with a dark blue pin-dot sashing. (Photograph courtesy of J.C. Penney.)

J.C. PENNEY
CELEBRATES
AMERICAN STYLE

◆

*Southeastern Region. 1986. 66
inches square. Sixteen 12-inch
hand-appliquéd and machine-
pieced blocks. Assembled and
hand-quilted by the Gwinnett
Quilters Guild, Lilbuin, Georgia.*

*This quilt from the southeast
is a pictorial ode to Mom's apple
pie and everything it stands for.
Miss Liberty perches proudly
upon a festive cake, while a
wound-up baseball player in a
neighboring block appears to
take aim at her. Meanwhile, in a
far distant square, Betsy Ross
calmly executes her famous
stitches. Luscious landscapes en-
circled by traditional piecework
are separated by a regal eagle.
The set of this quilt is almost a
negative of the previous one. The
two, side by side, provide a fascinating comparison of the effects of opposite uses of dark and
light fabrics for sashing and borders. The Gwinnett Quilters organized these winning blocks with
simple sashing strips in a light
blue print. They established a
stable and concrete external
boundary with the wider dark
blue border. Many districts incor-
porated the extra non-winning
blocks into quilts, pillows, pictures, etc., for auction or dona-
tion to charity. (Photograph
courtesy of J.C. Penney.)*

J.C. PENNEY CELEBRATES AMERICAN STYLE

•

Southwestern Region. 1986. Approximately 66 inches square. Sixteen 12-inch hand-appliquéd and machine-pieced blocks. Assembled and hand-quilted by the Quilter's Guild of Dallas, Texas.

This group of winning squares represents wonderful local, regional, homestyle, and patriotic interpretations of the contest theme, "A Celebration of American Style." One block contrasts urban and rural America, while another condenses the history of American transportation within its nutshell borders. A barber shop quartet sings the National Anthem, as an astronaut plants the American flag on the moon. In honor of the Statue of Liberty Centennial, Miss Liberty is dressed in both traditional and contemporary guises. The combination of red, white, and blue is the moderator for these fabric pictures; dark blue and white variable stars intersect the pale blue sashing; reds of different widths and shadings highlight the warm tones in the blocks. Contest organizer Madeline Guyon gave the groups diagrams to help them determine the size and assembly of their assigned blocks. Somehow, despite uniform directions, this Texas quilt is just a little bit bigger than the rest of the nation's. (Photograph courtesy of J.C. Penney.)

J.C. PENNEY CELEBRATES AMERICAN STYLE

•

Western Region. 1986. 66 inches square. Sixteen 12-inch hand-appliquéd and machine-pieced blocks. Assembled and hand-quilted by the Friendship Quilt of Whittier, California.

The block in the lower right-hand corner says it all: Made in the U.S.A. As the flag unfurls over amber waves of grain, a tenacious cowgirl gets a good grip on her hat. Bison amble, prospectors sift for gold, traditional pieced baskets overflow with goodies. There's even a hamburger with all the fixin's! The Whittier quilters turned an unexpected, asymmetrically colored sashing idea into a well-balanced montage. Each block is stripped with red fabric at the left and bottom, and pink at the right and top. The left and bottom blocks are completed in a thin strip of pink and a wide panel of red. This sequence is reversed at the right and top borders. Yellow and white pieced stars tumble in all the intersections. Dark blue binding contains the whole shebang. (Photograph courtesy of J.C. Penney.)

THROUGH CHILDREN'S EYES

•

Staten Island, New York. 1986. 72 inches square. Quilt Contest For Children ages six to ten, sponsored by Laura Ashley, Inc. Sixteen 12-inch picture squares translated from children's prize-winning sketches. Machine-pieced, hand-appliquéd, and hand-quilted by the Staten Island Quilters Guild, under the direction of Susan Frye.

This red, white, and blue quilt hails the Statue of Liberty on her one hundredth birthday with childlike renditions of herself and several Manhattan landmarks—the World Trade Center, the Empire State Building, and the George Washington Bridge. Maintaining the young artists' flair for design, the Staten Island Quilters Guild successfully re-created into fabric squares the winning drawings from sixteen New York State children, and assembled them into a simple but striking, asymmetrical setting using filler stars and striped blocks. The quilt retains the childlike naiveté of the original artwork. Raffle money for this quilt will benefit the Foundation for Children with Learning Disabilities. Laura Ashley contest quilts from seven other participating states were exhibited along with Through Children's Eyes *at the Great American Quilt Festival, April 1986. (Photograph courtesy of Laura Ashley, Inc.)*

QUILTERS' NEWSLETTER MAGAZINE 15TH ANNIVERSARY FRIENDSHIP SAMPLER

♦

Wheat Ridge, Colorado. 1985. 52 inches square. Nine 12-inch blocks entered in QNM contest. Pieced, appliqué, embroidery; assembled by Diane Sprague of Wheat Ridge, Colorado. Unquilted.

Ever since its first issue in 1969, Quilters' Newsletter Magazine *has chronicled the traditional quilt's contemporary revival. The editors decided to celebrate the magazine's fifteenth anniversary by asking contributors to submit an original twelve-inch block that "commemorates the development of the quiltmaking art and/or QNM from 1969 to the present." In "Fifteen Years of Inflation," top left, the balloons are executed in every technique from nine-patch to strip piecing. "Finish the Bloomin' Block," bottom left, spells "Quilts" with the poem:*

> *Quietly our dreams*
> *Unfold*
> *Ideas bloom in shapes*
> *Lovingly sewn*
> *To QNM happy 15th and*
> *Simply thank you.*

The silhouette in the rocking chair, "Yesterday Reconsidered," suggests that the quilt has evolved "from quiet necessity to aesthetic adventure." (Collection of Quilters' Newsletter Magazine.*)*

GREENHAM COMMON PEACE CAMP QUILT

•

Boise, Idaho. March 1984. 96 inches square. Thirty-two 12-inch blocks pieced in crazy style by the Boise Peace Quilt Project. Hand-quilted.

Jolted by the horror of nuclear war, two Boise women decided to do something: to "wage peace from a quilting frame." They made a patchwork quilt in 1981, and sent it to citizens in Russia as a gesture of friendship. Its people-to-people peace-quilting idea has since inspired fifteen more Boise quilts, and twenty more projects spawned in different cities around the world. Some of the Boise quilts have been sent to Japan, England, the Soviet Union; others serve as quilted peace prizes to honor activists, such as Charlie Clements, Norman Cousins, and Helen Caldicott. One is being passed around to all one hundred U.S. Senators with an embroidered invitation to "rest beneath the warmth and weight of our hopes for the future of our children." Another is being used to raise consciousness and money for humanitarian aid in Nicaragua.

This crazy quilt was given to the women of Greenham Common who surrounded a U.S. nuclear base outside of Newbery, England, weaving symbols of life into its ten-mile fence. Bound boldly in black and solid Amish-colored piecing, this webbed quilt was presented to a founding mother of the Greenham Women's Peace Camp. (Photograph by Heidi Read.)

SISTER MARJORIE TUITE'S PEACE QUILT AWARD: "CELEBRATE THE PEACEMAKERS!"

•

Boise, Idaho. February 1985. 108 inches square. Thirty-two 12-inch blocks appliquéd, embroidered, and reverse appliquéd by the Boise Peace Quilt Project. Hand-quilted.

This field-of-doves design was awarded to Sister Tuite, a Dominican nun and activist in the arenas of peace, justice, and women's rights. Included among the peacemakers' names embroidered on each square are Dr. Benjamin Spock, Rev. Jesse Jackson, Mary Baker Eddy, and Bishop Desmond Tutu. Sister Marjorie Tuite, who died of a disease she contracted in Nicaragua, gives us hope in the power of cooperative action. Her quilt now resides at Church Women United in New York City. Pete Seeger, the first Peace Quilt Award Winner, writes that "the patchwork quilt is a symbol of the world that must come; a new pattern made of many old patterns. We'll stitch this world together yet. Don't give up!" (Photograph by Heidi Read.)

THE JOINT
SOVIET-AMERICAN
PEACE QUILT

◆

Boise, Idaho. March 1986. 108 inches square. Cooperatively designed and stitched by Boise Peace Quilters and the Soviet Women's Committee as a gesture of friendship between the two nations. Forty 12-inch blocks depicting twenty American and twenty Soviet children. Hand and machine appliqué, hand and machine embroidery, fabric paint.

After five years of visiting each others' countries, quilters from Idaho and the Soviet Union decided to create a project together. This red and gold beauty is the result of their international vision. American women stitched the faces, using photographs of the real children from both nations. It's impossible to tell which children are Americans, which are Soviets. Russian women sewed trees, animals, suns, and words of peace into the quilt's borders; the central motif is adapted from a Soviet poster. The project, which is batted with "Peace Fleece" made from both Soviet and American sheep, was displayed in the conference room in Geneva, Switzerland, during the fourth round of arms talks between the super powers. This message in fabric "encourages people everywhere to insist that world governments mediate conflict with justice and respect for life," said Barbara Herbich, who is planning a documentary film about the quilt. (Photograph by Stan Sinclair.)

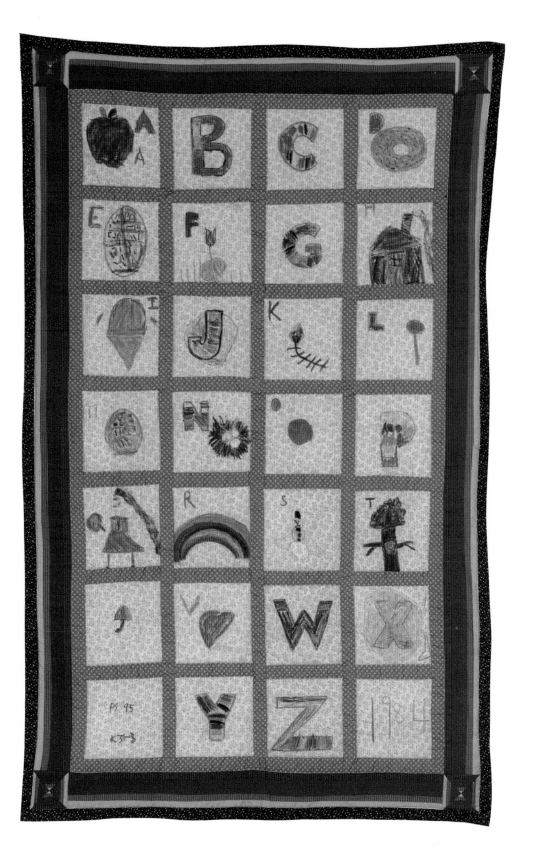

ALPHABET QUILT

•

Bronx, New York. 1985. 34 × 54 inches. Twenty-six blocks made by Elaine Greenfield's kindergarten students at Public School 95 as a class art project. Coordinated, machine-pieced, and machine-quilted by Paula Nadelstern.

Inspired by a kindergarten teacher who seemed eager to incorporate all kinds of creative projects in her curriculum, and by her daughter, Ariel, who, at age five, seemed willing to try anything, Paula decided to help the class make a quilt with fabric crayons. Every child picked a letter in the alphabet, and drew a symbol on light blue fabric to illustrate it. For those kids who weren't yet able to draw a design, she outlined a big fat letter and they colored it in. At home, Paula sashed the little masterpieces and strip-pieced fabrics of primary colors for the border. Rather than let the stripes butt each other at the corners, she connected them with blocks of four striped triangles. (Photograph by Bobby Hansson.)

HEBREW ALPHABET QUILT

◆

Hunter, New York. 1970. 47 × 69 inches. Twenty-four 8-inch blocks made by high school seniors as a summer camp project, under the direction of Paula Nadelstern.

This represents Paula's very first group quilt project. As a young counselor at a Leadership Training camp in beautiful up-state New York, she decided that quilting for campers was an ac-ceptable way to while away the allotted hobby time. A collection of high school seniors from around the country appliquéd and embroidered each Hebrew al-phabet symbol with an appropri-ate illustration. Hint: the quilt must be read from right to left, just like the real thing. Because the Hebrew alphabet has only twenty-two letters, this alphabet is buttressed by a sun block in the upper right and an owl block in the lower left, representing day and night, the beginning and the end. (Photograph by Bobby Hans-son.)

PUZZLE QUILT

◆

Bronx, New York. 1986. 58 × 58 inches. Sixteen 12-inch blocks with 2-inch sashing, machine-pieced by fourth grade students at P.S. 95, Bronx, New York. Directed by Paula Nadelstern, an artist in residence sponsored by the Amalgamated Housing Cooperative.

Hidden patterns and the magic of color were some of the lessons learned by thirty-two fourth-graders who made this brilliant visual game quilt. Each square has an identical twin in terms of its pattern. Only the colors, chosen by the students from a palette of fourteen traditional Amish solids, are different. The children worked in pairs on each block, sharing the cutting and machine-stitching, and conferring on design decisions in tandem. Paula attached the black sashing, and all the children helped baste and tie their masterpiece. One boy said he would "jump up and down, and show it to my cat and my parents" if the quilt were ever featured in a book. (Photograph by Bobby Hansson.)

INTERNATIONAL YEAR OF THE CHILD

◆

Jamaica, New York. 1979. 62 inches square. Twenty 7½ × 10½-inch blocks, depicting children from around the world. Block frames, 1½ inches; border, 4 inches. Made by fifth graders at P.S. 48, Jamaica, Queens, under the direction of their librarian, Jean Linden.

Jean Linden, a devoted elementary school librarian, now retired, was undaunted by the urban blight that surrounded P.S. 48 in Queens. She lifted the spirits, and the defeated egos, of her students by using quiltmaking to entice them to read. "Our quiltmaking is a cooperative effort," writes Jean, "and we avoid the 'That's my block' approach. The children who are working that day continue on whichever block needs finishing." "International Year of the Child" is one of twenty-odd projects inspired by her slogan "Read It and Quilt It." Expanding on Ruby Drake's "Children of Many Nations" patterns, a group of fifth graders researched costumes and atlases to make this multinational quilt authentic. "Personally," Jean writes, "I believe happy children learn better." This quilt now hangs in Jean's grandson's room. (Photograph by Amanda Moody.)

WE'RE ALL EQUAL
LET'S GO FOR IT!

•

*Quincy, Massachusetts. 1983. 85
inches square. Sixteen 17½ ×
17-inch blocks appliquéd and
embroidered by three hundred
students at Furnace Brook elementary school. Coordinated and
assembled by Carol Anne Grotrian. Hand-quilted and tied by
parents and staff.*

*A mustachioed nurse, a blond-
haired firefighter, a dinosaur, and
a rainbow of races inhabit this
idealized quiltland of sexual
equality. Each class, from kindergarten through sixth grade,
jointly designed one square that
reflects the project's chosen
theme. Sixth graders made "Role
Reversal," which consists of two
clasped hands—behind the
woman's is money, behind the
man's is a bag of groceries. Third
graders made "Equality Round
the World"—a globe, on which
the Falkland Islands (a current
event at the time) are virtually as
big as Africa. Children brought
fabric scraps from home, and
parent volunteers helped to cut
and safety-pin the appliqué
shapes to the muslin squares.
Large-eyed tapestry needles
threaded with yarn were used to
overcast fabric pieces without
turning the edges. The project,
designed to further sex equity in
Quincy public schools, was
funded by the Women's Educa-
tional Equity Act with the help of
NETWORK, a nonprofit research
service. (Photograph by Carol
Anne Grotrian.)*

FACES AND
FIFTH GRADE
AND FRIENDS

Houston, Texas. 1983–86. Made by fourth and fifth graders, respectively, in the Kinkaid School.

The Kinkaid School in Houston, Texas, incorporates quilting into its curriculum for all age levels. Every three years, preschoolers through twelfth graders produce a class quilt per grade for auction to benefit the school. One of the most ambitious quilts, Fifth Grade and Friends, *was stitched around the theme "my favorite animal." Each student translated a picture of his or her favorite animal into an appliqué picture block. The art teacher noted that "the students were encouraged to express their own individuality and were only assisted in technique. They were very proud of the result." The gathering of happy pink faces is a collection of fifty-six fourth graders' self-portraits. In 1986, all fourteen quilts were auctioned for a total of close to $80,000, with the fifth grade quilt going for $14,000. The real winners are the children. Mary Reddick, who teaches quilting in the school, writes of the experience: "Sharing our joy and knowledge with the children in our communities will enrich us all and further quilting as an expressive art form for the future." (Photographs courtesy of Mary Reddick.)*

WEAVER OF DREAMS

•

Atlanta, Georgia. 1985–86. 8 × 10 feet. Various sized blocks, made by elementary through high school students from network schools across the country, illustrating Dr. Martin Luther King's philosophical legacy. A joint venture of the Martin Luther King, Jr., Family of Schools Network, the Martin Luther King, Jr., Center for Nonviolent Social Change, and the American Can Company. Initiated by Carolyn Jones. Coordinated and designed by Marie Wilson. Quilt-as-you-go.

Children's dreams of racial equality are woven together in this appliquéd tribute to Dr. Martin Luther King, Jr. The "Round the Twist" pattern framing each block symbolizes the unified goals of the network of schools affiliated with the civil rights leader. Principals and community representatives selected three blocks from each of the thirty-five network schools on the basis of workmanship, historical significance, and creativity. In New York, volunteers from the Gotham Quilters' Guild and the Manhattan chapter of the Embroiderers' Guild of America completed the project. In Atlanta, Coretta King added the final two stitches on January 14, 1986, at the quilt's dedication. It now hangs in the Rosa Parks Room of the Martin Luther King, Jr., Center for Nonviolent Social Change, Atlanta, Georgia. (Photograph by Theobald G. Wilson.)

BARBARA'S BOWEN
NURSERY SCHOOL
QUILT
•

Newton Centre, Massachusetts. June 1985. 84 inches square. Sixteen 9-inch picture blocks made by nursery school students for their teacher, Barbara Quebec. "Trip around the world" pattern in rainbow colors is strip-pieced, machine-pieced, and tied by parents of Bowen Cooperative Nursery School, under the direction of Janet K. Springfield.

Using fabric crayons on paper, a class of four- and five-year-old preschoolers drew pictures of gifts they wanted to give their teacher, Barbara, which were then transferred by ironing onto muslin squares. The idea for the setting is simple, Janet says. "I took a traditional quilt pattern which could be easily pieced, and substituted the children's drawings in a symmetrical arrangement for certain elements of the original pattern." Other suggested patterns are Log Cabin, Double Irish Chain, Ohio Star, Churn Dash, or Nine Patch. The inscription on the back of the quilt says,

> *for Barbara,*
> *With love and thanks*
> *for a wonderful year!*

> *—made by the children,*
> *with a little help*
> *from a friend.*

(Photograph by Janet K. Springfield.)

BILLIE'S BOWEN NURSERY SCHOOL QUILT

•

Newton Centre, Massachusetts. June 1986. 56 inches square. Sixteen 12-inch blocks, embroidered and machine-pieced by parents of the Bowen Cooperative Nursery School for teacher Billie Foster. Designed and coordinated by Janet K. Springfield; tied by Janet Springfield and Nadia Maddens.

When a teacher at a Newton cooperative nursery school announced he was moving to New Hampshire, parents secretly planned a personalized going-away quilt. Since his students were all of three years old, the mothers decided to forego crayon pictures in favor of children's handprints and "signatures." Wee hands were traced on paper, transferred to muslin, and then outlined in embroidery by each mother. Log cabin frames in pinks, purples, and blues were machine-pieced in "assembly line" fashion. The entire soft, elegant work, bordered in a large floral pattern, took just three weeks to complete. Janet Springfield imparts the following words-to-the-wise for anyone attempting this pattern: "Since all the hands needed to point to the center, and the blocks had to be turned so the barn-raising pattern would appear, I would recommend sewing the blocks together first, and then embroidering the hands." (Photograph by Janet K. Springfield.)

PROGRESSIVE
PICTORIAL
STAGE 1

◆

Flushing, Michigan. 1986. 42 inches square. Hand-appliquéd and embroidered. Initiated, co-ordinated, and hand-quilted by Caron Mosey, who will donate it to the American Quilters' Society Museum, Paducah, Kentucky.

Caron Mosey invented a chain letter project that operates much like the telephone game we all played as children. Armed with the lists of names and addresses of all the quilters featured in her book America's Pictorial Quilts, *Caron outlined a simple house on a 42-inch square piece of muslin and sent it to the first name on the list. Each participant was asked to add one fabric detail to the evolving scene, sign the border in pencil, and send it to the next person on the list within five days. Every fifth stitcher was asked to send Caron a postcard to let her know where the quilt was hiding out; every tenth was asked to return the work-in-progress so that Caryn could document its progress with her camera. (Photograph by Caron Mosey.)*

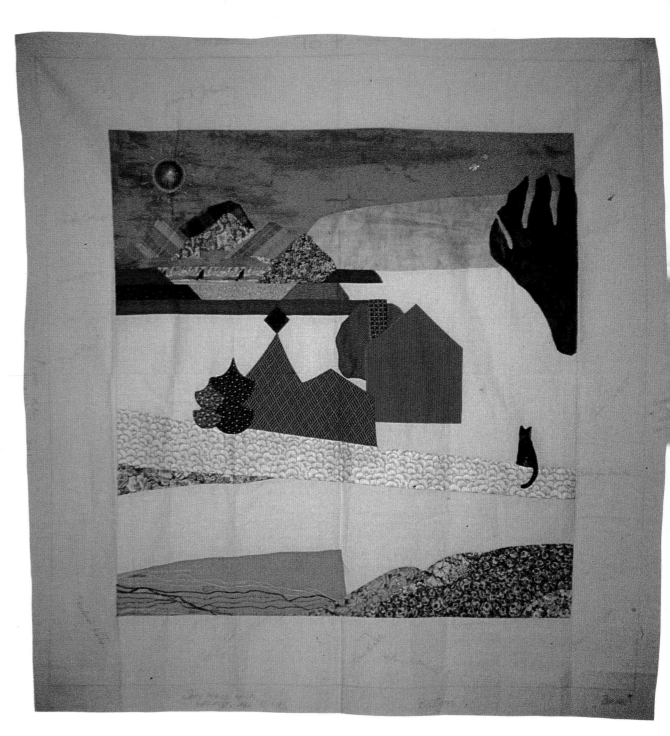

C·H·A·I·N
L·E·T·T·E·R
Q·U·I·L·T·S

**PROGRESSIVE
PICTORIAL
STAGE 2**

◆

(Photograph by Caron Mosey.)

**PROGRESSIVE
PICTORIAL
STAGE 3**

◆

(Photograph by Caron Mosey.)

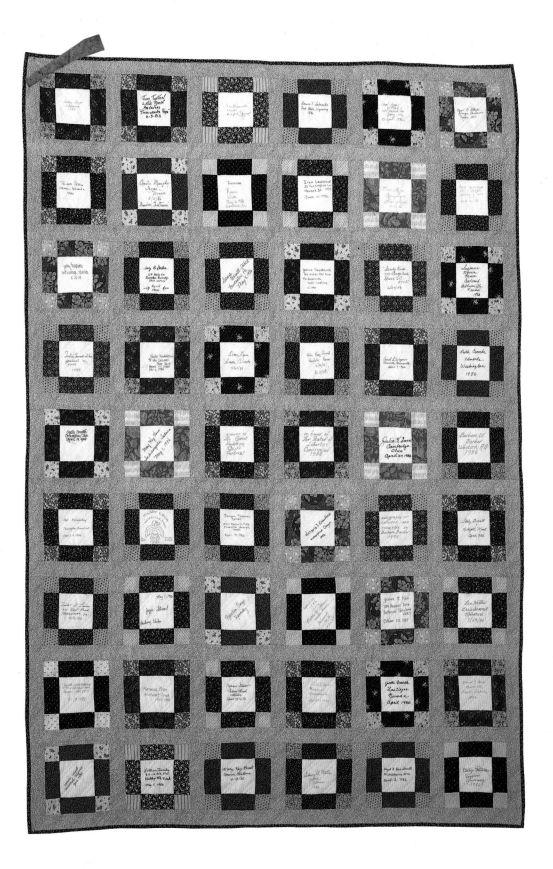

LIBERTY WINNERS

◆

Westerley, Rhode Island, 1986–87. 46 × 72 inches. Fifty-four 6-inch blocks signed by winners of the 1986 Great American Quilt Festival. Designed, strip-pieced, and channel-quilted by Barbara Barber. Sashing: 1⅜ inches wide.

History dictates that American craftswomen are called to the quilting frame to help commemorate important national events, and the 1986 Statue of Liberty Centennial was no exception. Fifty-one state winners of The Great American Quilt Festival convened in New York City in the spring of that year to participate in the Statue of Liberty's birthday, and to witness each other's prize-winning expressions of freedom in fabric. For many it was a very moving experience. Barbara Barber, the Rhode Island state winner, decided to create her own keepsake of the event within the framework of another American tradition—the signature quilt. She asked all the winners to sign a four-inch muslin square, then pieced the results together using a variation nine-patch design in antique blues and browns. The colors were chosen specifically to remind us of scrap quilts made one hundred years ago—the year Miss Liberty was erected. In order to make the quilt symmetrical, Barbara filled in three additional squares with explanations about the quilt's purpose. (Photograph by William Hays II.)

P·A·R·T

2

DESIGNING THE QUILT

Background
·
MORNING, NOON, AND NIGHT

Getting Started

*S*tart with a collection of enthusiastic people who want to create a quilt, for whatever reason. From that point on, anything is possible. There is no right or wrong way to select a framework. Your choice is determined by:

- the group's objective
- its time limits
- its collection of personalities.

All we can suggest is that you talk and plan before you take your first scissor snip. And be flexible. Whenever a group of people tries to do anything, expect surprises.

Every group quilt has its own evolutionary history. Some projects grow naturally out of old friendships, ancient scrapbags, and time-tested talent. Others bring a mixed bag of strangers to the quilt frame to commemorate a concrete occasion—like a neighborhood's facelift. (See *House on the Hill,* page 50.) One quilt evolved from a single person's passion for the piano, and a list of recruits willing to play along with her. (See *Me and My Piano,* page 88). The process of making the quilt is just as important as the quilt itself. A pleased group of stitchers produces a pleasing quilt and a passel of memories.

The initial order of attack is to gather the group, determine the theme, pick the quilt type and size, and draw up a time frame. Then see what happens . . .

PICKING THE THEME

◆ ◆ ◆

Usually, when it's least expected, the idea to make a group quilt flashes like a cartoon light bulb in one person's head. Perhaps a best friend is moving, a favorite teacher is getting married, a charity group needs a raffle prize for its big fund-raising bash, a town is having a birthday. Some like-minded people may be looking for a perfect visual gesture toward world peace, or, maybe you and your scrap pile are just very lonely—there are hundreds of reasons to gather a group and make a quilt.

If the quilt is for a specific person, the theme will probably sprout up automatically. If it's for a town or neighborhood, you may want to take a trip to the library first, to collect illustrations of significant events, past and present. Ideas for fund-raising projects may be a little less obvious. The same nursery school may raffle an audacious circus quilt one year, a traditional patchwork house quilt the next—with equal monetary and aesthetic returns.

Literature has even been known to inspire a block or two. *The Crown Quilt* (page 76), designed for the publishing company's chairman of the board on his birthday, is dedicated to best-sellers. Each square is one employee's rendition of a famous Crown title. Scenes from Alice Walker's *The Color Purple* are peppered amid feminist symbols in *Mothering America* (page 95), a college class project quilt. Look in Chapter 9, "How to Make the Group Work," page 212, for more ideas. Once the topic is set, the size, type of group, techniques, and time frame will fall into place.

If a theme doesn't jump out and grab you and your group, try roaming through the color plates of this book to get the mental threads spinning. At this point, it is a good idea to decide if your quilt will be pieced or appliquéd, since certain ideas work better with one than the other.

Subjects can be limited or large. One project within these pages is dedicated to the quilter's singular obsession with Miss Sue and Overall Bill, old-fashioned country patterns; another celebrates joy and life, in all their personal permutations. The point is to let your imagination run loose.

Quiltmaking is people's art. It's functional art. The techniques required are simple, the hardware accessible, and the results are always original. No two people have the same color sense, the same needlework skills, the same design ideas. Quilts are large fabric canvases that allow potent imaginations to roam the seams freely. Personalities, idiosyncrasies, senses of humor, Bertha's penchant for purple, or Franny's obsession with lunch boxes all dance on quilt tops made by many hands. And if they dance in rhythm, the end product looks terrific.

PICKING THE SIZE

◆　◆

BASE BLOCK SIZE

◆

After theme, the next decision is base block size. The base block is the unit of fabric completed by each participant and then combined to make a quilt top.

The simplest quilts, and some of the most creative, contain square blocks all the same size. Eight- to ten-inch squares work well for appliquéing pictures, since they don't present an overwhelming space to fill. Twelve-inch squares are better for pieced blocks. They can be easily divided into an even-sized grid for drafting patterns. They also allow enough space to incorporate manageable shapes. The quilts in this book have blocks that range from five and one-half to eighteen inches.

QUILT TOP SIZE

◆

Don't be tempted to draft a detailed blueprint of the whole quilt at this stage of the game. You never know how many blocks you'll actually receive. Some people get carried away and begin churning out squares at assembly-line speed. Others prick their fingers once and give up. Remember, if you receive a paltry few, you can always expand the quilt with sashing, borders, and simple filler squares.

The quilt's function dictates its size. A wall hanging can be any size, depending on the number of blocks received. A fund-raiser should always be twin-sized (see "Fund-raisers," page 221). Keep in mind that your quilt will have to be quilted. The bigger the project the more time-consuming the quilting stitches. If you don't have seasoned quilters in your group, keep it twin-sized or smaller. Of course, a practical bed cover should fit the bed.

Size	Mattress Dimensions
Crib	27″ x 52″
Twin	39″ x 75″
Full	54″ x 75″
Queen	60″ x 80″
King	76″ x 80″

To determine the correct size for a specific bed, you must consider the drop—the distance from the top edge of the mattress to the floor. A bedspread falls to the floor, usually a distance of twenty-two inches, while a comforter just covers the side of the mattress, a distance of about ten inches. After calculating the correct dimensions, add a couple of inches to both the length and the width to account for the inevitable shrinkage that occurs when the quilt is stuffed and quilted.

ORGANIZING YOUR TIME

◆　◆　◆

There is no question that group quilts take time, but it's time greatly appreciated. People *cry*—routinely—when they receive these fabric gifts of love. Friendship quilts become treasured family heirlooms, community displays of pride, cherished expressions of love. Who knows, future folk art historians may even research your group quilt for a book.

I'm a firm believer in deadlines. Without them, the quiltmaking process can drag on indefinitely. Some quilts come equipped with natural deadlines: birthdays, weddings, retirement parties, fund-raising events. I find the devious two-deadline strategy very useful, with or without a pressing event: one deadline is communicated to the group; the second is known only to the organizer. Allow for human error, car failure, fabric store bankruptcy, tornadoes, and civic disturbances when you calculate your hidden agenda.

The following is a general time frame for an average appliqué pictorial block quilt. The first stages are divided between two types of groups: local groups that can meet regularly, and out-of-town groups that communicate exclusively through the postal system. For local groups, give yourself five to six months from beginning to end. Add about one month for mail groups.

1. ORGANIZATION TIME:

1 month—local   1 month—mail

◆

The idea is hatched. Do whatever you must to draw a group together. Tack up notices in your church, school, neighborhood fabric shop. Phone potential contributors, get addresses of others. A core group can help make initial decisions: theme, basic colors, fabric, techniques. Buy, prewash, and distribute base blocks.

2. DISTRIBUTE BLOCKS WITH RETURN DEADLINE:

1 month—local   6 weeks—mail

◆

Experts who study Type A/Type B personalities should really have a look at group quilters' attitudes toward deadlines. Some panic if their square isn't finished a week early. Others think April really means two weeks into July. From California, the laid-back state, we received this humorous complaint: "Stitchers were given one month to complete their blocks, most came back within two months, some took ten months, and some never came!"

One month is really ample time for a local group to meet, share skills, doodads, ideas, and good fun. The blocks that are nurtured in these quilt consciousness-raising sessions always seem to sparkle with a special inspiration.

Groups by mail take a bit more nudging. Your initial letter should include clearly written instructions. Invite all contributors to contact you for ideas and resources. Two weeks before deadline, send a friendly "how's it going?" postcard, or maybe a letter ballyhooing the stitching accomplishments of the group's pre-deadline fanatics.

Most of the blocks in this book took one to three months to be collected. One notable exception is the New York Lourette Quilt, where blocks collected between 1941 and 1967 were not put together until 1985!

3. COLLECTING THE BLOCKS:

1 week—local   2 weeks—mail

◆

Think of this step as double insurance. It's just another mind-game designed to make sure your quilt is completed on time without having to get angry at anyone, including yourself for poor planning.

4. DESIGNING AND PIECING
THE QUILT TOP:

1 month

◆

It probably makes more sense to describe what goes into this stage than to pretend that everyone uses his or her time the same way. The timing will depend on whether the following steps are being done by one person or a group.

- Press finished blocks and cut them to correct size
- Move blocks around like a puzzle to determine the best layout
- Make up extra blocks if needed
- Design dimensions, color, and fabric for lattice and borders
- Buy fabric
- Prepare and cut templates and fabrics
- Piece the top by machine or hand
- Attach batting and back to quilt top

5. QUILTING:

1 to 2 months

◆

This depends on the quilt's size, whether it will be machine- or hand-quilted, whether it will be done by novices, experienced quilters, one lone nut, or a group of mixed nuts.

6. PHOTOGRAPH:

as little as 1 day

◆

Most people ignore this important stage and regret it. So many quilters we contacted for slides had to search the ends of the earth for a picture of their masterpiece. Every stitcher who has given his or her time and talents will certainly want a souvenir of the finished product. Photos of fund-raising quilts can also be turned into postcards or posters to help sell raffles. Take a picture of the entire quilt, plus details, straight on, in good light. Bobby Hansson, a New York crafts photographer who specializes in good pictures and better jokes, says it's best if you photograph a quilt outside on a bright and sunny day. That way you will have a better chance of having equal distribution of light on the quilt's surface. Tack the quilt up to the side of a house, tape it to a brick wall, "or find two large NBA basketball players to stand behind it and hold it up." You can baste the quilt to a large sheet first to protect it from getting dirty. Make sure there are no tree branches or roof overhangs casting unwanted shadows.

Creating the Design

INTRODUCTION
TO COLOR AND FABRIC

* * *

A group quilt is a little like a marriage. Compromises must be made along the way, but the key to success is the mood of the whole. Color and fabric send the strongest mood messages from your quilt to the world at large. The wedding of the two will determine your work's overall impression: whether it is traditional, contemporary, simple, elegant, happy, subtle, splashy—or, ultimately, incompatible.

Look for a balance of contrast and harmony when you make your selections. Colors should contrast without competing for attention, fabrics should blend without boring each other. Keep these deceptively simple maxims in mind and your quilt will live happily ever after.

COLOR

*

Color preferences are a very personal thing. Some people get all dewy-eyed over a quilt pieced in shades of one color. Others go instantly to sleep. But realize that before viewers even notice what the quilt is all about, they will respond to the atmosphere created by your chosen colors.

Your choice will depend on:

- the collective color-consciousness of your group
- the recipient's tastes
- the general feeling you want your quilt to convey.

The final decision should be one that unifies the group. We can give a few guidelines here, a little color theory there. But in order to make the task more congenial, you must choose combinations that please you.

How can you tell what colors you like? Stroll through the quilts in this book and ask yourself why you like one quilt's colors, why you don't like another's. Attach concrete adjectives to your reactions: boring, vibrant, muted, rich, plain, elegant, dense, daring. You aren't writing a critique for an art journal, so it doesn't matter if anyone else understands what you mean.

Where should you begin with your own color selection? First, it's a good idea to understand the effects of various contrasts in color design. You can experiment by breaking out your kids' crayons (or your own, don't be proud) and coloring various combinations of your proposed design on graph paper. But keep in mind that crayons barely hint at the tactile dimensions of textiles.

The Spreading Effect. When my daughter was in kindergarten, she was intrigued by the "what's your favorite" question. Everything was fine until she asked me, "Mom, what's your favorite color?"—a can of worms for an obsessive color personality like myself. Even though I remember being five years old, and putting my prized box of sixty-four crayons in meticulous order according to popular taste (shoving the browns and gray-blues to the rear), I just couldn't hand her a "pink" or a "purple" to make her happy. I had to confuse her with: "I like all the colors for different reasons."

Colors are never isolated entities—especially on a quilt. *The spreading effect* refers to the way colors change depending on what colors and fabrics they are next to. In the quilt sample pictured here, the magenta diamonds are identical in size in rows A and B, yet each block appears different depending on the diamond's various background colors. Magenta looks muted next to forest green, but bright beside brilliant yellow. The less the triangles contrast with magenta, the more it "spreads" out of its boundaries. Row A begins with a gray square to highlight magenta's true value, then continues with cool colors—greens and blues—that blend and contrast with the center diamond, creating a tranquil effect. Row B looks much more vibrant. Its contrasting triangles are made from warm colors—reds, yellow, and oranges—producing a stimulating effect. Study the two rows to determine which color combinations look discordant to you, which look harmonious. Maybe you'll be pleasantly surprised.

When you are in the fabric store, drape your chosen bolts next to each other, stand back, and squint. Only then will you see the interaction of colors as they play side by side.

Black and White. A quick glimpse at the antique quilts in the history chapter will show you that white is a very traditional and very beautiful choice for base blocks and sashing on friendship quilts. White is still often considered the simplest choice because it "goes with everything." However, I find it very tricky to use in an appliquéd group quilt.

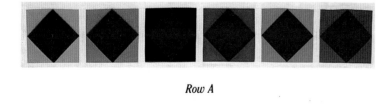

Row A

Row B

White has a tendency to expand and overflow its boundaries. Adding white to a color lightens it and produces a tint. The "spreading" of white affects its adjacent colors by creating a slightly washed-out or tinted effect. Black achieves the opposite effect. A black outline makes the enclosed colors seem richer and clearer in tone. The dark line controls the spreading effect, letting each color show "its true colors." An outline in white (or a high-value color) will make the enclosed colors less dynamic. The effect of black and white is illustrated in Row C. The black diamond looks smaller than the white. It's contained and clear in tone. The white diamond almost "spreads" out of its borders, looking larger, more airy than the black.

White or light sashing will pull light-colored blocks into one visual whole, dark sashing will separate them. If your group quilt has a variety of quite busy picture blocks, you may be happier if each square is set off from the others, rather than blended together. I find it easier to contain the vibrancy of each individual block with a black frame, and subtly weave them together with sashing.

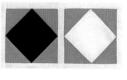

Row C

Light-Dark Contrast. *Value* is an artist's term for light and dark. Our ability to perceive something is based on contrasts and comparisons between light and dark. Every color has a certain value, determined by its position on the scale between white and black. Adding white lightens a color, producing a high-value color. Adding black darkens it, producing a low value. Powder blue has a high value; navy blue has a low value. The interaction of dark and light on the same surface stimulates interest and creates texture and depth. Closely related values have a calming effect; sharp value contrasts are more dramatic. Use the old squinty-eye technique to perceive a color's relative value in relationship to its neighbors.

Basic Colors. The color wheel system of organizing basic colors dates to the early eighteenth century. Any pair of the three primary colors mixed together makes a secondary color. Red and yellow make orange, yellow and blue make green, blue and red make purple. The six tertiary colors are mixtures of a primary and an adjacent secondary color. For example, red and purple make red-purple, red and orange make red-orange. Row D illustrates the primary and secondary colors.

Row D

Row F

Complementary Contrast. Try an experiment: Stare at a green square and then close your eyes. The after-image will be red. The mind's eye always seeks to restore balance, to find a color's complement, or its harmonious opposite. This is the physiological basis of the color wheel. Complementary color schemes combine two colors opposite each other on the color wheel. The contrast of complementary hues of the same value will be overwhelming. When placed next to each other they intensify each other's brightness and appear brighter than in any other context. Row E illustrates vivid complementary contrast by using red and green solid fabrics of the same value. Using various shades of complementaries may be equally pleasing.

Cool-Warm Contrast. Greens and blues are considered "cool" colors because they have a tranquil, airy, faraway feel. Reds and oranges are "warm" because they provide a stimulating, opaque, earthy effect. Yellow-green through violet is the cool side of the color wheel; yellow through red-violet is the warm side.

Cool colors tend to recede into the background. Warm colors catch the eye and advance from the ground. Row F shows green diamonds contained within a warm orange background and blended into a cool blue background. A combination of warm/cool colors can be used to establish a feeling of depth and volume. Of course, identifying colors in this way is subjective; the warmth or coolness of a color is relative to its surrounding colors.

Contrast of Proportion. Please don't think that balancing your quilt means providing equal *amounts* of two complementary colors, equal *amounts* of warm and cool colors, or equal *amounts* of dark tones and light tones. You have to tip the balance in each category, favoring one color over another, one contrast over another, or else the contrasts will cancel each other out. Too much contrast makes the eyeballs spin. Too much harmony makes a dull quilt.

Color Discord. Discord has a negative connotation. Synonyms for the word are conflict, disagreement, dissonance. When we say that colors clash, we mean that they seem to pull away from each other rather than relate harmoniously. Discord is not always a bad thing. In fact, mild color discord can be exciting, eye-catching, unexpected. Look at fashion. Look at graphic posters. Value is an important consideration when you look at the impression made by discordant combinations. Discord is greater when the value of two colors is similar. It will be more subtle when two colors have a great light and dark contrast.

Everyone has a different opinion about which colors are discordant and which are not. Look at Rows A and B of the color examples. One person may be appalled that magenta is next to chartreuse, another may never in a million years think of pairing magenta with red because they "don't go together." Approach color choices freely; seek the unexpected.

Row E

FABRIC

We can talk about color until we are various tonal values of blue in the face, but it's really fabric that makes the quilt canvas so special. Fabric is what we wrap ourselves in. Fabric provides the main appeal. Color takes on a whole new meaning when it's combined with the tactile dimensions of textiles. Prints change in color depending on what they are next to. The internal shades of color, no matter how subtle, serve to soften contrasts and provide depth and activity on the quilt's surface. Your choice will depend on:

- the quilt's function
- piecing and quilting techniques
- the skill of the stitchers
- your personal tastes.

See "Facts on Fabrics," page 148, for a detailed discussion of types of prints and their effects on design.

DESIGNING THE BASE BLOCK

Like color and fabric, design is highly individual. The best format for a group of unseasoned quilters is the ever-flexible block quilt—same-sized squares arranged in rows. It's amazing how this simple setting (complete with the perfect sashing) can make scores of wildly eclectic collages and color schemes seem perfectly orchestrated. The blocks provide a plain canvas for playing with preordained patterns or for applying boundless individual invention.

DESIGN STRATEGY

Once the theme is decided, you have two basic design strategies to choose from: stitcher's choice, where participants can create any image that comes to mind on their blank square, or the preordained option, where one image is chosen to be embellished or placed identically in each base block.

The stitcher's choice method often renders incredibly diverse results. Don't worry when the blocks return looking as if they've landed from different galaxies. Some will seem void and lonely, with a single image affixed to the center. Others' borders will be full to bursting with stories and images that span a lifetime. In the Elder Craftsmen's *A Friendship Quilt of Celebrations* (page 86), Gertrude Blaut depicts a tumultuous decade of her life. Her square shows how she escaped Nazi Germany and spent ten years in Shanghai, China, until she was finally granted an American visa. "I tried to put all this into my picture and the memories just flooded over me."

If you'd like centered designs to be in proportion to each other,

suggest a size guideline. For example, within a ten-inch block, some portion of the design should touch the perimeter of an imagined eight-inch square within the block. This will leave at least one inch of the ground fabric showing around the appliquéd shape.

All the blocks, no matter how incongruous, will be integrated by theme, fabric, and size of the base block. Skillful layout, sashing, and borders will also pull them together.

The preordained method lends a traditional, less busy look to your quilt. More initial planning and instructions are needed for it to work. A single image or scene is chosen to be placed on each block. Each member then adds his or her own personal touches to the block.

In Chapter Two, "An Album of Contemporary Quilts," we have organized three groupings of preordained quilts based on similar themes: the traditional schoolhouse block, the basket, and the ever-popular butterfly. These quilts, arranged from the simplest repeat patterns to the most gussied-up appliqués, prove that design possibilities are endless.

In *Basket of Flowers* (page 16), Mari Etta Fowler provided members of her South Dakota guild with the pattern and basket fabric and encouraged participants to stock them with their own choice of appliqué flowers. In *A House for All Seasons* (page 46), the third in a series of annual nursery school fund-raising quilts, stitchers were asked to furnish identical machine-pieced houses with a season and a personality. The scale of the houses is uniform, but the fabric and orientation is different.

BASE BLOCK COLOR AND FABRIC

Your next step will be to choose color and fabric for the base block. (See "Facts on Fabrics," page 148, for more details.) To guarantee visual continuity, I like to start the group stitching by supplying base blocks of the same fabric. I also find that by distributing precut squares, I've got a better shot at receiving on-grain blocks of the same size with right-angled corners.

I gravitate toward light values of "cool" colors for the base block. Transparent, airy, and calming are all good terms to describe the role I like the background to assume. The shapes and colors on a picture block shouldn't have to compete with a loud and boisterous background. A base block's presence should be felt, and not heard.

I find that light blue fabric, with an all-over print in minimal contrast, is very effective. The combination of pale blue with a simple print fabric acts much like a makeup base: it hides the flaws, it allows the other colors to step forward, and it blends with almost everything. Blue has the added advantage of subbing as sky or water in an appliqué picture.

I always instruct participants to leave part of the base fabric visible. This guarantees some continuity throughout all the blocks. Although one person always ignores my dictate altogether, most respond by dropping a central figure in the middle. Some inspired needleworkers have been known to work this rule right into their design, with ingenious results. In *The Crown Quilt*, Pam Thomas opened a window in her "Joy of Sex" square to reveal the blue base fabric, making it look like wallpaper in a bedroom. While exploring the fantastic in *Fantasies*, our nursery group manipulated the ground fabric in myriad ways. Annmarie Pitta-LaScala left a rounded slice of background on the bottom of her block to represent Planet Earth. A little girl with braids stands on top of the slice, contemplating the wonders of the solar system. In my contribution, the head of a fire-spewing dragon stands out at the left, against the light common base block fabric. The contrast of its smoky flames is eventually smothered into shadowy black.

"Staring at the Stars"

"The Joy of Sex"

"Dragon"

APPLIQUÉ COLORS AND FABRICS

•

Again, you have two choices: preordained color scheme or stitcher's choice. Some groups, such as the one responsible for the *Variable Star Scrap Quilt* (page 13), provide kits of fabric already cut up in shapes. Others simply identify a palette of colors to choose from (see *The Rose Quilt,* page 34).

The alternative is to allow each blockmaker to choose his or her own colors. I like this approach for group appliqué pictorials. The search for fabric and trimmings to translate into a picture connects the stitcher to her design and can be especially gratifying for the newcomer. Remind everyone to apply the theory of balance and contrast in their choice of colors and fabrics. Vary shades and tones, textures, and textiles. Consider the project's purpose: will it be washed often, or will it end up on a friend's wall, or (wishful thinking) behind glass in a museum?

Cottons and cotton-blends are the backbone of appliqué. A crisp, firmly woven fabric will hold its shape, and the edges won't ravel when they are turned under.

Ultrasuede is a colorfast, washable, and expensive material, available in a rainbow of delicious colors. It's perfect for tiny details, particularly for parts of the body. The edges don't ravel and it is easy to pierce with a sharp needle. Its only drawback is that ironing changes its texture. Remember to place a steam cloth over the Ultrasuede parts of a block.

Felt is fun for projects with children, although it doesn't have a good track record in the wash. What you cut is what you get, as in the *International Year of the Child* (page 110).

Bonded fabrics are constructed of two permanently joined layers that can provide interesting texture to your design. Check to see if the textile is colorfast, non-linting, and flexible. Experiment with edges to see if they ravel. Bonded fabrics are generally too thick to hem. If the edges are plagued with the ravels, consider fusible film to secure them.

Novelty fabrics require extra effort to secure the edges adequately, but their potential to entertain is worth it. For pictorial wall hangings, anything goes. Lamé can add the shiny three-dimensional touch you need for a skyscraper. An inch of mink on a hat in a crowd sparks a textured sense of realism. The wrong side of a brazen Chinese brocade may provide the antique look you covet for a picture frame.

Metallic materials and polished cottons reflect light, while other fabrics, such as corduroy and velvet, absorb light. The illusion of light, stitched into a quilt top, creates visual texture and depth. Depending on how it is cut, a single piece of light-reflecting fabric can glimmer in a variety of ways. The designer of "Country Weekends" interlaced the wrong and right sides of the same brown ribbon to make a realistic woven basket on *The Crown Quilt* (page 76).

"Under the Big Top"

TRIMMINGS AND FOUND OBJECTS

•

Trimmings are ornamental embellishments—things like ribbons, lace, braids, tassels, rickrack—that can be found in the trimming section of a sewing store. Found objects are not exactly gutter trash. They are decorative doodads—baubles, bangles, beads, rhinestones, feathers, sequins, parts of jewelry—that can be sewn onto a fabric picture.

My biggest problem with trimmings and objects is finding them when I need them. At the beginning of a project, I rummage through my transparent box of treasures looking for a remembered red ribbon, a longed-for looped lace, only to be diverted by a catchy piece of tiger skin that my daughter lovingly snatched up for me off her classroom floor. Such global problems!

With the proper peppering of the perfect objects, your design will transcend ordinary appliqué into unexplored realms of fabric collage. The only rules restricting creative use of rickrack and rhinestones are as follows:

· Consider the project's purpose. If the quilt will be washed, use trimmings manufactured specifically for garments, and check for colorfast and shrinking characteristics.

· Thin plastic ornaments that can be attached only with glue will either fall off while the quilt is being put together, or will bend out of shape when the quilt is stretched on a frame. If you've just gotta have it, add it *after* quilting, five minutes before the quilt goes on a wall.

· The trim you choose should serve its purpose. Some trims are more flexible than others. You can create curvaceous swirls to your heart's delight with bendable braids or rickrack. Restrict the use of inflexible trims —like wide, patterned ribbons—to relatively straight lines or mitered corners.

· Be forewarned: It's a rare person who can pass by a quilt filled with fun objects without copping a feel.

I bring my prized stash of trimmings and findings to early sewing sessions and watch people dive greedily into them, discovering creative impulses they never knew they had. I call it my collection of "raw materials," thus divorcing any preconceived notions one may have about the purpose of one particular doodad or other. I enjoy it when my accumulated finds are a source for inspiration. The designer of "The Rising of the Moon" sees angry waves breaking against the coast of Ireland in an inexpensive bunch of scalloped lace. A gaudy gem I've been hoarding for years becomes the perfect tacky touch for a billiard player's ring finger in "Pocket Billiards." Or, more literally, an itty bitty bead becomes an earring for "Baby Divine."

"Winter Scene"

"The Bridge of Sighs"

Glittery beads and multisided rhinestones are especially fun to incorporate into picture blocks. To avoid busyness, plot the inclusion of these shiny eye-catchers carefully. It's better to surprise the eye with a glint here, a sparkle there, than to jade the viewer with too much too soon.

Restraint and selectivity organize the composition. No matter how viscerally involved you become with your feathers and fur, try to hold yourself back. Don't succumb to trimming fever! (Common symptom: dumping all your favorite items on one block.) A composition made up of only beautiful objects can be as monotonous as a plain one. Remember to balance contrast and harmony in terms of textures and tonal values.

Sometimes your fingers fairly itch to manipulate an attractive material, even though you know it's probably too big, too thick, too loud, for your design. Consider how the rest of your design will be affected by this coveted object. If the novelty item doesn't stage a coup d'état, it belongs. If it stands out like a pumpkin in July, chuck it. The best way to understand the potential of trimmings is to see what others have done with them. "Treasure Chest" shows a creative use of well-attached sequins.

"The Rising of the Moon"

"Pocket Billiards"

"Baby Divine"

Thickly woven lace often contains a gallery of little designs that can be cut out for a picture—snowflakes, gargoyles, ghosts, as in "Winter Scene" and "The Bridge of Sighs" blocks in *Wedding Chupah* (page 66). Lace has a wrong and a right side. The right side has a visible cord around its designs. To make sure your lacy motif doesn't ravel, clip away the threads that hold the outlined design you want, keeping the cord intact.

"Treasure Chest"

DESIGNING THE BASE BLOCK

•

Here is your chance to breathe life into beads and brocades, to transform tweed into trees, to create a design with felt and feeling. This, folks, is fun. Your best resource is your sense of humor.

Work up a tentative sketch on graph paper and color it in various combinations, keeping in mind that crayons barely hint at the tactile textures of textiles. When choosing fabrics and trimmings, remember the aim is to translate the design into fabric skills, not just to make a carbon copy of a drawing in fabric. This means planning and analyzing the design so that your available materials can be used to their best advantage. For example, if you want to re-create a body of water, an ordinary print probably won't provide the movement and shading you want. Yet, if you layer waves of rickrack in shades of blue, green, and purple, suddenly the water comes alive with texture and movement as in "Deserted Island," from *Fantasies.*

"Deserted Island"

SOURCES OF INSPIRATION

•

If you hate to draw, have someone else do it for you. Or make a tracing from another source. Animals and human beings are particularly difficult to draw. You can borrow a posture by tracing from one source, dressing it appropriately for the occasion, and surrounding it with your own background. (See Chapter 6, "How to Make an Appliqué Base Block," page 170.)

Coloring books are great resources for tracings: their lines are bold, their colors vivid. One Oregon first-time blockmaker for *Cheryl and Dean's Wedding Quilt* (page 64) asked me to find silhouettes of two people talking on the telephone (she and Cheryl clocked in thousands of phone hours as teenagers). I sent her tracings of Bert and Ernie from a Sesame Street coloring book and she worked them into a successful design—complete with telephone wire.

Other resources are cookie cutters, greeting cards, wrapping paper, motifs cut out from printed designs, and children's picture books—especially illustrated fairy tales. Dover publishes a wonderfully versatile series of design motifs. See "Resources," page 229, for the address of its mail-order catalog.

Inspiration can be found in unlikely places, so keep your eyes open. Charlotte Warr Anderson, of Utah, writes about designing *Spacious Skies,* the second-place winner of the 1986 Great American Quilt Contest: "I searched all the local libraries to find a picture of the Statue of Liberty I liked, and could find none. I telephoned the Statue of Liberty Gift Shop in New York and had them send me $15 worth of posters and postcards and none of them were good enough. I finally found one at the grocery store on the back of a box of Kellogg's Corn Flakes."

Let your friends know what you're looking for. With your need in mind, they may make a connection when flipping through a magazine in a dentist's office or looking through card racks at a stationery store. When I was in the market for butterfly ideas, a friend lent me a pillowcase fluttering with beautifully embroidered insects. The colors were off, but the scale was perfect.

BASIC ELEMENTS OF DESIGN

•

I can't tell you what to draw, but I can point to some helpful elements of design as they relate to simple pictorial blocks. These elements are physical properties: visual unity, focal point, color, texture, line, scale, placement, space, and balance. Put together the individual components and you've got a well-balanced composition.

A successful design looks like *one visual unit,* not an assembly of bits and pieces. The viewer should first notice the whole picture, and then gradually home in on the little details—the designer's clever use of found objects, or an amazing collection of quilting stitches in the corner.

Decide what you want people to *focus* on in your design. The focal point should catch attention first and compel the viewer to have a look around. Without an emphasized center of interest, the design might be boring, or the eye might be led off the edge of the design. The simplest solution for pictorial designs is to place one figure in the center of your square, then embellish it so that it stands out.

In more complicated designs, the element that contrasts with, rather than continues, the overall pattern automatically attracts the eye because of its difference. For example, when most of the elements in a design are about the same size, one that is much larger will become the focal point; when most of the elements are irregular or abstract, one geometric or recognizable image will attract attention; when most of the elements are shades of beige, the royal purple one will stand out the most. The viewer's eye will move about the picture from points of greater contrasts to points of lesser ones.

We've already discussed how *color* can be used to establish a general mood and set up a relationship between the parts. We perceive forms and satisfying images through contrasts in value (the lightness and darkness of a color in relationship to what's surrounding it). Minimal contrasts in value produce subtle, quiet effects. Sharper contrasts in value are dramatic. Dark and light contrasts will emphasize or create a focal point.

Texture is also important. Even if we are not actually running our fingers over the surface, certain visual clues help us touch, with our eyes, the various sensations. Textures can be smooth or rough, soft or hard, heavy or light. They can be overlapped to create an illusion of depth, contrasted for visual interest, or combined so that the center of activity stands out sharply. When the differences in colors are subtle, the viewer will concentrate on the textures.

Strong contrasts, whether of colors or of textures, tend to attract attention immediately, while gradual changes lead us progressively from step to step. If your design is finished and your figure doesn't stand out from the ground as much as you'd like, define it by outlining the contours with a couching stitch in one or two strands of black embroidery floss. This worked in "The Nutcracker," from *The Crown Quilt.*

"The Nutcracker"

Line can be used to control and collect attention. Realize that when we talk about line, we are also talking about shapes; lines describe the edges of forms. A line actually is a form, with both a width and length. It can be thick and announce its presence, or be slight and whisper of restraint.

Sometimes an element in a design is an actual line. Sometimes points in a design create imagined lines—ones that aren't actually delineated, but are inferred by the eye as it moves from point to point, connecting the dots. Lines can be straight or curved, delicate or bold, graceful or nervous, even or uneven. Linear movement

expresses a sense of feeling and character: sharp and twisting lines seem restless, straight lines move quickly, curves are slow, and lines that meander are the most peaceful and leisurely of all. Horizontal lines are quiet, vertical ones more active, diagonals blatantly announce motion. If you want your horizontal or vertical lines to suggest stability, make sure they are parallel to the sides of the block. Lines emanating from the center carry the eye to the outer boundaries.

Scale and *placement* play a part in creating actual or illusory *space.* We pay attention to a strongly marked form and judge the rest of the space in comparison with it. We may find ourselves either in a crowded space, or lost in an empty one. We may feel ourselves close to the subject or far away from it. The location of a shape organizes the space around it. The shape becomes a positive element and the background is referred to as negative space. If your negative space is flat and empty, your shapes will look as if they are glued on. For more interesting designs, the positive and negative space should be integrated. If you can't think of a way to integrate them now, consider the potential of future quilting lines.

A sense of depth and perspective can be created by the arrangement of shapes and contrast of values. Shapes that are supposed to be far away should be smaller, in muted cool colors. Shapes that are supposed to be closer should be larger, in bright, light, or warm tones, and should overlap the far-away shapes.

Size is another consideration. Just because an object is large doesn't automatically mean it's the central focus of the picture. It depends on where it's placed in the design. Forms can be deliberately but subtly positioned to create and direct interest. So if you're adding a Christmas tree, make sure it isn't so huge that it casts shadows on your main man, Mr. Nutcracker.

Balance is hard to define; it's easier to sense when it doesn't exist. Think of your block as having a vertical axis right down the middle, and assess the visual weight on either side.

Human beings are symmetrical creatures; if our parts weren't evenly balanced, we wouldn't be able to stand up straight. Consequently, we tend to seek out symmetry. It's comforting to us, and it is the simplest element of balance to create and to recognize. A symmetrically balanced design has equal visual weight on either side of the invisible axis. Probably because of our sense of gravity, human beings are also comforted when there is more visual weight toward the bottom of a picture.

But designs can also be balanced asymmetrically. This involves weighing elements that aren't identical but have equal visual weight, and distributing them appropriately on the block. Balanced asymmetrical designs may look more natural, less contrived, than their perfectly even counterparts, but they are really more complicated to achieve. Color: a small area of bright can balance a larger area of a neutral. Value: a small amount of black can balance a larger area of gray. Shapes: a small, irregular shape can balance a larger, regular, defined one; and a small textured shape can balance a larger untextured one. Consider the seesaw factor when you're trying to balance your block. Say you have one chunky kid and one skinny kid on a seesaw. In order for it to be any fun, the fat kid will need to be closer to the center. So when you're designing your block, see what happens if you balance a large shape close to the center axis with a smaller shape near the edge.

All these theories may sound overwhelming to you now, but you'll see when you get down to doing your own picture that many of them are automatic. Design really isn't so difficult. Just make yourself aware of these few design elements. Try to arrange them in such a way that the viewer's eye moves comfortably around the picture and your design will be pleasing. The completed block's balance and strength will depend on the proportions of each element. Harmony is achieved when everything works together.

IF A DESIGN ELUDES YOU
•

If you don't have a clue where to start, browse through the blocks in this book for inspiration. Mentally dissect their parts. For example, in *The Crown Quilt* do the mountains in "The Rising of the Moon" have depth because they are made of layer upon layer of brown-toned shapes? Does the night sky in "The Hitchhiker's Guide to the Galaxy" fairly sparkle because of just the right splashing of shiny sequins?

Don't despair if a design eludes you. Remain open to new inspirations and you may find that your block takes off in a pattern all its own. Pam Thomas suffered from stitcher's block with "The Rising of the Moon." For weeks, she stared at one big yellow moon basted in the corner, and waited for the midnight fairies to finish the rest. Then she discovered a swatch of whorly, shiny black and silver silk that was perfect for the night water. A piece of scalloped lace became the ocean waves crashing against clifflike layers of green and brown prints. There was no stopping her. The night before deadline, Pam stayed up embroidering a tiny Irish flag (albeit inaccurate), adding stars in the sky, flowers on the hills.

"The Hitchhiker's Guide to the Galaxy"

"The Rising of the Moon"

Even if you send out instructions to your stitchers at the outset, expect the final blocks to be a mixture of the meek and the mighty. Some will be prizewinners, some will be primitive. This eclectic collection of quirks and skills provides the main attraction on a group quilt. The whole can be pulled together with the right lattice and the right attitude. Appreciate all the blocks for what they are—labors of love and ingenuity.

DESIGNING THE LAYOUT
•   •   •
STRATEGY
•

The layout is the arrangement of the base blocks. The simplest set displays square blocks in *rows*. When you are faced with sixteen entirely different picture blocks, row arranging is the easiest and most flexible solution for a balanced, symmetrical quilt. Just sixteen blocks yield more than twenty trillion different possible combinations.

Anytime you diverge from the row method, you are building in a little more planning to your effort. Blocks can also be set on the *diagonal*, or "on point," meaning that a corner, rather than a straight side, is on top (see *Friendship Cactus Baskets*, page 14). Since stitchers will have to know which direction to point their treetops, pictorial quilts must be designated as "on point" from the beginning. Otherwise you'll receive people and pets turned in a whole slew of cattywompus directions. It's more difficult to perceive the center of a diamond-shaped block, which makes it more difficult to create a balanced picture. We don't recommend attempting this configuration through the mail or with a group of first-timers.

There are as many layout options as there are billboards on the nation's highways. *Under the Big Top* (page 92) is an unusual example of a *super-predetermined schema* that tosses all our warnings out the window. Each block is a different shape and points in a different direction. (There is no sashing between blocks, so the shapes are difficult to perceive. Each block contains one figure.) Stitchers were handed every possible configuration found in advanced geometry textbooks and asked to apply one particular circus creature, be it beast or Bozo, in the center. Even though the level of quilting experience among its participants was almost zero, the overall result is an amazing testament to the tenacity of beginners.

Now, assuming that you've decided to go with square blocks in rows, we will get on to the business of arranging them so they look terrific.

ARRANGING THE BLOCKS
•

All the blocks are in. It's time to figure out which blocks will serve as the quilt's cornerstones, and which will fill up its insides. Give yourself lots of time. Spread out the blocks on a white sheet. Pin them to the living room curtains. Attach them with magnets to the refrigerator. Take Polaroid shots of the puzzle-in-progress. Pack the blocks up and look at them next week. Diagram your configurations on paper before you make a move. You want it to be perfect.

If a lone juggler hasn't been delegated, it's very satisfying to play with the puzzle pieces as a group. Bring out the champagne and celebrate (saving some refreshments for the "It's finished" hoopla later on). Party in a big room with an abundance of clean floor space.

How can you approach perfection when you have work by Picasso and The Little Rascals all on the same surface? The first thing you *don't* do is worry. It can be done and it can be beautiful.

Dark and dense designs can be made to rock and roll with the silly and the transparent. Lumbering squares can be made to waltz with the shy and demure. The goal is equality, symmetry, balance, visual appeal.

Think of the quilt as having a horizontal and vertical axis, and try to balance the left side with the right. Forget about your first impressions of each block and begin by artificially categorizing all of them in terms of density, orientation, color, and types of fabric. Look for pairs of sameness, then split them apart.

By *density,* I mean the amount of exposed background fabric. Dense blocks reveal next to none and are loaded with heavy textured fabrics and are often thick with embroidery foliage. Alternate them with more sparsely populated designs. Pay particular attention to the four corners of the quilt where blocks can get lost. Dense blocks can act as heavy cornerstones, anchoring your quilt to a solid foundation.

By *orientation,* I mean the direction the design causes the eye to go (left or right, up or down). Often pictorial blocks contain figures looking in one direction, or "action" that travels off-center somehow. Pair them up (one looking right, one looking left) in an arrangement that directs our eyes to the quilt's center. Try not to put blocks on the outside that have figures looking into never-never land, wishing they were somewhere else.

Blocks can be teamed up by *color.* I often find that many blocks will use a lot of the same colors or fabrics. Don't put them side by side. (Of course, there's always the inevitable oddball that whispers p a s t e l or screams RED!)

Keep in mind the *fabric* that has been tentatively chosen for the sashing and borders. Some of the blocks will inevitably look better with this choice than others. Place squares that threaten to clash away from the outside rows. Color in the sashing is most noticeable in the exterior strips.

I feel most comfortable putting pretty terrific blocks in the top row. (Michelle Sidrane, a vice president of Crown Publishers, Inc., tells us that readers begin scanning a page from the top right-hand corner. That's where the *New York Times* lead story always is, and that's where advertisers always want their ads.) After quilt viewers take in the whole masterpiece in one glance, they then start "reading" it from the top right. Encourage them by putting your best blocks forward. Intersperse the eye-catchers.

Having said all this, we will now share Judy Kellar Fox's completely unorthodox solution to a particularly long and drawn-out layout dilemma. "I had a miserable time figuring out how to assemble my squares," she says, referring to nine patchwork Christmas exchange blocks designed and made by members of her California stitchery group. "For over a year they hung pinned to my sewing room drapes. Meanwhile, others in the group put together really nice quilts with interesting settings.

"The idea struck me to slice up the squares on the diagonal and reassemble them. After photographing all the squares intact, doing a mock-up with photocopies, and working through the emotional impact of the cutting up, I came up with a piece I like. So do my friends who made the originals. Only a real friend would encourage you after you cut up something she had spent hours creating!"

Judy Kellar Fox's *Consensus: With a Little Help from My Friends* can be seen on page 33, following three other totally different layout variations designed by members of her group.

DESIGNING SASHING

❖ ❖ ❖

Sashing (also called lattice or stripping) is the tie that binds multifarious, multinational blocks together. Some groups opt to go without it for a very simple look (*Mothering America,* page 95) or for a classic look (*Baltimore Friendship Album,* page 36). Plain blocks will often alternate with pattern blocks like a checkerboard, in lieu of sashing (*Apple Box Labels,* page 80). Plain blocks provide small showcases for quality quilting stitches.

I think that sashing is essential for a quilt of creative picture blocks. It acts both as a border, providing each little masterpiece with its own gallery space, and as continuous, flowing corridors, tying all the units together into one museum. Sashing works best when it contrasts enough with the blocks to set them apart without competing for front center stage.

SASHING SIZE

❖

In a traditional-style quilt, sashing is one-eighth to one-quarter as wide as the block.

> 8-inch block = 1- to 2-inch-wide sashing
> 10-inch block = 1¼- to 2½-inch-wide sashing
> 12-inch block = 1½- to 3-inch-wide sashing

But you can't go on calculations alone. You must consider the diverse contents of your blocks when you think about sashing width. The best way to do this is to spread out a large sheet of chosen sashing material right in the fabric store and lay your blocks on it, experimenting with width. Place four blocks on the fabric two inches apart, and another four blocks one and one-half inches apart. Stand back and see which you like better. If your blocks tend to be dense and busy, the sashing should probably be wider. If they are light and breezy, a wide sash will make them bland. Remember also that wide sashing demands more quilting.

SASHING TYPES

❖

Beginners will be happiest with:

- one-strip, same-color sashing
- small, all-over prints
- color that contrasts with base blocks.

One-strip sashing, used in *Rabbi Alfred Wolf's Quilt* (page 60), is just what it sounds like: one continuous gridwork strip all in the same fabric. It is simple and very effective. (Diagram 1).

Detail can be added to create *pieced sashing.* The simplest method is to insert a plain or little patchwork square at each of the intersections (Diagrams 2, 3, and 4). I used several decorative sash-

Diagram 1. One-strip sashing using a dense, all-over print.

Diagram 2. Sashing with plain squares at intersections.

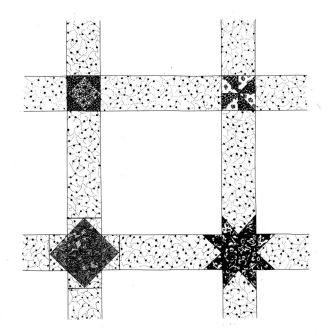

Diagram 3. Sashing with four different patchwork squares at intersections.

Diagram 5. Sashing strips pieced from two very different patterns of uneven widths with simple, all-over print squares at intersections.

Diagram 4. Sashing strips pieced from two different all-over fabric prints with nine-patch pieces at intersections.

Diagram 6. Narrow all-over print mat next to border print frame with mitered corners. Both are encased in a dark, overall sashing. This treatment is used to enlarge the quilt.

Diagram 7. This border print doesn't look the same from the top and bottom. Since the right strip was joined upside-down, the bottom strip doesn't meet in the left and right corners in the same way.

ing additions for a quilted wedding canopy project, *Wedding Chupah* (page 66). Dark blue sashing separates each picture block. Squares of an even darker blue are set into the intersections, giving the illusion of transparent stained glass. Black twill tape outlines the sashing for an Art Deco look. Appliquéd vines with soft Ultrasuede leaves float throughout the lattice to entwine the top and bottom panels visually.

In *The Crown Quilt* and *Fantasies* (pages 76 and 90), I created a more complicated scheme using several sashing strips, thereby creating a *frame* around each of the base blocks, which are then unified by sashing.

In *The Crown Quilt,* each base block has three frames. First is a one-and-one-half-inch black print frame that acts like picture matting. Next is a one-quarter-inch frame of a small printed muted color that is almost impossible to describe (somewhere between beige and mustard). Last is a one-way border print fabric that acts like a fancy frame. Its design matches exactly on each block. The tiny muted mustard in between breaks up the darkness and subdues the contrast of the two. If you like this effect, remember that I had to miter eighty corners to make sure the border print flowed continuously around the corners.

SASHING FABRIC

•

Sashing was traditionally cut from solid fabrics to show off quilting. Since most beginners would rather disguise their stitches, a small, all-over print, with very subtle internal color contrast on a firmly woven fabric is a much better choice. Little prints are easy to mark, they are not infected with directional sheen disease, they hide seams, they hide mistakes.

Unless you've had lots of experience, you should probably stay away from one-way designs in the sashing. They demand a lot of planning, careful stitching, and mitering—a very time-consuming but very necessary process to avoid visual World War III on your quilt top. One way to get around mitering border prints is to piece squares at the corners so the print's pattern never meets itself (Diagrams 5, 6, and 7). See the bustling *Fantasies* quilt, page 90.

SASHING COLORS

•

Sashing color should *contrast* enough with your blocks to set them apart, without clashing with them. Color can also influence the mood you want your quilt to convey. Susan Schwarting in her *Me and My Piano* (page 88) uses stark contrast for a keyboard effect. The skillful quilters of *Morning, Noon, and Night* (page 43) chose subtle contrasts—dawn-to-dusk sashing colors that blend into the houses—for a painterly effect.

When in doubt, remember that colors change in different contexts. Consider the effects of various color contrasts: light-dark, complementary, cool-warm, proportion. Colors can contrast to a minimum or maximum degree. For example, I chose red and green complements for *The Crown Quilt* (page 76)—but not primary reds and greens. I mellowed the contrast for a more elegant look by using mulberry and forest green—colors that are almost equal in tonal value.

Lest you think I chose the perfect colors right off the bat, I must confess that I fought using mulberry down to the last minute. For hours and hours, I kept looking hopefully at bolts of beiges to lighten up my green, systematically rejecting poor mulberry because it seemed too dark. In the end, I'm glad I chose it. I wanted the blocks to appear as a unit and to be the focal point, with the panels surrounding them on three sides to complement but not compete. Using a lighter value in the grid would have created too stark a separation.

Using the same color sashing as the base blocks creates a wide-open, floating look.

A Note on Black. I often separate varied picture blocks by framing them in a low-contrast small-scale all-over black print, and then melding them back together with a lighter color sashing. Black contains each block's vibrant action. It allows the internal shapes and colors to dance at their liveliest, without having to worry about what's going on next door. Since each block is usually created by one solitary person, it deserves to be observed separately inside its cozy black house first. White lattice has the opposite effect. It tends to allow each block to flow into the next, and should probably be used only on a quilt with similar style pictures.

DESIGNING BORDERS

♦   ♦   ♦

Borders are a place to play with patterns, a way to expand a quilt's dimensions. Group quilts don't necessarily need them. The frame provided by outer sashing or by contrasting binding often suffices. In fact, tried-and-true border axioms stressed in quiltmaking books don't always apply to communal appliqués.

By its very nature, a group appliqué pictorial quilt is filled with a medley of designs, of textures, of workmanship. A border collects the chaos, composes and defines it. It contains, but doesn't conquer. A change of color or a different pattern around the edges of a quilt can set off the design the way a frame sets off a painting.

Borders for free-form picture quilts come complete with a built-in dilemma. They must be designed at the end because you never know until the last minute how many blocks you'll actually have, or what they'll look like. But, a border should neither seem like an afterthought, nor should it compete with the quilt's inside designs. The outer frame should look as if it were born attached to your quilt.

The border around our first Amalgamated Nursery fund-raiser, *Scenes of Childhood* (page 89), was included just because we thought a quilt had to have one, and because we needed a slightly larger quilt. Even though it is a design that's entirely separate from the rest of the quilt, it happens to work because it's not overwhelming. The color scheme reflects the juvenile theme without resorting to primary colors. Remember, our aim was to create a project that would appeal to the adults who would buy the raffles.

A NOTE ON CORNERS

♦

In order to understand types of borders, you should first understand what happens in the quilt's corners. For whatever type of border you choose—solid, pieced, printed stripes, or appliqué—the way you treat the corners must be a focal point. All four corners must match if the border is to be symmetrical. The pattern should flow around them gracefully, not stop abruptly. There are two basic ways to deal with the corners: butt or miter.

Butting the ends is when shorter strips fit and meet longer strips at a right angle (Diagram 8a). Mitering is when the two borders are joined with a diagonal seam (Diagram 8b). See also "How to Piece Borders," page 189, and "How to Miter a Corner," page 166.

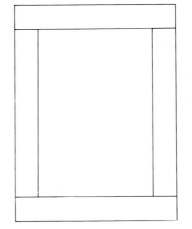
Diagram 8a. Butted border corners.

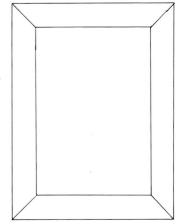
Diagram 8b. Mitered border corners.

BORDER TYPES

♦

Whole Piece Borders. Long border bands provide a calm and effective place for the eye to rest. If you choose a solid fabric as opposed to a print, they also provide a showcase arena for elaborate quilting as in *J.C. Penney Quilts* (pages 96–99) and *Sailors' Snug Harbor* (page 51). Whole piece borders can be made either of a single band of fabric or a series of different bands of fabric. The various strips can be of equal or varying widths (see *Alphabet Quilt*, page 105, and *Apple Box Labels*, page 80). Whole piece borders can be butted at each corner (Diagrams 9a and 9b).

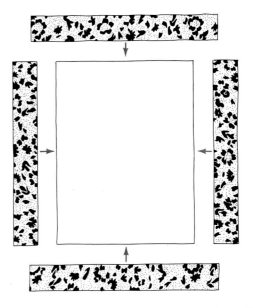
Diagram 9a. One whole-piece border band is attached to quilt top.

Diagram 9b. A series of three bands of different whole-piece fabric is attached in sequence to the quilt top. Note that the corners are butted.

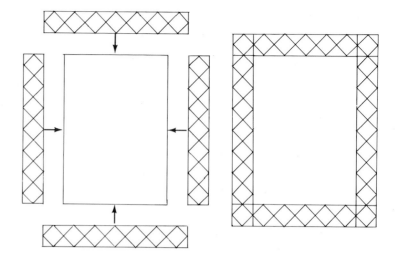

Diagram 10. Pieced border designed from a single pieced block, repeated from end to end, with one full patchwork block filling in each corner.

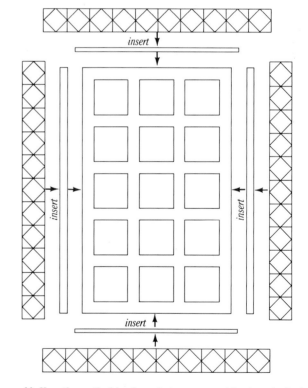

Diagram 11. Here the vertical border strip inserts are wider than the horizontal strips. Adding inserts adjusts the quilt's dimensions.

*P*ieced Borders. Pieced borders are usually designed from a single pieced block or unit, repeated from end to end, with one full patchwork block filling in each corner. The pattern of the patchwork unit should meet the corner unit in exactly the same way. The more complicated the fabric or design, the more difficult this perfect meeting (Diagram 10).

Begin by measuring and planning a border from edge to edge. To determine a manageable width for a repeating pieced unit, which will allow you to fit the same pieced unit into each corner, find a number that can be divided into both the horizontal and vertical measurements equally. If this calculation doesn't yield a nice round number, the dimensions can be increased by inserting strips of fabric between the quilt top and the border (Diagram 11). See also "How to Piece Borders," page 189. When this unpieced insert is made from the same fabric as the sashing, it will blend into the quilt top and not be noticed (Diagram 12); if it is a similar color to the border, it will blend into the border design and act to expand the border's width (Diagrams 13 and 14); if it is of a contrasting color, it will look like a separate border around the quilt (Diagram 15).

Another alternative is to plan a separate corner unit that either links the border fluidly or is totally different (Diagram 16). And still

Diagram 12. Unpieced insert made from the same fabric as the sashing.

Diagram 13. Unpieced sashing made from the same fabric that's in the border.

Diagram 14. Unpieced sashing made from fabric similar to border fabric.

Diagram 15. Unpieced sashing made from a fabric contrasting with both sashing and border fabrics.

another method is to design a totally different unit at the border's center either to expand or diminish the border's length, so that a full border unit can be installed gracefully at the corner (Diagrams 16a and b).

Some pieced blocks look different from various angles. Either the pattern is not symmetrical, it has been colored asymmetrically, or it has a direction. *Cheryl and Dean's Wedding Quilt* (page 64) is an example of a quilt with an asymmetrical border pattern. In such cases, you will probably have to make some creative adjustments. With a directional border unit, the direction can be reversed in the center of each side in order to create symmetry in the four corners. To do this, you will need an even number of units in the border to start with. For example, if you're using a a Wild Goose Chase pattern (Diagram 17), start two triangles pointing in opposite directions right in the middle of each side of the border (Diagram 16c). Repeat the pattern out from both directions and see if they all meet in the same way at all four corners.

B*order prints and stripes.* An effective way to frame your project is to use a stripe or border print. You will need quantities of the same fabric in order to make it all around the quilt's perimeter; and you will need a little extra patience in order to make the pattern flow. Choose a design that runs along the lengthwise grain of the fabric. Be careful to match motifs and lines when you piece strips of a printed stripe or border print together.

Playing with beautiful border prints is certainly a creative endeavor, but it's not the easiest solution. I don't recommend using them if you have a group of beginners on a very tight schedule. Here are the complicating factors (Diagram 18): The design on a border print should be in the exact same place on each side of the quilt. (See Diagram 7 for an example of an unsuccessful meeting of border print corners.) Some border prints look the same whichever way you

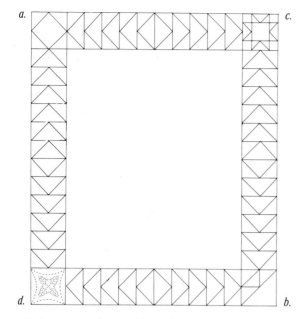

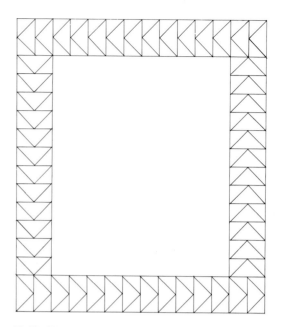

Diagram 16. Corner units (a) and (b) link the border strips fluidly by connecting the points. Corner unit (c) repeats the triangle shape from the border strip, yet is a totally different pattern. Corner (d) is made from one solid block square on which an intricate quilting pattern can be sewn.

Diagram 17. The Wild Goose Chase pattern has a direction. Because the strips are butted, the triangles don't turn the corners fluidly.

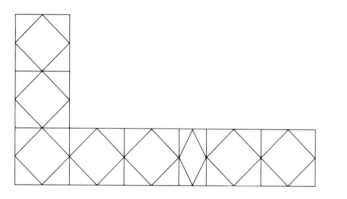

Diagrams 17a and 17b. Diamond border pattern adjusted two different ways in order to end up with symmetrical corners. In 17a, the center diamond is shrunk to half its size.

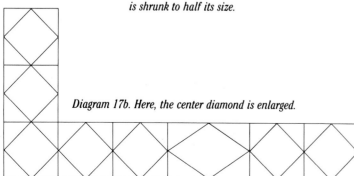

Diagram 17b. Here, the center diamond is enlarged.

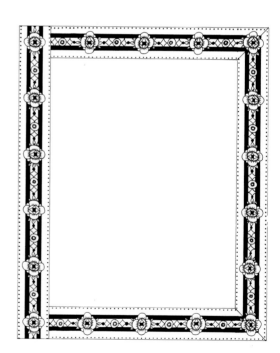

Diagram 18. Border print design meets in the exact same place on each side of the quilt. The left strip is butted so the design ends abruptly in the corners. The right strip is mitered so the pattern flows more smoothly.

turn them (Diagram 19). Others do not (Diagram 20). You must be very careful to attach the same side to the edge of the quilt consistently.

Border prints that butt into each other in the corners are really noticeable. If you would rather not have your fancy prints crashing into each other at every bend, you may want to miter them, or piece an additional block in each corner. (See Diagram 18, right strip, for an example of mitering.) If your quilt is square, and if you've been careful to place your border print symmetrically around the quilt's edges, then the print's motifs should match up nicely in a mitered corner. (Notice the meandering floral print frame around each block in *The Crown Quilt,* page 76.)

If your motifs are to meet and miter happily ever after on a rectangular quilt, you will need more yardage on the vertical sides. Fool around to see how the ends will match. You may have to forgo perfectly balanced designs all around the edges in order to achieve the perfect miter.

*A*ppliquéd borders. Appliquéd borders help to unite appliqué in the quilt. In the *Wedding Chupah* (page 66), the floral border softens the geometric lines in the pieced squares. In the *Baltimore Friendship Album* (page 36), the festoon border uses the same lines and motifs as the internal squares.

ELEMENTS OF BORDER DESIGN
◆

Deciding what border to use on a group appliqué pictorial quilt is rarely obvious. Perhaps the easiest place to begin is to try to repeat shapes or motifs already in the quilt. Look at the design elements that unite your quilt so far, such as theme, neutral base block fabric, contrasting sashing fabric. Can any of its colors or fabrics be repeated, or highlighted with contrasting colors in the border? Think about the principle of variety within unity: shapes can be repeated in various sizes, colors can be repeated in different values.

Is there a way to incorporate the theme? A sampler gift for Pearl (see *Pearl's Quilt,* page 38), a beloved second-grade teacher, is double bordered with two meaningful patterns. First is a Wild Goose Chase motif to commemorate Pearl's running around in the classroom. Second is a diamond pattern, reflecting Pearl's precious status in the eyes of her quiltmakers. *Under the Big Top* (page 92), a fund-raiser circus quilt, is bordered by pink and red streamers at both sides, bannering the raucous revelry inside the tent.

If you have some crack quilters in your group, a solid border may be their only chance to show off.

Browse through the quilts in this book for ideas. There are no set rules for the width of your border. The width depends completely on the quilt, the kind of mood you want to convey, and the amount of quilting you want to do. Susan Frye's *Sailors' Snug Harbor* (page 51) has a huge floral border that works beautifully, adding a dimen-

Diagram 19. Border print that is the same on each edge.

Diagram 20. Border print that is different on each edge.

sion of grace and flourish to the static buildings inside. The Schoolhouse Quilters of Newington, Connecticut, added a relatively narrow border around their enormous *Variable Star Scrap Quilt* (page 13). It uses the same color pieced triangles in the border that were used for the stars' points.

To find out what you like, look at framed pictures in your house, or in a museum. Do you prefer the effect of a matting between the picture and the frame? Do you like wide matting, narrow or dark borders? Or do you like a hint of mat inside an ostentatious frame, or a self-effacing frame outside a glorious mat?

Should the border be attached directly to the lattice? An elaborate border pieced right to the sashing might not provide enough contrast. If that's the case, consider inserting long strips of one whole fabric between the sashing and border, in the same way you would place a mat inside a frame. A strip of a different color or fabric can add another dimension, even an illusion of depth. If you use the same fabric as you did for the sashing, your total quilt will look like one big sheet with blocks laid on top. See what happens if you set off a border with a strip different from the sashing, then use the same strip after the border to end or bind the quilt (see *Scenes of Childhood,* page 89).

If your quilt needs to be expanded by quite a bit, add a couple of borders of different widths. Insert strips between them. To make the border wider, add a strip that blends into the border fabric. To set the two borders apart from each other and to add an additional color band around the quilt, use a contrasting strip between them.

During the metamorphosis of *The Crown Quilt* (page 76), when I was particularly discouraged, I was tempted to use the dark green fabric all over the quilt—as sashing for the blocks, as well as the background for the various panels. This would have made the book blocks look as if they were placed on top of one big sheet of green. It was not the effect I wanted. I'm happy with the contrasting mulberry sashing that establishes the unique blocks as the center, and sets them apart from the background.

BORDER COLORS

◆

Colors in the border help to accent colors in the quilt. Is there a particular hue you would like to highlight? Will it throw off the color balance of the quilt if you do? Consider the effects of contrasts as they interact with each other. Dark colors in the outer frame pronounce a definitive end to your quilt. They contain the internal action, safely, completely. Light-colored borders whisper of intangibles beyond the quilt surface. I pieced five sample borders to demonstrate the techniques and considerations I've discussed here:

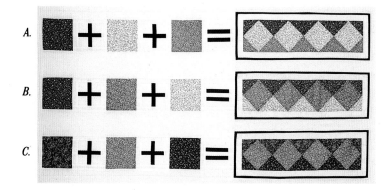

Three small, all-over prints in subtle light, medium, and dark shades.

The first two of these delicately muted, textured border examples show how the same three fabrics can cause different effects depending on how they are positioned in the design. In A, the largest piece—the center diamond—is made from the light print. Because it's surrounded by medium and dark prints, it creates the most contrast of the triplets. In B, the effect is more subdued, with the dark shading into medium, shading into light. C is subtler still. Two dark prints, one of which has a medium-sized, more distinct pattern, encase the diamond.

The paisley design creates a special effect much like a stained glass church window in each of these borders' diamonds. It changes in effect—from standing out to receding—depending on its encompassing fabrics. In D, E, and F, the smaller triangles are made from tiny, overall prints in light, medium, and dark tones, respectively. This type of print looks and acts almost like solids, but provides more texture. G uses the same paisley motif in the center, but with different fabric patterns in each row of triangles. The black print is a two-way pattern. Care was taken to use it symmetrically in each triangle.

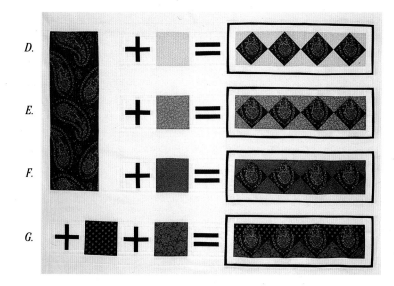

The same large paisley motif in the diamond used over and over again with various contrasting color prints.

In example I, the center paisley pattern is cut differently from all seven other border examples that use the same print. The motifs lie on their sides, pointing toward each other in pairs, creating a flowing effect across the border. In example J, the small triangles are made from a simple dark red brick stripe. In the right corner, the stripe continues along its previously scheduled course. In the left corner, the triangle is divided in two, helping the stripe to make a neat turn around the corner.

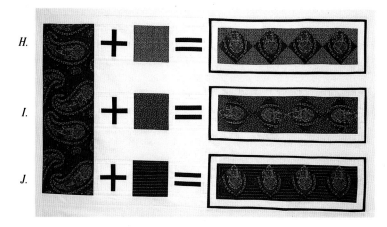

Three shades of red prints (light, medium, dark) subtly combined with the same paisley motif.

Border K is whimsical, border L is elegant. Both are made from prints in green, periwinkle, dark blue, and shades of maroon through pink. Mama Penguin and Baby Penguin wait patiently smack dab in the center of each diamond in the top example, while an appropriate wavy print floats by in the little triangles. The bottom border diamonds are made from a periwinkle medium all-over print, its little triangles cut from a fancy stripe border print with two distinctly different edges. The top triangles use its top edge; the bottom triangles, its bottom edge.

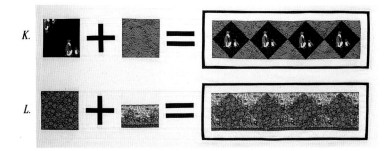

Two entirely different moods conveyed using the same kinds of colors on different prints.

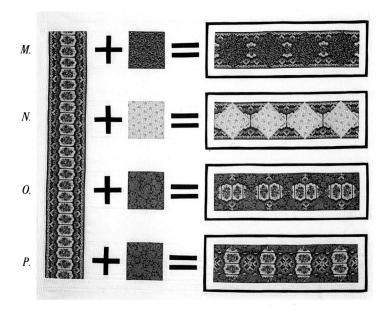

A brightly colored border print used four different ways, all against a different overall pattern.

In examples M and N, the little triangles are cut from different parts of the border print. Look closely where the triangle points meet on each example. They create different patterns. The center diamond in M is a black and gray, medium all-over print that gives a solid impression. The diamond in N is made from a yellow all-over that doesn't resemble a solid because it's printed with red, blue, green, and black contrasting colors. In example O, the border print, cut from the same part each time, provides the center diamond. The triangles are made from a large overall-patterned forest green print. The same concept is repeated in example P, in a much more elaborate manner. Its triangles are strip-pieced from both the green and the border fabric. As the triangle points, consisting of two diamonds and two triangles, meet, an intricate pattern emerges.

For a pieced border, draft a small section to scale on graph paper. Color in the patches. Duplicate it reversing the colors. Which patches stand out, which blend together? Cut out the shapes of one unit from the actual fabric without seam allowance, and fit them together like pieces of a jigsaw puzzle. Do you like the effect?

BORDER FABRICS

◆

For a simple quilt with just sashing and blocks, bordertime means creative playtime. My only advice is to choose prints or solids you feel your expertise can handle. If you decide to make a pieced border

in a one-way print, remember to mark and piece with the utmost precision, or else you'll be very unhappy with your skewed, off-balance border. I usually don't stitch two complicated directional prints together. If I choose a border print for one frame, I often choose an all-over pattern for the adjacent one. Wherever two border prints connect, they must first be basted together carefully.

Pick combinations of prints that complement each other in some way. Remember the effects of contrasts: maximum degree grabs the eye first, minimal degree beckons the eye gently, progressively. Similar-size prints in similar colors produce a mellow, muted look. Medium prints next to small prints in similar colors are also subtle.

*S*ome parting words as you embark on your communal journey... By nature, a quilt is put together in many stages; it's a whole made up of many parts. Of course, it's the whole that gives the final impression. But if one of its parts looks terribly wrong to you, an error of color or fabric judgment, or whatever, it will be a magnet for your eyes, and will ruin your enjoyment of a project that took many collective hours. (No one else will notice, I promise.)

It's difficult to conjure up a whole quilt from the few swatches you were playing with in the fabric store. Build enough time into your schedule to allow for making amendments. Pull the offending piece apart, replace it, toss it out, buy new fabric. In retrospect, some of my most effective compositions have been invented at a late-night panic point in the quilt. The thrill of creating is in the process.

P·A·R·T

3

SEWING
THE
QUILT

Background
·
THE GILBERT HOUSE
QUILT

Fabric, Tools, and Techniques

FACTS ON FABRIC

♦ ♦ ♦

Consider the quilt's function and your piecing and quilting techniques when you choose your fabrics. A baby blanket, which may be more abused than used by its well-meaning toddler owner, must be constructed of easy-care fabric guaranteed to survive teeth marks and long journeys down gravel driveways. A bed cover should be assembled from similar-weight, durable fabrics. A never-to-be-laundered wall hanging can incorporate a creative array of fabrics in a multitude of weights.

For beginners who are choosing fabric for a bed quilt, I would recommend looking for:

- light- to medium-weight cotton (or cotton blends)
- firmly woven materials
- solid-colored fabrics or small to medium all-over prints.

You can be more flexible if your quilt is going to be displayed on a wall, but don't make problems for yourself by choosing the most elaborate, flimsy, wildly patterned materials you can find. When in doubt, simplify. Look in Part 2: "Designing the Quilt," for more specific fabric details concerning base blocks, lattice, and borders.

Now that you are finally making something much more interest-ing than an A-line apron for home economics class, here is the basic fabric information your teacher probably tried to drum into you back in junior high school. You'll need to know this when you place templates and cut your material—so please pay attention. There will be a quiz at the end.

WOVEN FABRICS: HOME EC 101

♦

Woven fabrics are composed of two sets of threads that run at right angles to each other. Each fabric begins its life as strands of yarn threaded lengthwise on a weaving loom. Next, filler yarn is woven crosswise, over and under the lengthwise threads. (Kind of like making those polyester potholders at day camp.) The extreme outside finished edges, parallel to the lengthwise yarns, are called *selvages*. Don't ever use selvage fibers in a quilt because they are woven very tight and shrink at a different rate than the interior fibers.

Threads running parallel to the selvage are called the *lengthwise grain* (warp) of the fabric. There is very little "give" in the lengthwise grain (Diagram 21). The *crosswise grain* (weft) runs from selvage to selvage and has some "give."

Bias refers to any diagonal on the fabric. True bias is the diagonal edge formed when the fabric is folded so that the crosswise threads run in the same direction as the lengthwise threads. Fabric cut on the true bias has the maximum give.

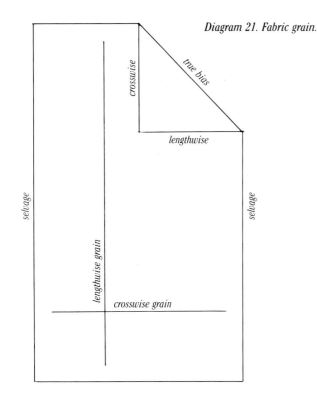

Diagram 21. Fabric grain.

A fabric is *on-grain* when the lengthwise and crosswise threads run exactly at right angles to each other. Fabric is *off-grain* when the two thread sets don't run at right angles. In order for your quilt to lie flat, it is important to cut as many sides of a shape on the grain as possible; with certain printed fabric motifs, however, you will have to choose between following the print route or the grain-line route. Fabric is often pulled a little off-grain just from sitting on the bolt in the store (Diagram 22). You can pull it back on-grain by stretching it in the appropriate direction.

*C*ottons. Purists believe that 100 percent cotton broadcloth is the only way to go. The pliable nature of its weave makes pure cotton ideal for hand-piecing, hand-quilting, machine-piecing, and machine-quilting. It's also a good choice for children's projects because it's easy to control when you are marking and cutting it. However, if you box yourself into only one kind of fabric, you will be limiting your choice of color and designs.

*C*otton blends. The person out to have a good time will be content to use natural cottons alongside man-made blends of the same weave and weight. If in doubt, compare the weave of the blend to 100 percent cotton goods. If you're still in doubt, read the label on the bolt and only accept a blend of at least 65 percent cotton. If by this point you have fallen hopelessly in love with a flimsy polyester

and it pains you to leave it behind in the store, buy a quarter of a yard and put it away for a later project.

WEIGHT

◆

Medium-weight, firmly woven fabrics such as calicoes and broadcloth are coveted by quilters. Functional quilts should be made of similar weight, easy-care fabrics. Beware of very tightly woven fabrics. They are fine for machine-piecing, but slow and frustrating during appliqué and hand-quilting. What's more, pulled-out stitching errors leave nasty, tattletale holes.

Heavier weight fabrics create globs of material at the seams, globs that will cause clunky quilting problems. Use them only if you plan to tie the quilt.

When it's least expected, a certain fabric may sabotage quilting skills. As I was writing this book, I received a phone call from Lynn Della Posta. She had just finished the quilting on *Cheryl and Dean's Wedding Quilt* (page 64) and her fingers had really taken a beating. Lynn informed me that one of my main fabric choices—a versatile firmly woven print that I had proudly rescued from a remnant pile—was a quilter's nightmare. The beautiful sections of luscious color print acted as if they were painted onto the fabric and reacted like barricades against Lynn's quilting needle. Instead of being able to load the needle with stitches, she was lucky to manage two stitches at a time. I thanked her for waiting until the end to tell me.

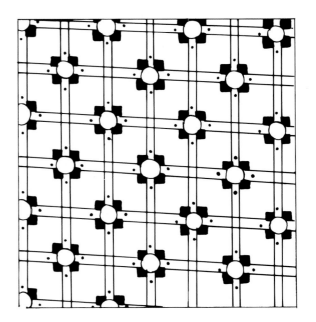

Diagram 22. Print pulled off-grain.

PRINTS

◆

All-Over Patterns. An all-over print is the fabric of choice for base blocks and lattice. It looks exactly the same from any angle. Scrutinize the fabric on the bolt from far away to see if the pattern, say, a tiny pin-dot print, has even the slightest directional pattern. Within this category the prints differ in scale: small, medium, large.

Simple, small, all-over patterns are very "forgiving." If you end up a little off-grain, no one will notice. You don't have to worry about matching flower petals in the sashing or having someone accidentally appliqué his or her picture upside down. There is no upside down on an all-over pattern. You can place templates on it quickly without wasting fabric. It creates a flat surface without bends, curves, or irregularities. All-overs are also the easiest fabrics to blend, and therefore to piece—important assets when you are seaming them to blocks created by many different people (Diagrams 23, 24, 25, and 26).

Two-Way Patterns. Some fabrics have two-way designs that can be used in two directions of the fabric, but not four. Simple same-color stripes and rows of same-color polka dots are examples. A little more fabric is necessary because the templates cannot be placed just anywhere. If you want to cut an angle that's anything other than 90 degrees, you may not be able to follow the print. You may have to follow the line created by the print, not the grain line (Diagrams 27 and 28).

Diagram 24. Medium all-over pattern.

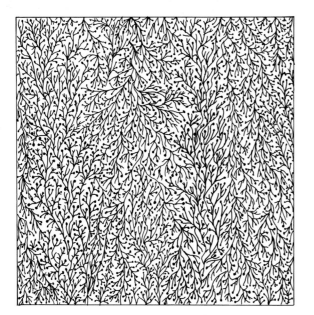

Diagram 23. Small all-over pattern.

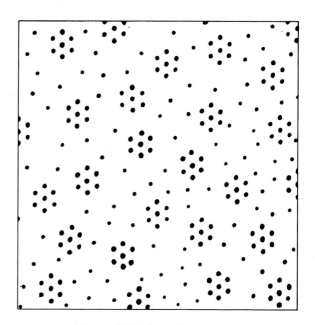

Diagram 25. Medium all-over pattern.

Diagram 26. Large all-over pattern.

Diagram 28. Large two-way pattern.

Diagram 27. Medium two-way pattern.

*O*ne-Way Patterns. One-way patterns, also called border patterns, can be used only in one direction. These are often border prints, stripes, or geometrics. They can be used with very pleasing results, but require lots of extra time, extra care, and extra fabric (Diagrams 29, 30, 31, and 32).

*D*irectional Sheen. Corduroy and velvet have a very obvious directional sheen; their appearance changes depending on the direction of the nap. Solid cottons and cotton blends also have a directional sheen, although it's more subtle. To find the sheen, rotate the fabric in good light.

If you cut light-reflecting fabric in a variety of directions, you will have pieces that shine every which way. This effect may be very intriguing within your appliqué picture, but it will be disconcerting in the border or lattice. My advice is to stay away from directional sheen solids in the piecework of a group project. If you must use them, take one of the following precautions:

1. After prewashing, lightly pencil an X across the entire wrong side of the fabric, making sure it doesn't show through to the right side.

2. As you are marking templates, pencil in a small, clear consistent arrow on the back or in the seam allowance of each piece. Arrange all the pieces in the quilt with the arrows pointing in the same direction.

Diagram 29. Medium one-way pattern.

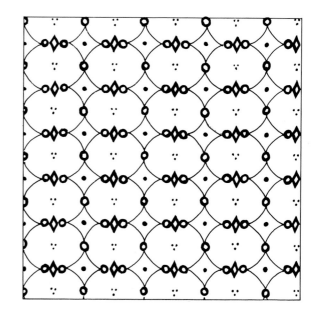

Diagram 30. Medium one-way pattern.

Diagram 31. Large one-way border print.

Diagram 32. Large one-way border print.

FABRIC FOR QUILT BACKING

◆

The fabric used for the back should be similar in fiber content, weave, and weight to the fabrics used in the quilt top. A firmly woven fabric is easy to quilt. Quilting stitches are much more visible on a solid-colored fabric than on prints. Keep this in mind if your stitches will be better off camouflaged than displayed for the world to see. If you've had it with making so many decisions, pick a fabric that's already in the quilt, even the same as the sashing. If you want a fling with a wild print, go for it, as long as its colors match those in the quilt. I often choose a medium-print backing fabric with lots of different colors in it. I figure it will hide the long pieced seam, and it won't get dirty.

Don't be duped into buying bedsheets for backing because they look easy to use. Sheets are made of tightly woven percale, which is impossible to quilt.

TOOLS OF THE TRADE

◆　　◆　　◆

You can really tell the difference between a quilt made with a decent pair of scissors and one made with gardening shears. Good tools make a huge difference. Of course, professional stitchers (a small class of people who suffer acute fabric-deprivation pangs when they haven't seen the insides of a sewing store for a couple of weeks) are expected to have an impressive collection of equipment that may seem excessive to most. Beginners, for example, do not need sixteen shades of blue embroidery floss, a dozen strange-shaped hoops, and boxes of needles and pins in all shapes and nationalities.

Beginners do need, however, a few basic tools of the trade. If your group is communicating through the mail, send them a condensed list of implements at the project's outset. Write them out. Verbal instructions tend to be remembered in the middle of the night when the damage is already done.

SCISSORS AND CUTTING TOOLS

◆

Precision tools yield precision results. Three good pairs of scissors separate the women from the Huckleberry Finns in drag. Buy one pair of quality dressmaker shears for cutting fabric. Buy a second smaller, lighter-weight pair for snipping threads and small appliqué pieces. Buy a third for cutting paper and plastic. Then—and this is important—hide them! Hide them especially from the under four-feet-tall set in your family. One well-meaning school project can give a good pair of scissors the incurable spurs.

THREAD

◆

For hand-sewing use standard cotton or quilting thread. For machine-piecework, 100 percent cotton or cotton-covered polyester can be used. Select a neutral or white-colored thread, except for seaming dark color fabrics. Try your best to match dark color thread to dark fabric.

Appliqué is a different story. Always match thread color to appliqué patches, not ground fabric. This simple attention to detail will yield amazing results. When in color doubt, go with a thread slightly darker than the fabric. Thread wound around a spool looks darker than it really is. For basting, keep a spool of strong light-colored thread close by.

BEESWAX

◆

I use beeswax to lubricate and strengthen thread; for example, to prevent snarls and knots on a thread to be beaded. It is available in a grooved clear plastic holder. To coat the thread, pull it through the groove several times.

Beeswax, which can be bought in most notions departments, can also be used to smooth the bottom of your iron.

HAND-SEWING NEEDLES

◆

People who say they hate to sew are probably using humongous needles for delicate tasks. Number 8 "sharps," an all-purpose medium-size needle, are commonly recommended for hand-piecing and appliqué. (Note: size 1 is the coarsest, size 10 is the shortest.) The shorter and stiffer "betweens'" (also called quilting needles) are used for fine sewing and hand-quilting.

I generally go for the shortest needle, whose eye is just big enough for the thread I'm using. I often use "betweens" for appliqué techniques; the sharp point is good for piercing tightly woven fabrics and man-made ones like Ultrasuede.

If your needle seems to stick, change to a smaller size. Keep your needles in the package so they won't rust.

Extremely long and fine beading needles are available for delicate beads with teeny openings—openings that help you empathize with a toddler trying to force a square peg into a round hole.

THIMBLES

◆

Thimbles have a bad rap. I won't tell you that a thimble isn't awkward —at first. But once you adjust, you'll wonder how you did without one. I, a one-time thimble-hater, now find I'm still wearing the little finger-casings when I run out to the supermarket. Try it (for at least half an hour)—you'll like it.

For hand-sewing, use a metal thimble that fits snugly onto the middle finger of the dominant hand. It should have a flat top with grooves or ridges.

MACHINE NEEDLES
◆

The weight of the fabric determines the size of the needle. If the needle bends, or makes a large puncture hole in the fabric, it's either too thin or too thick for the kind of material you're using. General-purpose needles are available in sizes 9, 11, 14, 16, and 18. For medium-weight fabrics, use an 11 for machine-piecing and a 14 for machine-quilting. Keep extra needles on hand to fend off the evil eye (a broken needle in the midst of a whirlwind sewing session) and make sure they're neither bent nor dull.

PINS
◆

Use fine, nonrusting pins that pierce the fabric quickly, don't make noticeable holes, and won't trip up the sewing thread. Pins with brightly colored heads are good for children—they're fun, easy to handle, and easy to find on the floor before they find the soles of your feet.

SEAM RIPPER
◆

A seam ripper is used to take out unwanted stitches. A long handle provides better leverage.

MEASURING TOOLS
◆

Here are two helpful hints from someone who often becomes stuck in the middle of a quilt with carefully measured pieces that still don't fit together:

1. Make sure your graph paper, ruler, and tape measure all create the same dimensions.

2. Use the same tools from beginning to end. Some instruments are either printed or calibrated differently. If you have twenty shapes, and each one is off by one-sixteenth inch, you'll end up with one and one-quarter inches of excess fabric.

*R*uler. Use a see-through plastic ruler with accurate one-eighth-inch grid lines, preferably at least eighteen inches long and two inches wide. The grid makes it a breeze to add seam allowances without measuring. If you have a choice, buy see-through plastic in red—it's easier to read.

*T*ape measure. Use a reversible sixty-inch, metal-tipped, plastic-coated tape measure that can be read from either end.

FABRIC MARKING TOOLS
◆

The new marking utensils on the market add a stroke of magic and a touch of controversy to the act of quiltmaking. Some skeptics in the business claim that these newfangled pens with inks that disappear either by themselves, or with a drop of water, have been known to reappear mysteriously after a while to haunt the quilt top. On the other hand, other skilled and knowledgeable quilt artists swear by them.

The solution is to be aware of how each marked line functions. You will be making marks on fabric for seam lines, sewing lines, embroidery lines, appliqué guidelines, and quilting lines. I ask myself the following questions: Will the marked line be visible on the quilt top? Will it be on the right or wrong side of the fabric? Will it be a line that may be erased later on when I change my mind or make a mistake?

Accuracy for all of these lines is imperative, so the pen's point must always be fine and precise. This cannot be stressed enough. Lines don't have only length, they also have width. When you outline a shape, you increase its size with the width of your marking. You'll understand why this isn't just nit-picking when you get down to sewing your shapes onto fabric. A marker should glide smoothly, without stretching the fabric, leaving a thin but visible mark, without dulling its point quickly.

I use vanishing marking pens for drawing details on appliqué blocks that will be embroidered fairly quickly. Their purple lines disappear within forty-eight hours, all by themselves—in fact, they may perform their vanishing act even quicker if it's very humid.

Water soluble pens serve the same purpose—their lines disappear in a drop of water—but you have to remember to wash out the marks before pressing. White washout pencils are good for marking dark fabrics, as long as they fit in a pencil sharpener.

Many quilters use a well-sharpened #2 lead pencil for everything. When marking quilting designs or embroidery lines that should never show on the quilt top, they use very thin, light lines. They say that if the pencil mark doesn't rub off on its own, it can either be washed out or erased with an art-gum eraser. But just as some quilters won't let a disappearing pen touch the surface of their quilt, I'm paranoid about using a graphite pencil on the front of fabric or on the quilt top. I use pencils only when I'm marking a cutting line that will end up shrouded in the seam allowance. I make too many mistakes, or, to put it more positively, I'm constantly reassessing my designs.

For darker fabrics, some people recommend an artist's white or colored pencil, as long as the lead is not so soft that it doesn't stay sharp. Tailor's chalk pencils, which come in light colors, can be sharpened in the pencil sharpener. But because the point gets dull quickly, they can run up your expenses on a big quilt.

Always test your marking tools on a scrap of prepared fabric. Never use felt-tipped or ballpoint pens that might run all over your design. And while we're on the subject, hide a couple of #2 lead pencils from the rest of the family: you'll need ones with nice clean erasers when you're drafting graphs, pattern pieces, and templates.

GRAPH PAPER
◆

Look for two qualities in your graph paper: accuracy and size. Make sure the lines are printed precisely and the measurement is consistent with your other tools. You want a grid that is easily divisible by four because it makes it easy to add the one-quarter-inch seam allowance. Use either 4 × 4 or 8 × 8 to the inch graph paper.

Use graph paper when designing a base block or template shapes. You'll also want to be able to draft the entire quilt on one sheet, so you'll need a large piece with fairly small squares. One graph square should equal one square inch of the quilt top. Graph paper that's 8 × 8 to the inch is available at art supply stores in 17 × 22-inch sheets or in pads. The one-inch line is generally marked in a darker color.

TRACING PAPER
◆

Thin paper can be used to trace a design for appliqué, or a complete appliqué pattern that will be cut apart for templates.

TEMPLATE MATERIALS
◆

A template is a durable pattern piece used to copy a shape. It *must* be accurate. Templates are made out of material that can be precisely cut and marked with fine lines. You can use oak-tag, layout boards (available with a useful grid), index cards, or sheets of see-through lightweight plastic, preferably with a one-quarter-inch grid.

Transparent plastic is the most versatile choice. It won't get dog-eared from constant use, and it's excellent for seeing your way along special border prints or two-way prints. By using a transparent template material that is superimposed on the shape and then traced, you are making only one cut, thus reducing the risk of making an inaccurate template. Transparent template material is available at craft and quilt supply stores or through the mail. It is packaged in 8½ × 10¾-inch, or 12 × 36-inch sheets, with or without a grid.

Denril, a transparent vellum material intended for drafting, is a cinch to cut accurately. It's very versatile, resilient, and durable, and combines the best properties of paper and film. It's also forgiving. You can actually erase ink markings on it. Just lick your eraser first. Denril is available in pads or sheets at art supply stores.

FABRIC ADHESIVES
◆

Fabric glue sticks are useful for temporarily pasting appliqué shapes onto a base block to see how they look before sewing them down. Children can use them instead of basting. They're particularly convenient when working with tightly woven fabrics, leather, synthetic suede, and teeny-tiny pieces that would either distort, or show puncture marks, if they were anchored with a pin. Fabric glues wash out when the quilt is washed.

Fusible film is good for securing the raveling edges of textiles that would be unsightly, bulky, or difficult to turn under and hem. These bonding materials join one fabric layer to another. The bonding agent is made of heat-sensitized material that melts when ironed. They withstand washing and dry cleaning, and are suitable for trimmings as well as woven fabrics.

PRESS CLOTHS
◆

Press cloths protect vulnerable fabrics from giving off a telltale shine after ironing. It is always a good idea to use them while pressing an appliqué block—especially one that is embellished with many kinds of fabric. Cheesecloth (grade 70) is recommended for general use. Dampen it slightly to create steam. Press cloths are also available for specific purposes: to prevent crushing nap fabric, to raise details so they don't flatten, to improve application of fusibles. Transparent cheesecloth is available to help you see delicate materials and trimmings while you press.

EMBROIDERY FLOSS
◆

Embroidery floss comes in as many flavors as ice cream these days, and it's almost as much fun to buy. Floss is usually packaged in strings of six strands each. They can be used individually, or separated into combinations of two to six threads, depending on the effect you want.

EMBROIDERY HOOPS
◆

An embroidery hoop is used to keep the fabric taut, smooth, and on-grain. People resist hoops the way they resist thimbles. The undisputed fact remains—blocks done on-hoop look much more polished than their off-hoop companions.

These controversial gizmos are either round or oval and come in various sizes. Use what you're comfortable with. Oval-shaped hoops are useful in awkward places, such as near the edge.

BASIC TECHNIQUES

• • •

HOW TO PREPARE THE FABRIC

•

Test all your fabrics for their *colorfast* and *shrinking* tendencies. It would be criminal if a mere drop of water caused colors to run and ruined the entire project.

Unless the quilt will be encased under glass as soon as the last stitch is in place, it is always a good idea to prewash the fabric. By *prewashing,* you are testing to see if the fabrics are colorfast. My tried and true, highly technical method is called "sloshing"; it's accomplished by simply sloshing the textile in a sink of mild water and squeezing gently. If the water runoff is even slightly discolored, hold the fabric under the tap until the water runs clear. If the color continues to run, repeat until the water stays clear, or until you decide to bench this wimpy fabric and look for a healthier replacement.

Next, *machine-wash* the fabric in warm water with detergent, and line-dry or tumble dry using medium heat. Fabrics that pass the first-round colorfast test can be washed together. If a fabric performs poorly during this second test (too much wrinkling, raveling, or shrinking) bench it. All-cotton fabrics tend to shrink.

Cut off one-half inch from each selvage and press.

HOW TO CALCULATE YARDAGE

•

A *cutting layout* is a master plan showing how a piece of fabric can be dissected into the proper shapes for a quilt. To figure out how much fabric to buy, you must make a cutting layout for each different textile that will be used in your quilt.

Don't forget to add seam allowances to both length and width dimensions in your calculations. The usual seam allowance in a pieced quilt is one-quarter inch. Multiply that times two to represent both sides of the block. This creates a sturdy patch and minimizes bulky seams that make quilting an unhappy chore.

Draw a rectangle that represents a piece of background fabric forty-three inches wide. Most Made-in-the-U.S.A. cottons come in forty-four- to forty-five-inch widths. You'll need to subtract about one inch from the width to account for the selvages you will have to trim off—they are too tightly woven to be used for patches.

Beginning along the imagined straight-grain edge of fabric, mark off shapes in a row—as many as will fit. Don't be stingy: plan for a few just-in-case pieces. Patches can be aligned edge to edge. Mark the largest and longest first, and sneak smaller pieces economically in between. Arrange triangles and diamonds efficiently by fitting them together, but make sure that they are all placed on the correct grain line according to the piecing pattern you have in mind (Diagram 33). See also "How to Piece Borders," page 189.

Let's say you want to estimate how much background fabric you'll need for a quilt of twenty ten-inch-square base blocks. The cutting size for each block will be $10 + \frac{1}{4} + \frac{1}{4} = 10\frac{1}{2}$ inches. Divide the number of patches you need by the number of pieces of fabric, including seam allowances, that will fit across the width: $20 \div 4 = 5$. Multiply this number by the size of the patch: $5 \times 10\frac{1}{2}$ inches $= 52\frac{1}{2}$ inches. Divide by 36 to convert inches to yards, rounding off to a larger number to get $\frac{1}{4}$ or $\frac{1}{2}$ yard: $52\frac{1}{2}$ inches $\div 36 = 1\frac{1}{2}$ yards. The result: you will need to buy $1\frac{1}{2}$ yards of base block fabric.

HOW TO MAKE TEMPLATES

•

A template is a sturdy pattern piece used to make an accurate copy of a shape. Templates must be extremely precise—I can't stress this enough. The mere act of outlining a template can enlarge your shape. While this may not matter for free-form picture blocks, it makes a huge difference for piecing and repeat appliqué designs. The template is held firmly on the fabric and outlined carefully with a fine mark. (Cut the fabric on the *inside* of the marked line for the sake of accuracy.) You will need one template for every different shape that cannot be drawn freehand. See "Template Materials," page 155.

Constructing Templates. Outline the pattern piece on template material using a well-sharpened pencil. I prefer sturdy see-through templates. Sheets of template plastic can be bought in a quilting supply store. Superimpose the plastic over the paper sketch. Trace each shape directly onto the plastic. Use a ruler to trace straight lines. Add the seam allowance on all sides using the quarter-inch delineation of a see-through ruler. Cut the template with utility scissors just inside your line. Between these acts of marking and cutting, the original size of the template is reestablished.

Find your errors before you begin cutting the fabric. Check the template's dimensions by remeasuring or superimposing it on a full-sized pattern.

It's wise to mark the grain lines right on the templates. To determine which sides of the shape should be cut on the straight grain and which should be cut off-grain, these two guidelines should be followed whenever possible:

1. Outside edges of a block should be cut on-grain.

2. Avoid sewing two off-grain edges together because they will have a tendency to stretch out of shape.

To accomplish this, first mark arrows on the templates that represent the outermost edges of the shape. After these lines are marked, you'll be able to see which edges will end up on the bias. If placing two bias sides together is unavoidable, try your best to keep those two bias edges from coming together in an area that will receive a lot of stress, such as the center of a pieced block.

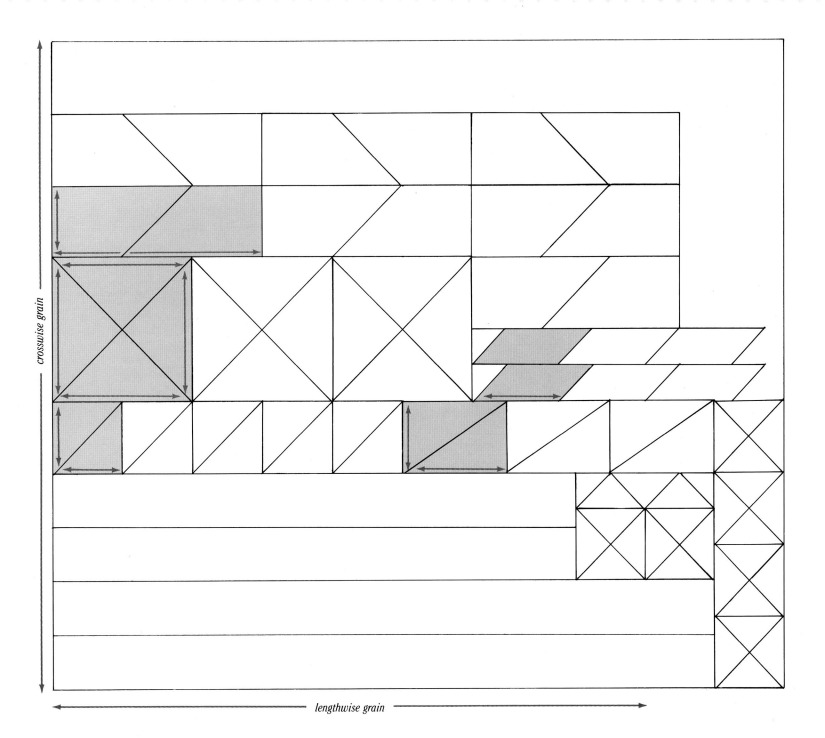

Diagram 33. Cutting layout.

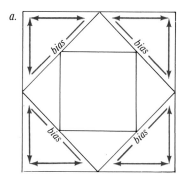
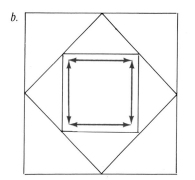

a.   *b.*   *c.*

Diagram 34. Placing fabric shapes on the grain lines.

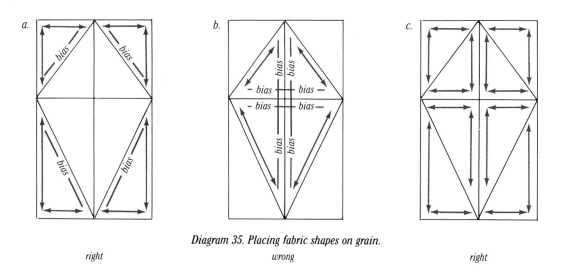

Diagram 35. Placing fabric shapes on grain.

   right   *wrong*   *right*

In Diagram 34, these guidelines work beautifully. First the outside edges are marked on-grain, then the center square is marked on-grain, and finally the inside triangles are marked. Bias edges meet grain line edges every time. In Diagram 35, the directions don't work out as smoothly. If you (a) first mark the outermost shapes on-grain, and then (b) mark the interior triangles on-grain, with the grain lines on the outside edges, you will end up with bias lines joining right at the stress points in the shape—the axis. So in this case, it's better to mark the outside edges of the internal triangles on the bias (c).

DIFFERENT KINDS OF TEMPLATES

•

Templates for Hand-Sewing and Appliqué. For asymmetrical shapes mark grain-line and orientation arrows on the templates. You may also find it useful to indicate how many shapes you want of each.

Hand-sewing templates should be the exact size of the finished pattern; they do not include seam allowance. The outline of the template marks the line you will use to stitch (Diagram 36).

Templates for Machine-Sewing. Machine-sewing templates include a precise one-quarter-inch seam allowance. The stitching line is not marked. The crisp edges of the fabrics are used to determine the line to be stitched. An even seam line is created by aligning the patches' edges, and using a guage on the sewing machine (Diagram 37).

Templates for Machine-Piecing Acute Angles. An acute angle is a point that is less than 90 degrees. If you align the cut edges of two differently angled triangles (two diamonds, and in some cases a triangle and a square), the finished product will be distorted (Diagrams 38a and b). This is because the stitching lines, one-quarter

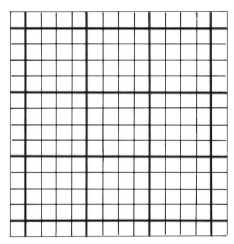

Diagram 36. Hand-sewing template

Diagram 37. Machine-sewing template

Diagram 38a. The hoped-for result when you piece together a diamond and a square with two different angles.

Diagram 38b. Wrong. This is what happens when you line up the raw edges instead of the stitching lines.

Diagram 38c. Correct. Extend the point ¼-inch from the sewing edge of the other patch.

inch from the cut edge, don't match. In order to match up the stitching line, the point has to extend exactly one-quarter inch from the sewing edge of the other patch. (Diagram 38c). But since only the cutting line is marked, there is no guideline to judge how to position the triangle perfectly. The sharper the angles to be pieced, the more difficult it is to eyeball the correct alignment.

The solution is to mark the quarter-inch seam allowance (the stitching line) one-quarter inch in from the cut edge of both templates. Then, matching the stitching lines, fit one over the other as if you were going to sew them together. Trim away extending points so that the templates fit each other perfectly (Diagrams 39a, 39b, 40a, 40b, 41a, and 41b).

Templates for Asymmetrical Shapes. Asymmetrical shapes are those that are nonreversible. In other words, the back and the front of the shape are mirror-images of each other. Symmetrical

shapes (squares, circles, etc.) are reversible; for example, a square is a square from the back and from the front.

If you have an odd shape, pay close attention when you cut it out, or you may get it backward. You can either flip your template over when you mark on the *wrong* side of the fabric, or carefully mark on the *right* side. When you need to create a pair—the one-way shape and its mirror-image—mark the template first right side up, then flip it over and use it wrong side up. See Diagram 47.

Templates for Repetitive Special Effects. A stripe or a motif printed on a fabric can be used identically in repeated patches to achieve a special effect. The repetition of a printed basket, a penguin, or the same geometric creates instant unity in your design. Perhaps you want to center the same basket of flowers in a diamond-shaped patch in the border, or use a border print to frame each base block. To achieve visual unity, the elements that repeat have to be

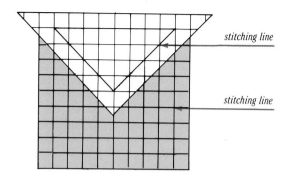

Diagram 39a. For piecing differently angled pieces, match stitching lines of templates.

stitching line

stitching line

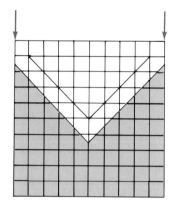

Diagram 39b. Trim away extending points so that the templates fit each other perfectly.

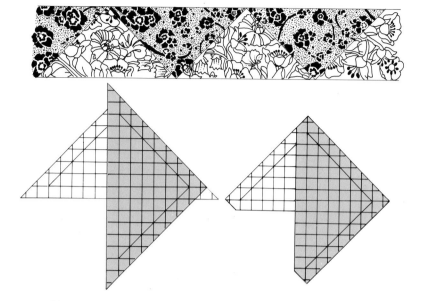

Diagram 40a. To make the above pattern, place two same-sized triangle templates over each other. Match stitching lines.

Diagram 40b. Trim extending points.

Diagram 41a. To make the above pattern, place two same-sized parallelogram templates over each other. Match stitching lines.

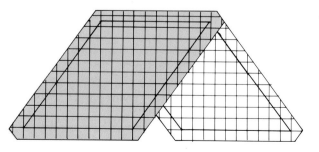

Diagram 41b. Trim extending points.

identical. If one basket is missing half its handle and another is tilted with its flowers threatening to spill out, the effect will be jarring instead of smooth and unified (Diagrams 42 and 43).

Cut the template accurately out of transparent plastic and place it over the motif on the front of the fabric. Trace either the whole motif or just a few of its lines onto the plastic template. Now, superimpose the template over the same motif when it occurs again on the fabric, tracing it repeatedly in exactly the same way.

I used this method to create some of the border ideas shown on page 145. In one example, I isolated the same portion of a large printed paisley fabric several times. In another, I centered a pair of cute penguins. And in a third, I used the same border pattern in four different ways. By marking the seam allowance lines on the template, I was able to identify the area of the motif that would be visible in the patch. The paisley diamond-shaped patches are not cut on-grain. This was a case when I had to sacrifice having the shape on-grain, in favor of getting the special design effect I was looking for.

Diagram 42. Templates for repetitive special effects.

Diagram 44. Window template.

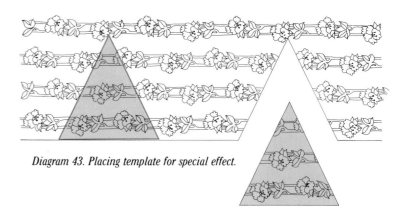

Diagram 43. Placing template for special effect.

*W**indow Templates.* If the fabric has to be cut in a certain way for a special effect, and you don't have any transparent material available, don't despair. Trace the finished shape onto any template material. The traced line provides the stitching line. Now add and mark the one-quarter-inch seam allowance. Cut along both of these markings. You will create a window the size of the finished shape, with the seam allowance framing it. Place this window template on the right side of the fabric. You only have to mark the outside edge of the seam allowance (Diagram 44).

HOW TO MARK AND CUT FABRIC

•

Above all, be precise! Hold the template firmly in place; mark with a pencil, applying just enough pressure to produce a visible *thin* line, without stretching the fabric. For darker fabrics, use a white or light-colored pencil. Take care to mark corners and points precisely. For the most part, mark shapes to be pieced on the *wrong* side of the fabric. Only appliqué shapes and special motifs from a decorative print should be marked on the *right* side of the fabric. Cut accurately with dressmaker's shears. Aim the scissors down the middle of the marked line.

Beginning along an edge of the lengthwise grain of fabric, place the template so that grain lines match, or so that the maximum number of sides are on the straight grain. Arrange the shapes in rows so you don't waste fabric.

*H*and-sewing. Outline your templates, leaving at least one-half inch of fabric between each one. Cut them out so that each shape has an approximate one-quarter-inch seam allowance outside the marked line, which is the sewing line, not the fabric edge (Diagram 45).

*M*achine-piecing. Do not rip fabric, or cut it with pinking shears. For machine piecework, a precise fabric edge is needed in order to match each patch perfectly. This edge is used to gauge seam allowance for piecing. Ripping creates an on-grain shape that may happen to be the correct size, but is edged with lots of unruly threads.

Line up templates next to each other without leaving any space in between. The marked line is both the cutting line and the alignment gauge for the other raw edges (Diagrams 46 and 47). See also "Fabric Marking Tools," page 154.

HOW TO HAND-PIECE

•

Align patches, right sides together, so that the points where the seam lines end match. Pin at each of these corresponding points, then at the junctions of the seams, then add additional pins in between for long seams.

Thread a #8 sharp needle with an eighteen-inch single strand of 100 percent cotton or cotton-covered polyester thread. Make a small knot. Using a small, even running stitch, sew from one end of the marked seam line to the other—not from raw edge to raw edge. End with a couple of back stitches. You can take one stitch at a time, or you can load the needle with three to six stitches before pulling the needle through (Diagrams 48 and 49).

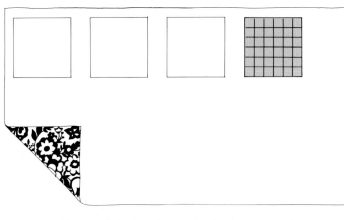

Diagram 45. Marking fabric using hand-sewing template.

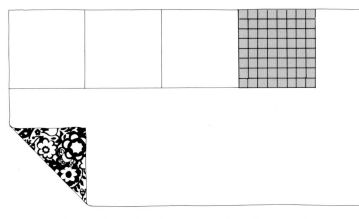

Diagram 46. Marking fabric using machine-piecing template.

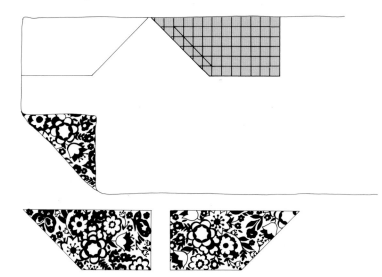

Diagram 47. Marking fabric with asymmetrical template.

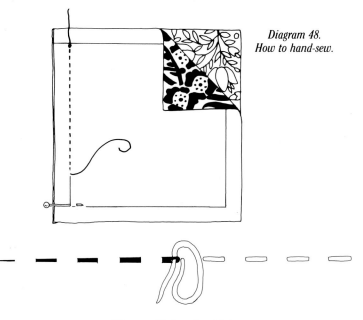

Diagram 48.
How to hand-sew.

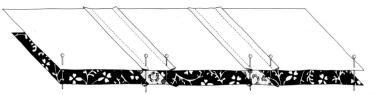

Diagram 49. Running stitch.

HOW TO MACHINE-PIECE

Templates for machine-piecing include a quarter-inch seam allowance. To achieve a perfectly straight seam line, match up the fabric edges and sew, letting your machine be your guide.

On some machines, the edge of the presser foot is exactly one-quarter inch from the needle. Others have a one-quarter-inch mark etched on the throat plate. Still others come with a magnetic or screw-on accessory to indicate sewing lines. Some have no markings whatsoever, in which case you can make your own with a piece of masking tape on the throat plate. Measure from the needle using the same rulers or graph paper you used to cut and measure pattern pieces. Check it a few hundred times—this is important. Compulsiveness now will lead to well-behaved rows later on. The fabric is kept in line with the left edge of the guide as you stitch.

Don't feel you need to go out and buy an expensive, state-of-the-art sewing machine. Just dust off the antique you inherited, oil it, and put in a new needle. I use a sturdy thirty-year-old secondhand portable.

Seam joints must look as if they were destined to meet each other on this particular quilt surface. *Pin the right sides together.* Begin by aligning and pinning the ends. Then match and pin through corresponding joints. Ease in fabric and add additional pins, working from the center pin to each raw edge. Insert the pins at right angles to the seam line. Some people like to remove the pins before the needle stitches over them. That is really a matter of preference and machine capabilities (Diagrams 50 and 51).

When piecing one on-grain edge of a patch to one off-grain edge, put the on-grain shape on the bottom. This will keep the end result from stretching or somehow distorting.

For medium-weight fabrics, adjust the stitch length to ten to twelve stitches per inch. Use a size 11 needle. White or neutral-colored polycotton thread can be used throughout, or you can match thread with the predominant dark fabric color. Start with a full bobbin and have a spare one close by. It is rather irksome, to put it mildly, to run out of bobbin thread in the middle of a full-blown stitching storm.

With the presser foot up, place the units to be pieced under the needle, aligning the edges with the seam guide. Release the presser foot and manually put the needle in the fabric. Hold a couple of inches of top and bobbin thread tails out of the needle's way as you begin to stitch.

Sew from raw edge to raw edge, with the smaller unit on top. When sewing a shape with a skinny point (an acute angle less than 90 degrees), begin from the side with the greater amount of fabric and end at the point (Diagram 52).

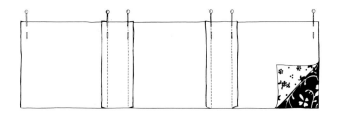

Diagram 50. For machine-piecing, align and pin right sides together. Match pins through corresponding joints. Insert pins at right angles to seam line.

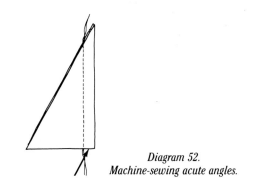

Diagram 51. For machine-piecing, match pins through seam joints.

Diagram 52.
Machine-sewing acute angles.

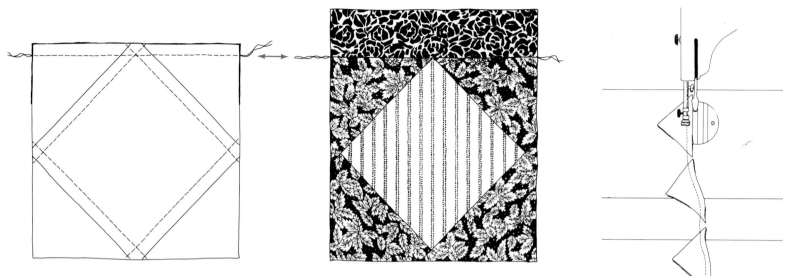

Diagram 53. Machine-sewing points. The needle must travel through the intersection exactly.

Diagram 54. Assembly-line machine-piecing.

Make sure the needle is in the fabric when you stop to stretch, to answer the phone, or to check or realign the fabrics. If you leave the needle up, there is nothing stabilizing the fabric during your break.

As long as the pieced patches are handled with love and respect, and you leave an inch of twisted top and bobbin thread, you don't need to knot each piece with backtacking. Each row of stitches will be anchored by a second intersecting line of stitches.

Squares and rectangles are easier to sew than pointed patches. Shapes with points have at least one bias edge and require accurate seaming. Where seams intersect in a pieced unit with pointed shapes, an X is created. In order to make a precise point when connecting this unit to the next, the needle must travel through the intersection exactly (Diagram 53). When joining two angles that are not the same, remember to align the seam lines, not the cut edges. Trim away any points that stick out.

Assembly-line approach. To save time, sew identical units all at the same time. Don't cut the thread after you've seamed a unit; keep guiding them through the machine so that they dangle like a string of sausages, leaving an inch of stitches in between. Snip apart after stitching a chain (Diagram 54).

Strip-piecing. With this timesaving technique, strips of different fabrics, in varying or similar widths, are seamed together to create a new piece of whole fabric. The result is now treated as if it's a striped piece of fabric. When shapes cut from this strip-pieced textile

are sewn together, the effect is textured and complex. It looks as if you've meticulously cut tiny patches and pieced them together perfectly.

Placing templates on strip-pieced material is just like placing them on a striped fabric. Make either a window template or a transparent template and mark with the finished dimensions of the various widths. Then when you superimpose the template on the front, you can align the strips correctly (Diagrams 55a, 55b, and 55c).

I used this technique in two different ways in the border on *The Alphabet Quilt* (page 105). For the long vertical and horizontal strips, I strip-pieced bands of solid-colored fabrics of equal widths. In each corner there is a square made of four triangles. Each triangle is created from strip-pieced fabric. Since strip-pieced fabric functions like a stripe, the border needed a barricade in the corners to keep the bands from getting too closely acquainted.

In *Cheryl and Dean's Wedding Quilt* (page 64), I used a more elaborate strip-piecing technique. The semicircle palm of God is an example of strip-piecing's unlimited potential. First, I joined shaded prints and solid fabrics into a new fabric. From this fabric, I cut four large triangles and a long band. Then I joined these shapes into a rectangle with the sewing machine and cut a semicircle from it. Finally, I appliquéd the semicircle onto the quilt top.

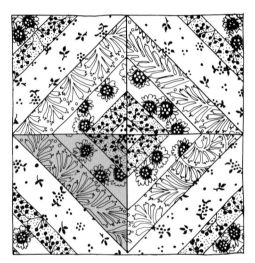

Diagram 55. Strip piecing. (a) Four fabrics of varying widths from which triangles are cut. (b) Triangles cut from both edges are joined into a square. (c) Different use of same fabric.

MADE A MISTAKE?

Don't hesitate to pull out mistakes. We all make them. My only advice is to use a seam ripper to remove stitches—don't pull the edges apart. Remove stitches every one inch on one side then pull out the thread on the other side; remove any leftover short threads on the first side. If the stitches you've removed were in the middle of a seam, overlap the leftover previous ones with the new ones when you restitch.

And try, try again. You'll be happy you did.

HOW TO DETERMINE
A PIECING SEQUENCE

Pieced blocks are usually made from rows of seamed-together patches. In order to avoid sewing into a corner, each pattern is analyzed and dissected into straight rows that can be horizontal, vertical, or diagonal. Rarely is anything but straight seam-piecing necessary. When piecing, work from the smallest to larger to the largest units. Single patches are pieced into units, which are then pieced to other units, and eventually joined in rows. Complete each type of unit before moving onto the next. The longest seam is sewn last (Diagrams 56, 57, and 58).

To ease in fullness on the sewing machine, put the larger unit, the one that needs easing in, underneath.

HOW TO PRESS PIECEWORK

Don't press each seam as soon as it's born. Wait until you've completed a group of similar units, then press before sewing to the next sequence.

In quilts, seams are not pressed open. They're pressed together and flapped over to one side of the seam line. This creates a strong seam and prevents batting fibers from sticking their prickly heads through the top later on. Press gently, on the wrong side first, in the direction of the straight grain of fabric. Then turn over and iron out the wrinkles.

Whenever possible, press the seam toward darker fabric. Think about your future quilting. Press seams away from areas that require close quilting. If you consistently press identical units in the same direction, you will eliminate as many layers of fabric that congregate at one point as you can. The antidote for a little pucker may be a touch of steam.

HOW TO MITER A CORNER

♦

A mitered corner looks just like a picture frame: the strips meet in a diagonal seam. The fabrics bend gracefully, creating a continuous, finished look. To determine the length of a strip to be mitered, here's the equation:

Finished length of side to be mitered
+ 2 × (width of border)
+ ½-inch seam allowance

For example, if your sixty-inch side will have a five-inch border, you add:

$$60'' + 10'' + \frac{1}{2}'' = 70\frac{1}{2}'' \text{ long} \times 5\frac{1}{2}'' \text{ wide.}$$

For a rectangular quilt, both the horizontal and vertical measurements must be determined.

On the strip to be mitered, mark a tiny dot one width measurement plus one-quarter inch in from each edge. Mark on the wrong side on the seam line. On the side to be mitered, mark a dot one-quarter inch in from each edge (Diagram 59). With wrong sides together, use pins to match the dots and center the strip onto the side to which it will be attached. The strip to be mitered will extend beyond each end by one width measurement. Beginning and ending at this dot, sew a strip to each side of the quilt or block. In other words, you are not beginning and ending, as usual, at the edges of the strip, but rather at the seam line (Diagram 60).

Working from the wrong side, lap one border over the other. Use a ruler to draw a line from the dot (the seam line) to the outside corner, creating a 45-degree angle. Reverse the borders, and repeat. Right sides together, match the lines, pin or baste, and stitch. Trim away excess fabric from seam allowance. Repeat at every corner. Press, seams open (Diagram 61).

Diagram 56. Three examples of piecing from smallest unit to largest.

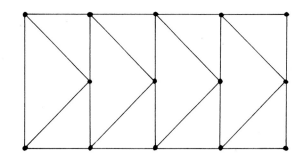

Diagram 56a. Simple border pattern that can be pieced vertically.

Diagram 56b. One unit separated into all its parts.

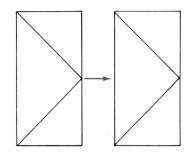

Diagram 56c. Piecing two units together with vertical seam.

Diagram 57a. Block pattern that can be dissected into horizontal rows for simplest piecing sequence.

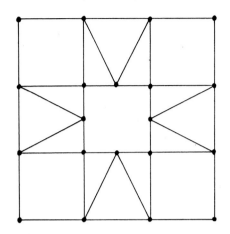

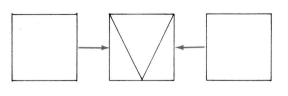

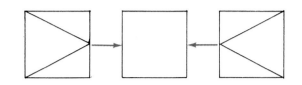

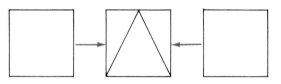

Diagram 57c. Each unit in a row pieced together.

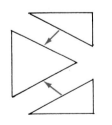

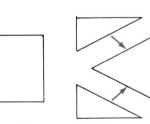

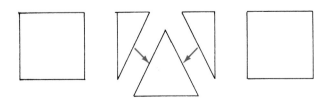

Diagram 57b. One block separated into three horizontal rows and broken down into its simplest shapes.

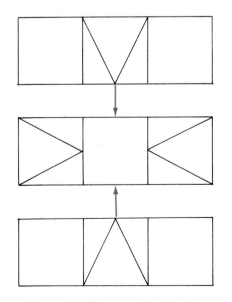

Diagram 57d. Three rows pieced together.

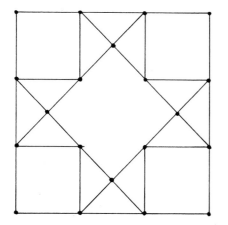

Diagram 58a. Block pattern that can be dissected into diagonal rows for simplest piecing sequence.

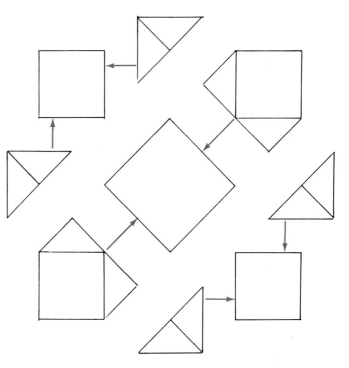

Diagram 58c. Smallest units in a row are pieced together.

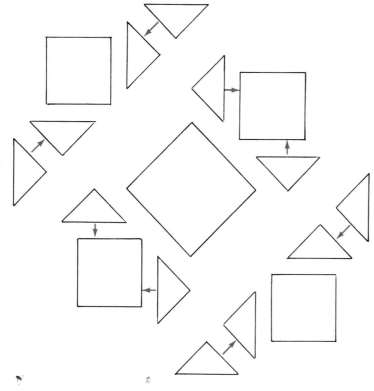

Diagram 58b. Pattern broken into three diagonal rows of its simplest shapes.

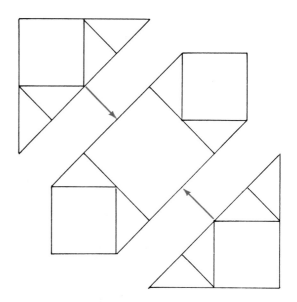

Diagram 58d. Units joined together in diagonal rows.

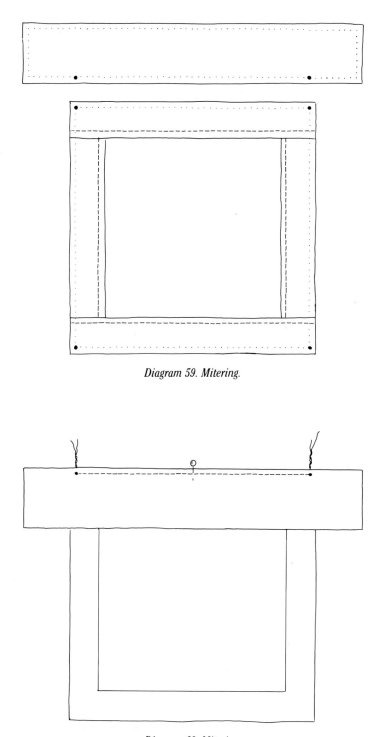

Diagram 59. Mitering.

Diagram 60. Mitering.

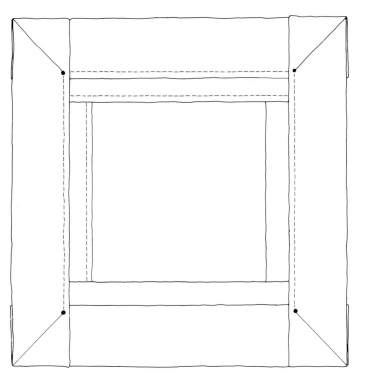

Diagram 61. Mitering.

How to Make an
Appliqué Base Block

BASE BLOCK FABRIC
◆   ◆   ◆

Begin by preparing your fabric according to the directions on "How to Prepare the Fabric," page 156.

CALCULATING YARDAGE
◆

To figure out how much background fabric you need, start with the finished base block size and add two full inches (one-inch seam allowance for each side). In other words, for an eight-inch block, you will need to cut a ten-inch square from your fabric: $8'' + 1'' + 1'' = 10$ inches. Don't forget to include a few just-in-case blocks in your calculations.

Refer to "How to Calculate Yardage," page 156.

THE IMPORTANCE OF A
"FAT" SEAM ALLOWANCE
◆

An appliquéd pictorial block is a spoiled version of its less demanding machine-pieced counterpart. Pieced blocks are happy with just one-quarter-inch seam allowance. Pictorials can't manage without a corpulent one-inch allowance—for the following reasons:

· A big seam will give you room to remeasure your block no matter what happens during appliqué time. The background fabric can get pulled off-grain or eaten up by layers of appliqué, dense embroidery, or a preponderance of protruding objects.

· Sometimes your design will take off on a course all its own. With the extra fabric, the stitcher still has time to read the clues, raid the trimmings box, and stretch spontaneous inspirations into the seams.

· Extra fabric allows for extra abuse. Most blocks will inevitably be shlepped around from meeting to subway to playground to work. Some may be shipped off to distant planets, or neglected for days in front of the TV, causing their delicate edges to fray.

MAKING BASE BLOCK TEMPLATES

•

Make a durable and accurate cardboard or clear plastic template for the base block. Remember to include a one-inch seam allowance all around. Even though it's not absolutely essential, I prefer to make transparent plastic templates at this stage, because I will need them later anyway when the blocks are ready for machine-piecing. To recycle for later piecing, just trim down the one-inch seam allowance to one-quarter inch.

Refer to "How to Make Templates," page 156.

MARKING AND CUTTING
BASE BLOCK FABRIC

•

Equipment: templates, dressmaker's shears, see-through ruler, graphite or light-colored pencil, water-soluble marker.

Beginning along an edge of the lengthwise grain, outline your block template on the *wrong* side of the fabric. Repeat until you have drawn all the blocks you need, plus a few extras. Working on a flat surface, cut the blocks accurately by aiming the scissors down the middle of the marked line.

Next, use the ruler to mark the one-inch seam allowance very clearly on the *front* of each block with a water-soluble marker. This is one time when your mark does not have to be excessively fine. But it must be visible and it must be able to be *erased* later on if the seam line has to be readjusted. Don't use pencil. Align the one-inch ruler delineation with the edge of the fabric, and zip a line across.

Or draw a line in pencil on the back of the fabric, one inch away from each edge. Using this line as a guide, run a basting stitch around the four sides.

If the fabric has a direction, mark "top" on the front in the seam allowance (Diagram 62).

Refer to "How to Mark and Cut Fabric," page 162.

DESIGNING THE
BASE BLOCK ON PAPER

• • •

Equipment: tracing paper, graph paper, reliable ruler, pencil, crayons or colored pencils.

DRAFTING THE DESIGN

•

Use tracing paper to copy a design from another source. Use graph paper if you plan to draw freehand. Graph paper makes it easy to locate the square's center, which helps to balance the design. If the paper doesn't have a grid and the design must be centered, gently

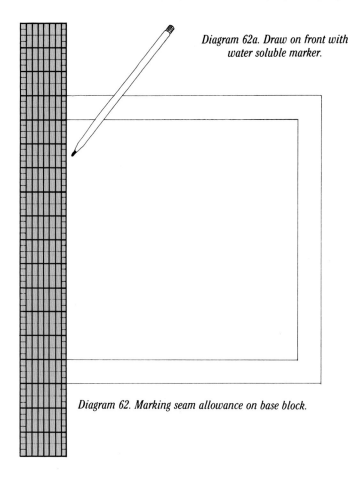

Diagram 62a. Draw on front with water soluble marker.

Diagram 62. Marking seam allowance on base block.

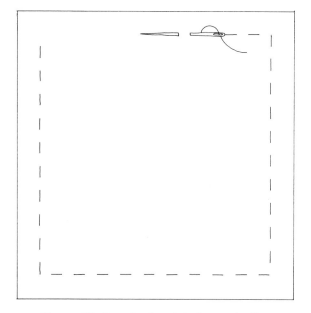

Diagram 62b. Run a basting stitch along sewing line.

fold it into quarters and mark the center with a dot.

With a reliable ruler, draw a square the size of your actual block (e.g., 8″ × 8″) on the paper of your choice. This outline represents the actual sewing line that will be used to piece the quilt top. Add a one-inch seam allowance frame.

Realize that blocks with perfectly centered designs may come back with an assortment of proportions: a moose-sized insect may have to reside next to a tiny elephant. If you want the designs to be fairly uniform in size, with the appliquéd shape taking up approximately the same amount of space and leaving equal amounts of visible background fabric, suggest to the blockmakers that some part of the design touch an imagined margin line within the block. For example, a nine-inch square within a ten-inch base block will leave at least an inch of background fabric showing around the appliqué. For a centered figure, mark and measure the perimeter dimension.

Draw or trace the design inside the square. If you're drawing a big picture, particularly a scene of some sort, spill the design into the seam allowance (Diagram 63). A scene that stops exactly at the sewing line can cause problems come piecing time. Unless the block matches perfectly to the connecting sashing, some of the background fabric may peek out of the corners and ruin your design (Diagram 63a).

Trimmings, especially those with raw edges that are tricky to tuck under neatly, should also be extended into the seam allowance whenever possible. This alleviates the need to turn them under and hem. Trimmings will be sufficiently secured when the block is pieced to the sashing. Don't worry. Most of the resulting bulk in the seams can be safely trimmed away after piecing. Quilting patterns can be created to bypass them.

My attitude with free-form designs is that this sketch is just a beginning. Once the paper design is translated into fabric, it may be totally transformed. Be flexible. Let the design muses speak to you. This is when humor, originality, creativity, and the endless possibilities of raw materials should be given free rein. Your aim is not simply to copy your paper design into textiles, but to translate it, play with it, revise it with fabric. A mountain may raise its fabric peak a quarter of an inch higher or lower, a tree stump may inch left or right. We talked a lot about using trimmings and fabrics to their best advantage in "Trimmings and Found Objects," page 130.

ADJUSTING DESIGN SIZE

◆

If you find a picture to trace but it's too small or too big for your block, ask your local photocopying outlet to enlarge or reduce it.

Otherwise, you can use the following grid technique to alter its size. Make a grid on a piece of tracing paper; the smaller the grid units, the more accurate the conversion will be. Superimpose the grid onto the picture of choice and trace the design. Use one color

pencil to mark the grid, and a second color to trace the picture. This will cause the figure (the design to be traced) to stand out from the ground (the grid) and eliminate confusion about which line to follow (Diagram 64).

Calculate the ratio between the actual size of the design and the desired size. In Diagram 64a, the size of the butterfly is two inches, and we need to enlarge it to four inches.

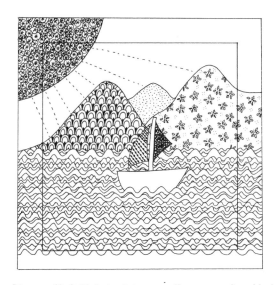

Diagram 63. Spill design into seam allowance on base block.

Diagram 63a. Note the background fabric visible in the upper left corner.

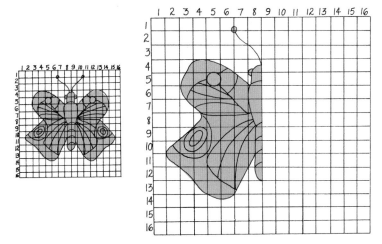

Diagram 64. Adjusting design size on base block.

$$\frac{\text{Size of picture to be traced}}{\text{Size of enlargement}} = \frac{2''}{4''}$$

Reduce the fraction to ½. The ration between the two is 1:2.

Make a second grid that has units that are in the same ratio to the size of the units in the first grid as the ratio between the size of the picture to be traced and the size it will be enlarged to. Let's expand our previous example. We have a ratio of 1:2, so the size of the units in the second grid should be twice as large as the size of the units in the first grid.

In Diagram 64b, the size of the units in the first grid is one-eighth inch.

$$\frac{\text{Size of units in first grid}}{\text{Size of units in second grid}} = \frac{\text{Size of picture to be traced}}{\text{Size of enlargement}}$$

$$\frac{1/8''}{1/4''} = \frac{2''}{4''}$$

In this illustration, the size of the units in the second grid should be one-quarter inch. Counting the units, copy each line of the design from the first grid onto the second grid. For a symmetrical design, you only need to draft one portion of the design. When drafting templates and transferring the design to the fabric, you can use the reverse side of the template.

Roberta Horton uses a no-math method for enlarging designs that are already on a square piece of paper. Fold the square so that you have sixteen equal divisions. Make a square representing the size of the finished block. Fold it into sixteen equal divisions. Draw the design onto the bigger paper, using the folded grid of lines as guidelines. Focus on one square at a time, paying attention to where the drawing intersects the folded lines.

APPLIQUÉING THE DESIGN ON FABRIC

♦ ♦ ♦

STRATEGY FOR APPLIQUÉ SEQUENCE

♦

Dissect your design into all its parts. Mentally peel away the top layers of the picture to imagine what is underneath; these under-pieces should be sewn down first. Label the appliqué pieces with a number and an arrow. The number is the order in which they will be sewn, from the ground fabric up. The arrow indicates the left-right orientation of the shape on the design. Many appliqué shapes are nonreversible, like the Nutcracker's boot or the Hitchhiker's thumb. The back and front are mirror images of each other. If your tiny little cutout trousers get separated from your pile, you may not recognize what they are, let alone which direction you intended them to go. The arrow will also provide a guide for matching the template to the correct grain of the fabric.

TEMPLATES

♦

Equipment: tracing paper, template material, pencil, util-ity scissors.

A template must be prepared for each shape that cannot be drawn freehand. Remember, you don't need to include seam allowance, since it is added to appliqué shapes as the pattern is cut from the fabric.

First, prepare two traced copies of the entire design. Include the sequence number and arrow notations. Cut one into its compo-nents to make templates, and keep the second intact; this "map" will be your guide.

If you are creating a *once-in-a-lifetime free-form design*, where precision matching is not essential, you can use the cut-apart shapes of tracing paper for templates. Otherwise, trace each piece carefully on the template material of your choice. Use see-through plastic sheets if you want to control the placement of stripes or motifs printed on the fabric. Cut carefully. This thin line represents the actual dimensions of the finished piece.

For a *symmetrical block*, construct a template of only one half the symmetrical design—one in which the size and position of its shapes are identical on both sides of an imagined center line. If you create a single template of the entire design, there's a chance the two sides will be different. After outlining it on the fabric, you can match at the center and flip the template to get its mirror image and the complete design.

Refer to "How to Make Templates," page 156.

MARKING AND CUTTING
APPLIQUÉ FABRICS
•

Equipment: templates, dressmaker's shears, graphite or light-colored or chalk pencil, water-soluble or vanishing marker.

Leaving one inch between shapes, match grain lines and carefully mark around the template on the right side of the fabric. Remember to compensate for the thickness of the marked line by cutting on the inside or down the middle of the line.

Add a one-quarter-inch seam allowance around the shape, and cut (Diagram 65). Seam allowances on underlying pieces are needed to tuck under overlapping shapes; the seam allowances of these top-lying pieces will have to be turned under and hemmed. As the pieces are stitched in place, some of the seam allowance may have to be trimmed away. This is especially true for teeny pieces, for bulky textured fabrics, or for areas that will be heavily quilted.

Refer to "How to Mark and Cut Fabric," page 162.

B*ias Shapes.* For curved contours, such as flower stems, rainbows, and basket handles, templates can be placed on the bias to take advantage of the fabric's natural "give." Cut bias strips the width of the exact size needed plus seam allowance for each side. A second method involves cutting a template for the curved shape in the same manner as all the other templates.

TRANSFERRING THE DESIGN
TO THE BASE BLOCK
•

Repeating or symmetrical patterns (such as the same butterfly on each block) need to be centered. To find the center, fold the base block fabric gently into quarters and mark the middle with a light dot. Use a pencil only if the dot will be covered by appliqués; otherwise use a water-soluble or vanishing marker, which can be used even to mark a central axis.

For the sake of consistency, you will need to transfer your repeated design onto the background fabric. There are times when you want to indicate directly on the block where each shape should go. Trace another map of the entire design, cut around the outline creating a template, center the template on the base block, and trace the design onto the fabric. I feel more comfortable using a disappearing or water-soluble pen than a light pencil that might show if I'm not accurate. Now you can mark off the individual butterfly shapes by outlining each template.

L*ight Box.* Use a light box to trace a design directly onto an opaque piece of fabric. A homemade light box can be devised in two ways. One way involves taping the original sketch onto a clean window,

taping the ground fabric over it, matching the center marks, and tracing the design (on a sunny day, of course) with a vanishing marker. If worse comes to worst, you will end up with a dirt-free window.

If you find it too awkward to draw from a vertical position, look around the house for materials to devise a substitute glass table. Get a sheet of Plexiglas, prop it between two chairs, and put a light underneath. Or place the clear plastic over a top-loading washing machine with a light source inside. The advantage of these methods is that you can work in a more comfortable position.

Diagram 65. Marking appliqué template on fabric.

Diagram 66. Clipping outside curves ⅛-inch in seam allowance.

HAND-APPLIQUÉ TECHNIQUES

• • •

It doesn't matter if you're slipping, overcasting, or whipping your stitches blindly into oblivion. The right way to appliqué is the way you like best. Remember, once the block is quilted no one will ever see the back. Your sewing goals should be smooth edges and politely obscure stitches.

Turn under and hem the edges of most woven fabrics and findings. Fabrics that don't fray, such as felt and Ultrasuede, can be cut out without seam allowance. They won't need hemming. Sewing can be made a little easier if you follow a few techniques for preparing fabric shapes.

PREPARATION FOR APPLIQUÉ

•

*C*urves and Corners. Before you turn under rounded shapes, make tiny clips with the point of sharp scissors in the seam allowance. Make as few as necessary, because they weaken the seams. For *inside concave curves and corners,* clip the seam allowance up to, but not through, the sewing line. Some *outside convex curves* must be clipped with little Vs one-eighth inch from the raw edge to remove some of the fullness from the seam allowance (Diagram 66).

Edges cut on the bias can be stretched, but they can't be "shrunk." For shapes cut out on the *bias,* stitch the inside curve first, to eliminate fullness. The bias shape can then be stretched to complete the wider outside curve.

*P*oints. To prepare shapes with *sharp points,* clip off some of the excess fabric at the tip. Working with the wrong side facing you, turn the point under, finger press, turn under one side of seam allowance, finger press, baste almost to the point, fold, finger press, and baste the second side.

*B*asting. You'll need a needle and thread matched to the weight and color of the fabric (usually a #8 "sharp" needle or a size 10 quilting "between"), thimble, scissors, straight pins, sharp scissors, fabric glue.

If your design needs precision stitching, the most rewarding (and most time-consuming) sequence is to baste the seam allowance, baste the shape in place, then appliqué the shape securely and neatly. Remove basting.

For basting, use an unknotted light and contrasting colored thread. Hold the right side of the fabric toward you and turn the seam allowance away from you. Using the marked sewing line as a guide, make a running stitch directly beside the line. Secure basting stitches with a single backstitch.

For free-form designs, it's usually sufficient to pin or fabric-glue (if the appliqué can be washed as soon as it's finished) the

shapes to the ground fabric. I never baste. Instead, I use the tip of my needle to roll under the seam allowance as I come to it, holding down the crease with my non-dominant thumb.

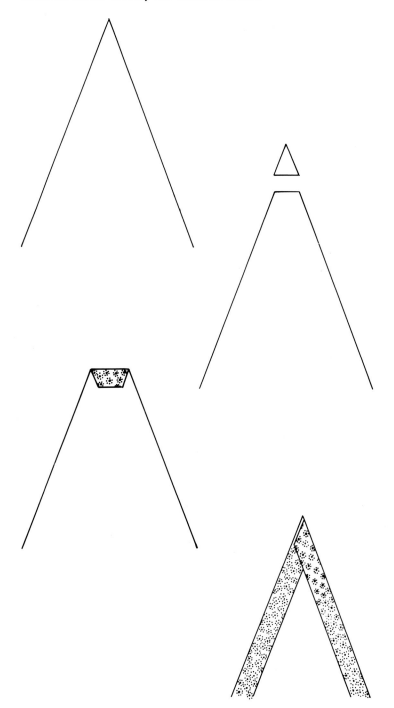

Diagram 67. Prepare shapes with sharp points by clipping off excess fabric at tip.

THE APPLIQUÉ STITCH

•

The appliqué stitch is similar to the slip stitch, whip stitch, and overcast stitch. It is a utility stitch, not a fancy one. It's used to secure shapes onto fabric, not to embellish them. Appliqué stitches should make the viewer wonder what magical ingredient is keeping that shape in place.

To begin stitching, cut the end of eighteen inches of thread diagonally. Thread the needle with the just-cut end, and knot the same end. This ensures that you will use the thread in the same direction as it was wound around the spool, keeping it from twisting and knotting a lot.

Come up from the back of the fabric, catching the folded edge of your appliqué shape, and pull the thread all the way through to the front, until the knot sits comfortably underneath the background. In one motion, put the point of the needle back into the ground fabric directly above its first entry into the folded edge, and then up from the wrong side to the front (no more than an eighth of an inch from the original stitch), pulling the thread all the way through. Repeat ad infinitum. To finish, make a few backstitches or knot on the wrong side (Diagram 68).

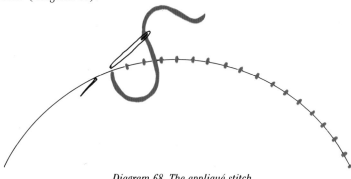

Diagram 68. The appliqué stitch.

Camouflage your stitchery by matching the color of the thread to the appliqué fabric, not to the ground fabric. When in doubt, choose a shade that appears darker on the spool.

FINISHING TOUCHES

•

When all stitching is complete, remove the basting carefully. Weave loose threads on the back into the seam allowance or under an appliqué. You don't want a dark thread to show through the quilt top once the batting and backing are attached.

If you intend to quilt on top of the appliqué shapes, trim away the excess ground fabric underneath. This will leave a single, more manageable layer of fabric to quilt through. Leave about one-quarter inch of fabric at the appliqué stitching line. You'll need to be wide awake when you attempt this delicate work. This is obviously not a job for gardening shears. If the quilting will follow the outline of the shape, then the ground fabric can be left as is. The double layers will provide texture.

ATTACHING BAUBLES, BANGLES, BEADS . . . AND BUTTONS

•

This is where the real fun begins—where your personal aesthetics dictate design. Baubles, bangles, beads, and other rummage items add texture, pizzazz, and uniqueness to your block. Remember not to get carried away with these tempting tidbits—too many can create eyesores. Use the correct implements to make things as easy as possible for yourself.

Hold the fabric taut with an embroidery hoop whenever possible. Select a fine and special beading needle that will slip through the holes easily. Try to camouflage your securing thread by selecting a color that matches the bead. Use silk, nylon, or cotton thread covered with beeswax, such as quilting thread. A waxed thread will be less likely to twist. Make sure your thread is not thicker than the hole of your bead. You don't want to feel as if you need the strength of Samson or the magic of Merlin to string on one tiny little bead.

Keep the thread relatively short. Begin and end by securing the thread on the wrong side with a knot or small backstitches. Don't pull the stitches too tight or the fabric will pucker. You can attach beads one by one, or in multiples on a long strand.

Sew on *large beads* with a regular running stitch. For extra security, make a small knot or backstitch after attaching several beads.

For a *line of beads,* begin by bringing the needle up through the fabric to the right side. String on several beads at a time and use a running stitch from group to group. The number of beads you will be able to string on at one time depends primarily on their size and weight. For curves, reduce the number of beads on each stitch. To apply *prestrung* beads, couch the thread between them at intervals.

Don't forget about the *shiny rhinestone doodads* that come with their own four-pronged metal fasteners. The beauty of these gems is that they require no sewing. If your fabric is thin, pierce through the block with the sharp prongs from the back to the front. Set the rhinestone between the prongs, using an eyebrow tweezer to bend them over the jewel. If the fabric is too thick and your prongs get lost in the bulk, sew the fastener onto the front, set in the rhinestone, and bend the prongs as before.

Be careful with *buttons* with shanks. There are many tempting children's buttons now on the market—little bunnies, choo-choo trains, elegant butterflies—that may seem perfect for your design. If they come with a shank, however, they will stand so far away from the block that they will be distracting.

Sew *sequins* on with a French knot or with a tiny bead in the center. Using a very fine needle and knotted thread, bring the needle through the fabric to the right side. Slide on a sequin and then a bead. Take a stitch over the bead and back through the sequin and fabric on the wrong side. Secure.

APPLYING TRIMMINGS

♦

How close do your stitches have to be? Let your conscience be your guide. Trims like rickrack, which have points, should get a stitch at each point. Laces can be attached at the edges. The trim should lie flat on the fabric surface and look as if it is adhered with glue.

SECURING NOVELTY FABRICS

♦

See if *deep pile* or *furlike fabric* have edges that will ravel. If they need to be hemmed, shear the pile from the seam allowances and stitch in the direction of the pile whenever possible. Don't clip curved edges too closely. Steam press without touching fabrics. Dee Gomez's courageous lion captured midair in a flaming hoop is made from a fake fur that didn't ravel, so it wasn't hemmed. For *real fur,* mark cutting lines on the skin side. Use a razor blade to cut from the skin side, raising the pelt to avoid cutting hairs. Sew through the skin with firm but unnoticeable running stitches.

Avoid marring the surface of *leather.* Use pins or cellophane tape only in the seam allowance. To sew through it, use heavy-duty mercerized thread with a very sharp needle; wedge-pointed needles are made especially for stitching leather. To press, use a dry iron on a warm setting and place brown paper or a press cloth over the leather.

FUSIBLE MATERIALS

♦

Fusible materials join one fabric layer to another without having to sew. The appliqué shape is cut without a seam allowance because the bonding process eliminates the need to turn under the edge. Call me old-fashioned, but I use these only when there's no other way: when a material is too bulky or too delicate, or when a cut edge will be appalling if hemmed. Usually I just banish the problematic fabric to the scrap pile.

Fusible films are available, with or without a paper backing, in two sizes: by the yard, or in prepackaged narrow strips. The nonpaper-backed type seems more durable. Read the manufacturer's small print. Brands vary in the amount of heat needed to apply them. Test them on a scrap of fabric before applying them to your design.

Here's the recipe for the nonpaper-backed variety: Cut a shape identical to the appliqué shape. It should not extend beyond the edges. Place it between the two layers. Bake by pressing firmly for ten seconds with a dry iron, at cotton setting. *Do not* slide iron back and forth. Pick up the iron and move it to the next section, overlapping areas. After letting the fabric cool, test an edge to see if it's

sealed. If at first you didn't succeed, press again for several seconds on each side. For fusing openworked lace, use a wet paper towel as you press to absorb the residue. Throw the used towel away and repeat with dry ones until no residue remains.

Two notes of caution: fusible webbing stuck to the bottom of your iron can be a headache, and don't use these materials in places that will be quilted closely. Heat-bonding creates a stiff surface.

EMBROIDERY

♦   ♦   ♦

Equipment: needles, embroidery floss, sharp scissors, thimble, embroidery hoop, removable or disappearing fabric markers.

Embroidery stitches add personality, profundity, and pizzazz to your design. They can also serve as elaborate Band-Aids for boo-boos. If your stitch has a name, that's very nice; if your stitch is a personal invention, that's fine, too. Embroidery patterns tend to stand out on a block. For a textured, finished look, I like to use a variety of stitches in a combination of both similar and contrasting colors.

Use an embroidery hoop, no matter how awkward it may feel at first, to keep the fabric taut, smooth, and on-grain while you're stitching. On-hoop blocks are much easier to piece together than their more skewed off-hoop relatives.

I'm of the unorthodox school that doesn't pay much attention to the back of my piece. My rationalization is that I use embroidery threads and colors in the same way a painter uses a palette. If I need a dab here, I just bring over my thread to the awaiting spot (within reason—I wouldn't make my thread travel more than about three inches). But I insist that the front of the piece look as if it had been born on the ground fabric.

If you'd like to draw your embroidery design onto the block, use a water-soluble or disappearing marker. I stay away from penciled lines that can't be erased. Another alternative is to use a "dead" ballpoint pen, orange stick, or a burnishing tool to mark guidelines on specially developed embroidery tracing paper. Be sure to remove these marks by "swishing" in cool water before you press or dry clean. Always test a swatch of your fabric to make sure the marks can be obliterated easily.

Choose threads and needles that are compatible both with each other and with the fabric they will pierce. Try to use the sharpest, most delicate needle you can get away with, with an eye just big enough for the thread. The threads should slip easily through the fabric surface so that a stitching rhythm can be established.

To create different textures, embroidery thread can be separated into two, three, four, or six strands. (After years of suffering with tangled threads, I have developed a rather unhygienic method of separating floss: place one end gently in your mouth, stretch the thread taut in front of you with two hands, separate and pull!)

Experiment with different thread thickness combinations. It's very upsetting to be almost finished only to discover that your thread looks too light, too bold, or the texture isn't right. Ripping out embroidery can create vicious little tattletale holes.

You don't really need to have an encyclopedia of stitches at your fingertips in order to create an effective design. Learn just a few, and play with them. Vary color: put together shades of the same color to provide texture and depth. Refer to "Introduction to Color and Fabric," page 125, with an eye to embroidery clues. Vary texture by using different yarns: thick, fuzzy, smooth, delicate. Make a stitch shorter or longer. Make a single stitch. Fan the stitches from a center. Stitch a stitch on a stitch. Combine one stitch with another. Relax. Have a good time.

EMBROIDERY STITCHES
· · ·

Working with eighteen inches of thread, I begin stitching with a knot on the wrong side, and finish by weaving the thread through other threads, on the wrong side.

COUCHING
·

I use couching (also known as tacking) a great deal. Like the more difficult classic outline stitch, couching creates a continuous-looking line. It is excellent for outlines, for details, for long flowing hair.

Couching is done with two needles: one is threaded with yarn or embroidery floss, the second with a single strand of the same-colored floss or regular sewing thread. (Feel free to experiment with different colors and thicknesses as well.) The thicker thread is laid on the surface of the fabric and tacked in place by the second more delicate thread. Both are knotted at the ends.

To begin, come up through the back of the ground fabric with the thicker floss and *lay* the thread on the line to be couched. Now bring the single threaded needle from the back, and *tack* the embroidery thread in place, at one-eighth- to one-quarter-inch intervals. The thicker thread comes up from the back in the beginning and reenters the fabric only at the end. To complete the stitch, return to the wrong side of the fabric with both needles, weaving the thread to secure it (Diagram 69).

Couching is great if you're using out-of-the-ordinary types of threads. Let's say you can't get your must-use metallic thread into the eye of the needle. Couch it, instead. Secure its raveling ends unobtrusively. Look for convenient hiding places. For example, begin or end in the seam allowance or tuck it out of sight under an appliquéd design. For delicate details, such as faces, I couch using

Diagram 69. Couching stitch. (a) couching (b) example of couching.

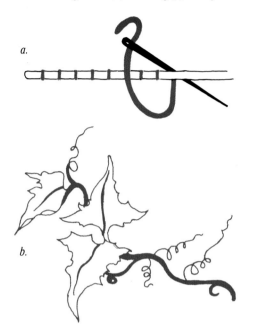

a.

b.

black silk thread (available at most sewing stores). It is also a wonderful way to create hair styles like that of "Baby Divine," from *The Crown Quilt,* page 78.

BACKSTITCH
·

The backstitch looks very much like a machine-stitched line. It can be used as the basis of more elaborate stitching. Variations: whipped, single or double; threaded, backstitched star, or sheath stitch (Diagrams 70, 70a, and 70b).

STEM AND OUTLINE STITCH
·

The classic difference between these two is all in the thread's position: in the stem, the thread is to the right of the needle; in the outline, it's to the left. In both cases one stitch touches the next, and the needle enters and leaves on the line (Diagram 71).

CHAIN STITCH
·

The chain stitch is extremely versatile and creates a smooth, continuous, textured line. Simple, but delicious flower arrangements can be made with combinations of the chain stitch in its many incarnations—whipped, single, groupings worked over a foundation. You can fill the middle of the chain stitch with a running stitch of a different color, or add a stitch to its tip (Diagram 72).

Diagram 70a. Backstitch.

Diagram 70g. Sheath stitch.

Diagram 70b. Whipped.

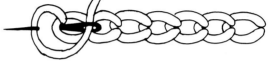

Diagram 71. Outline stitch.

Diagram 70c. Double whipped.

Diagram 72a. Chain stitch.

Diagram 70d. Threaded.

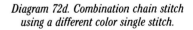

Diagram 72b. Backstitch worked down center of chain.

Diagram 70e. Two parallel backstitch rows, threaded.

Diagram 72c. Combination chain stitch creating a flower.

Diagram 72d. Combination chain stitch using a different color single stitch.

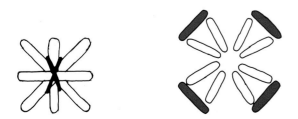

Diagram 70f. Variations of backstitched stars.

Diagram 72e. Grouping worked with single stitch in middle.

Diagram 72f. Chains on chains creating a double layer.

BUTTONHOLE

•

The buttonhole is also very adaptable and can be created open or closed. It's used as an appliqué technique. Variations: double, grouped, threaded, whipped (Diagram 73).

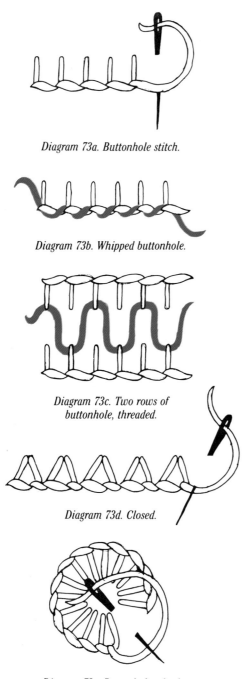

Diagram 73a. Buttonhole stitch.

Diagram 73b. Whipped buttonhole.

Diagram 73c. Two rows of buttonhole, threaded.

Diagram 73d. Closed.

Diagram 73e. Buttonhole wheel.

SATIN STITCH

•

The satin is used as a surface filler and for shading (Diagram 74).

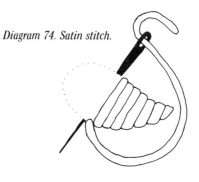

Diagram 74. Satin stitch.

FRENCH KNOT

•

These are cute little guys that can be used something like small beads. Don't attempt a French knot with only one strand of thread. You need several. Bring the thread to the right side and hold it taut above the fabric with your thumb and finger of the non-dominant hand. Then twist the needle twice around the thread (not the thread around the needle). The needle is then turned completely to reenter the fabric almost where it emerged. French knots must be tight (Diagram 75).

Diagram 75. French knot.

FINISHING THE BLOCK

♦   ♦   ♦

The blocks are collected and all accounted for. Now you must cut them down to the actual piecing measurement, which is the size of the finished base block, plus one-quarter-inch seam allowance. In other words, for an eight-inch block, you will be trimming the appliquéd masterpieces to eight and one-half inches.

Example: $8'' + \frac{1}{2}'' (\frac{1}{4}'' + \frac{1}{4}'') = 8\frac{1}{2}''$

TO FIX OR NOT TO FIX

♦

Look over the little masterpieces and fix what absolutely needs fixing —a string of beads that didn't survive the mail, a wild thread that won't be still. Clean off that dried spaghetti, hem down the fraying edges. Sometimes you can extend vulnerable shapes into the seam allowance, or snip a few hemming stitches and readjust a block that's pulled off-grain. Remove all washable pen marks and basting stitches before pressing.

I usually don't touch anyone's block beyond these security checks. If you have some block improvement suggestions, it's a good idea to run them by the creator before changing his or her labor of love. This is where your interpersonal relations skills come in handy. Somehow you always know who you can ask. I practice quilter's license generally in only two cases: when the main figure in the block doesn't stand out (a simple black embroidered outline works wonders), or when a quick something will help an oddball block harmonize with the others. Such minor improvisations usually make the blockmaker happier, too.

PRESSING

♦

Pressing is not the same as ironing. Ironing means moving your iron back and forth across the fabric surface. Pressing means literally pressing a portion of your iron onto the fabric area and lifting it up again, using steam when necessary.

Don't skip this stage, no matter how tempted you may be. Templates fit better onto well-pressed blocks, so the better you press, the more accurate the quilt. Have patience. If you have blocks with a cornucopia of textures, objects, and glitter, you may have to adjust your heat, your pressure, and your steam every inch of the way. Beware of dreaded iron shine, caused by overpressing with excessive heat and moisture.

For touch-ups on the right side, protect the design by using a dampened (not wet) press cloth. In a pinch you can substitute a heavy brown grocery bag. For fabrics that need extra moisture, place a dampened cheesecloth over the press cloth. For tinier touch-ups, use a small paintbrush to moisten either the press cloth or the actual fabric.

Different textile fibers have different pressing needs. For the majority of fabrics, light pressure and the iron's natural steam are plenty. Test any fabric you're not sure of: sheers that might pucker, naps that might flatten, swatches that might harden from excessive heat. Here's a list of helpful hints:

- Begin by seeing if pressing on the wrong side is good enough. Try to press only the background fabric so that appliqué shapes and raised surfaces aren't flattened. Maybe you'll be lucky and it won't need any more.

- If the base block is predominantly *cotton,* press it first with steam, then with no steam, until it's completely dry.

- Place a dry steam cloth over *dark colors* when pressing them on the right side.

- Don't touch *napped surfaces* (deep-pile fake furs, synthetic suedes, velvets) directly with the iron. These fabrics must be steamed rather than pressed to avoid permanently crushing the nap. On the delicate area, place either a piece of terry cloth, a bristled press cloth specially manufactured for naps, or a swatch of the same fabric. Hold your iron one inch above both layers, allowing the steam to penetrate, and move it slowly in the direction of the nap. Remove the protecting cloth. Softly brush the fabric in the pile's direction while it's still damp, and allow to dry thoroughly before handling.

- Use a light touch on *silk* and *man-made fibers.* Minimal moisture, pressure, and heat are all that's necessary.

- To avoid flattening a *raised design,* first pad your ironing board with a thick towel, place the block face down, and *gently* press on the wrong side.

- *Just in case you blew it,* here's our last helpful hint: to remove iron shine, to raise nap, or to eliminate an overpressed look, hold the iron one inch away from fabric and allow the steam to penetrate.

REDUCING THE SEAM ALLOWANCE

◆

Equipment: template material or transparent plastic template used to first cut out base blocks, fine-point marker or pencil, dressmaker's shears.

*T*emplate. The seam allowance must now be reduced to the traditional one-quarter inch for piecing. Making a perfectly accurate template will ensure that you have created matching dimensions with right-angle corners on the base block.

If you didn't make a transparent plastic template when you first cut out your base blocks, now is the time. Cut a square of plastic (preferably with a grid) the size of the finished base block, adding one-quarter inch around each side. Mark a bold horizontal and vertical axis on the plastic square. Refer to "How to Make Templates," page 156.

MARKING AND CUTTING

◆

Work on a flat, clean surface. Remove the coffee cups and cookie crumbs. Place the template on the *front* of an immaculate, complete, pressed base block. You checked the workmanship before you pressed the blocks. Now it's time to focus on the design. Place the template so that the focal point is centered or balanced pleasingly, and so that background fabric doesn't peek out where it's not wanted. Sometimes the block has to be off-grain a little bit. That's OK. At this point, centering the design is more important.

Outline the template with exquisite, thin precision on the *right* side of the base block. The line you mark is the seam allowance, not the stitching one. Hold your breath—and cut.

How to Make Sashing and Borders

HOW TO DRAW THE QUILT TO SCALE ON GRAPH PAPER

♦   ♦   ♦

Equipment: large sheet of graph paper, sharp pencil with clean and ample eraser, ruler.

*I*t's time to draft a quilt plan on graph paper. A picture drawn to scale will help you determine yardage and the smoothest piecing sequence. This drawing is the finished size of the blocks and sashes —it does not include seam allowance.

This is the simplest calculation to work with: one square on the graph paper equals one square inch of quilt top. Buy reliable graph paper that's big enough for you to draw the entire quilt on one sheet. Use a sharp pencil with an ample eraser.

The following instructions are for our old standby hypothetical quilt set: rows of blocks separated by sashing strips. (For variations on this theme, see instructions for sashing with blocks at the intersections, and frames around the base blocks, pages 187–188.)

When drafting the picture, calculate the blocks first, sashing second, borders last. Divide the number of actual base blocks into the number that fit into horizontal and vertical rows. For example: twenty blocks can be divided into four rows vertically and five rows horizontally. In our examples, the sashing width is the same, whether it's between blocks, between rows, or on the borders. If yours will be a borderless quilt, you may want to increase the width of the outside sashing to create a definitive ending.

Draft from left to right, top row to bottom row. Don't start in the immediate top corner of the graph paper. You'll need to leave a few inches at the top and left in order to add on sashing and borders. Counting the same number of graph paper squares as quilt inches, draw the top left base block. Add a vertical sashing strip to the block's *right* edge, counting graph paper squares for sashing width. Continue adding blocks, alternating with sashing width, to complete the first top row.

Do not add vertical sashing to the right of the last base block in each row. Draw a horizontal sashing strip running under the row of blocks, counting graph paper squares for sashing width. Continue adding rows of base blocks separated by vertical sashing strips, with a horizontal strip underneath. End with the last row of base blocks. Draw a long horizontal sashing strip at the top and bottom of the quilt picture. Draw a long vertical strip at the left and right sides of the picture.

This outlined area of graph paper represents the boundaries of the quilt top, without borders. Borders can now be designed and adjusted to achieve the desired quilt dimensions.

How to Estimate Yardage for Sashing and Borders

• • •

Refer to the graph to determine the number of pieces needed from each fabric. Refer to "How to Calculate Yardage," page 156, for more guidelines.

DETERMINING SASHING SIZE
•

Sashing seam allowance is one-quarter inch, so add one-half inch to each dimension ($\frac{1}{4}$" + $\frac{1}{4}$").

Width. For example: For one-inch-wide sashing you will need to cut one-and-one-half-inch strips. Two-and-one-half-inch sashing will require three-inch strips.

Length. To compute the length, follow these steps:

1. The length of the vertical sashes between blocks is the same as the side of the block to which it will be sewn.

2. To figure horizontal sashing length between rows, add:
   (Finished size of block) × (number of blocks across)
   +
   (Finished sashing width) × (number of sashes across)
   +
   $\frac{1}{2}$-inch seam allowance . . . .
       Total (Horizontal sashing length)

3. To figure length of two long vertical sashings, add:
   (Finished size of block) × (number of blocks across)
   +
   (Finished sashing width) × (number of sashes across)
   +
   $\frac{1}{2}$-inch seam allowance . . . .
       Total (Long vertical sashing length)

DETERMINING BORDER SIZE
•

Length. If you're going to butt the corners, four border strips must be made: one lengthwise (vertical) pair for the two sides and a pair for the top and bottom. The procedure for calculating border size is the same if the borders are cut from one cloth or created from repeated pieced units. The side borders are constructed the same size as the dimension of the quilt's finished length measure-ment, plus one-half-inch seam allowance. The horizontal (top and bottom) borders are constructed the same size as the finished quilt's width measurement plus double the width of the border, plus one-half-inch seam allowance. (For mitered corners, see page 166.)

Width. The border width is flexible. Remember to create symmetry in the four corners. For a pieced border, the easiest method is to plan a repeating border unit in a size that will divide evenly into both the horizontal and vertical measurements. This will make it possible to put a complete border unit in each corner.

If this division doesn't yield a nice round number, a pieced border can be made to fit the quilt top by inserting a plain strip of fabric between the quilt top and the border, creating horizontal and vertical dimensions that can both be divided equally by a practical measurement. Sew these strips by butting them to the quilt top rather than to the edge of the border.

In patchwork etiquette, the size of the strips added to the top and the bottom must be the same. The size of the left and right strips must also be equal to each other. But the dimension added to the top and bottom can be different from the side ones.

Here is how to determine the measurement of these inserted strips: First, calculate the dimensions of the strips that will be added to each side of the quilt top. The length is the same as the finished length of the quilt top without borders plus seam allowance. To find the width measurement, subtract the quilt's finished length measure-ment from the finished vertical border measurement. Divide the difference by two to find the width of the required strip; add seam allowance (Diagram 11).

Now calculate the dimensions of the strips that will be added to the quilt top at the top and bottom. The length is the size of the finished quilt width measurement plus double the width of the strips added to the sides, plus one-half-inch seam allowance. To find the width measurement, subtract the quilt's finished width measurement from the finished horizontal border measurement. Divide the differ-ence by two to find the width of the required strip; add seam allow-ance.

If this unpieced insert is made from the sashing color, it will blend and not be noticed. If you add a contrasting colored fabric it will act as another separate border around the quilt. If it is a color similar to the border, it will blend into the border's design and expand the border.

DETERMINING CUTTING LAYOUTS
•

Plan a cutting layout for each fabric. Piecing long sashes will be easiest if you cut one long fabric strip, preferably along the length-wise grain, which has a minimum of "give." You won't have to make any seams. If you prefer to save yardage by piecing the long sashes,

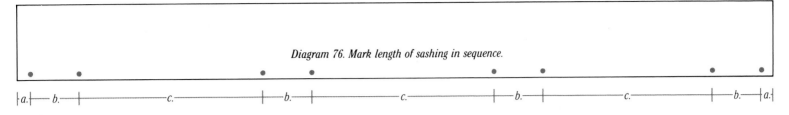

Diagram 76. Mark length of sashing in sequence.

| a. | b. | c. | b. | c. | b. | c. | b. | a. |

the seams must be made at evenly spaced intervals—for example, the halfway mark (Diagram 33).

Refer to "How to Calculate Yardage," page 156.

HOW TO MARK AND CUT SASHING

• • •

Measure, mark, and cut on the *wrong* side of the fabric. It is important that all the sashes in each row match each other. The sashing is a visual grid of continuity. If the sashes are pieced willy-nilly, the quilt top may end up cockeyed; if they are not measured carefully, they might wiggle where they should lie flat.

Templates cannot be made for extremely long sashes. In order to know exactly where a point on an unwieldy sash will meet other seams, I make marks in the seam allowance that correspond to these junction points. It is a little more time-consuming, but this precision step ensures that the viewer's eye will be carried smoothly from one block to the next.

This is how I mark and measure long sashes: First, measure the width from an on-grain edge. Use a ruler and a pencil to mark the width measurement with a small dot about every six inches. Connect the dots. Create right angles at the ends. If you have a ruler marked with a grid that is wider than the finished sashing by one-half inch, you can align the appropriate ruled marking on the fabric's straight edge and zip across.

Now measure the length. Begin at the left, and, in the seam allowance, mark in sequence: seam allowance, finished sashing width, finished block width, finished sash width, continuing to the last sashing at the end of the row and including seam allowance (Diagram 76).

Refer to "How to Mark and Cut Fabric," page 162.

HOW TO MARK AND CUT BORDERS

• • •

Prepare and cut templates appropriately for each shape. Border patterns are usually created from combinations of geometric shapes. The outside edges of squares and rectangles will always be on-grain. However, at least one edge of a triangle must be cut on the bias, even if it is not the true bias.

The outside edge of a quilt top or a pieced unit must be cut on the straight grain of the fabric. For crisp edges, the sides of a template that will become outer edges must be cut on the straight grain of fabric. If the outer edge is on the bias, it may wiggle, wave, and stretch. So pay close attention to which edges of your templates will be on the outside (Diagrams 77 and 78).

Refer to "How to Mark and Cut Fabric," page 162.

HOW TO DETERMINE PIECING SEQUENCE FOR THREE KINDS OF SASHING

• • •

As long as you're working with a simple block-block-block set, you will have only straight seams to sew.

Refer to your original quilt top graph as a map for piecing sequence. Remember to work from the smallest to the largest units. If you work consistently, from left to right, top to bottom, you won't get lost. For example, using the base block as a basis for orientation, piece all seams at the right and at the bottom of a base block.

Refer to "How to Determine a Piecing Sequence," page 165.

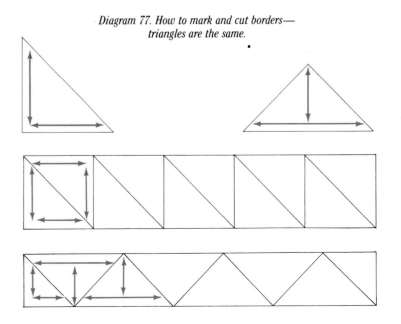

Diagram 77. How to mark and cut borders— triangles are the same.

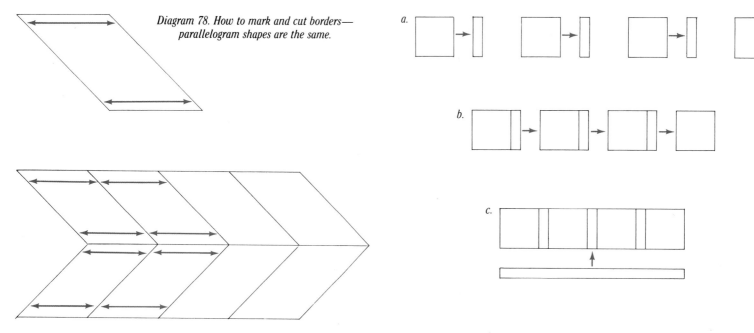

Diagram 78. How to mark and cut borders—parallelogram shapes are the same.

PIECING SEQUENCE FOR APPLIQUÉ BLOCK WITH INSERTED SASHING

•

See Diagram 79.

a. Add short sashes to the blocks: begin at the top row and work from left to right. Sew a sash to the right side of each block (except the one on the right end).

b. Join the sashed blocks together until you complete one row. Piece all of the block rows in the same way. Press seams.

c. Pin a long horizontal sash to the bottom of each block row. Don't pin one to the bottommost row. Match the dimensions marked in the sashing's seam allowance to corresponding seams in the rows of blocks. Put a pin at each joint. Use additional pins to ease in fullness. Sew the rows together and press seams.

d. Pin and sew the long sashing strip on the bottom of the first row to the top edge of the second row of blocks. Add rows until all the rows have been sewn together. The bottom row will not have sashing.

e. Add a horizontal sash to the top and bottom of quilt. Press seams.

f. Add long vertical sashes to the two sides. Press seams.

Refer to "How to Determine a Piecing Sequence," page 165.

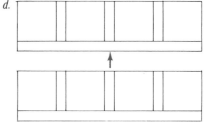

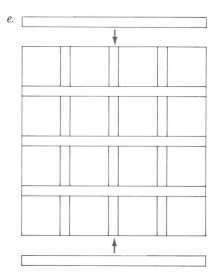

Diagram 79. Piecing sequence for inserted sashing.

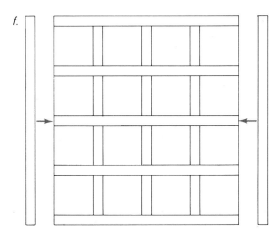

f.

Piecing sequence:

a. Begin at the top row and work from left to right. Sew a sash to the right side of each of the blocks in a row, and to the left side of the block at the left end.

b. Join units of blocks and sashes by piecing the right edge of a sash to the left edge of a block. Continue across until you have a row. Piece all of the block rows in the same way. Press seams.

c. For the long horizontal sashing bands, determine from your graph paper how many sashes need cornerstones pieced to the right. There will be as many as there are blocks in a row, plus two sashing rows more than rows of blocks. Sew a cornerstone to the right side of each sash. Press seams.

d. Join units of sashes and cornerstones, continuing to the end of a row. Add a cornerstone to the left side of the sash at the left end. Press seams.

e. Pin a long horizontal sash to the top edge of each completed row of sashed blocks, and one to the bottom edge of the bottommost row of blocks. Match and pin the sashing row's seams to the seams in the block row. Use additional pins to ease in fullness. Sew and press seams.

f. Join the rows, by pinning and sewing the long sashing strip that is attached to bottom of the first row to the top of the second row of blocks. Add rows until top is completed. Press seams (Diagram 80).

Refer to "How to Determine Piecing Sequence," page 165.

Piecing Sequence for Appliqué Block with Cornerstones at Sashing Intersections. Cornerstones are little squares placed at each sashing intersection (see *J.C. Penney quilts,* pages 96–99). Draft a blueprint on graph paper to determine the yardage, piecing sequence, and number of sashes and cornerstones. Alternate a short sash with a cornerstone. (Hint: For each sashing row, two more cornerstones are needed than the number of base blocks in a row. To calculate how many you'll need to cut, multiply this number by the number of horizontal sashing rows. There will be two rows more of horizontal sashing than the number of rows of blocks.)

Instead of marking and cutting long sashes of one fabric, the sashings must be pieced. All the long seams are pieced horizontally.

Two templates are needed. For all the sashing units, make one rectangular template the same *length* as the base block. The *width* measurement is whatever your heart desires. For all cornerstones, make one square template the same size as the sashing width.

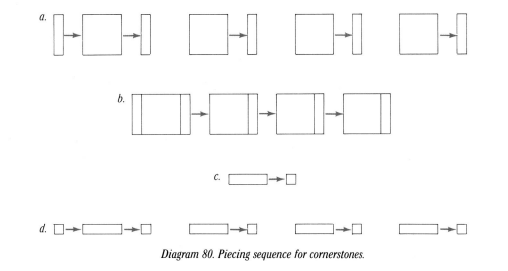

Diagram 80. Piecing sequence for cornerstones.

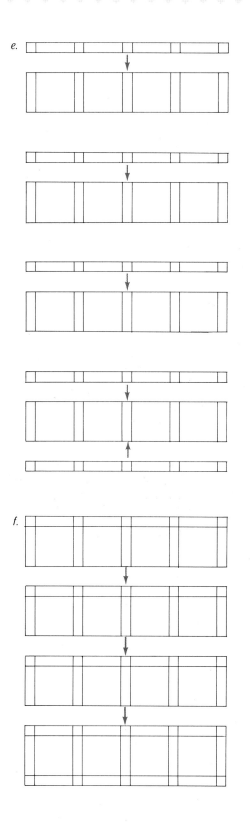

PIECING SEQUENCE FOR MATS AND FRAMES AROUND EACH BASE BLOCK

•

Draw a picture on graph paper to determine the yardage and piecing sequence for mats, frames, and sashing. Each base block is first pieced to the "mat" fabric with butted corners. The "frame" fabric is added next. In this example the corners are butted. If you prefer a mitered effect, read "How To Miter a Corner," page 166.

This construction is then treated in the same way as a base block with attached sashing, so the piecing sequence can be followed. (Steps a–f, page 187.)

Make three templates including one-quarter-inch seam allowance.

*M*at Fabric. For the horizontal strips, make a rectangular template as long as the base block. Cut two for each base block. For the vertical strips, make a rectangular template as long as the base block plus twice the width of the mat. Add one-half-inch seam allowance. Cut two for each base block.

*F*rame Fabric. Since the dimension is equal to the length of the vertical mat, use the vertical mat template for the horizontal frame strips. Cut two for each base block. For the vertical frame strips, make a rectangular template as long as the horizontal frame plus twice the width of the frame. Add one-half-inch seam allowance. Cut two for each base block.

Piecing Sequence:

a. Sew a vertical mat to the left and right side of each base block. Press.

b. Sew a horizontal mat to the top and bottom of each base block. Press.

c. Sew a vertical frame to the left and right sides of pieced unit. Press.

d. Sew a horizontal frame to top and bottom of the configuration. Press. Continue piecing sequence a–f, page 187.

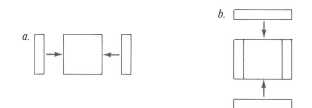

Diagram 81. Piecing sequence for mats and frames.

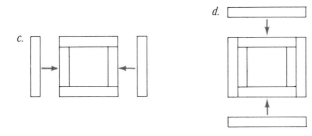

HOW TO PIECE BORDERS

* ◆ ◆ ◆

First piece individual units and then sew them together for each border strip. It's a good idea, however, not to piece the outer borders before the center is done. In a group effort, it's often tempting to divide responsibilities—delegating borders to one mini-group, sashing to another. But if you piece the cart before the horse, you may end up with more remeasuring headaches than you bargained for. Take it from a veteran of many unscheduled 2 A.M. sewing sessions—quilts pieced by many people are always full of surprises. Refer to "How to Machine-Piece," page 163.

Don't let long, unwieldy borders get you down. First, using your graph paper, calculate what the outside measurement should be. Then measure your quilt edge to find out what it really is. Now (and this is important!) measure across the *center* of the quilt. Fabric tends to stretch and pull itself out of shape; it's the nature of the beast. In order to prevent wavy quilt edges, use the center measurement to calculate the size of the border. You will need to ease in the quilt's edges to match the borders.

The procedure for piecing borders to the quilt top is the same if the borders are cut from one cloth or created from repeated pieced units. The following instructions will yield a butted corner. (For mitering, see page 166.)

Attach both side borders first, and then the top and bottom. With right sides together, pin the border to the quilt's edge at the halfway point and at both ends. Place the unit with the fullness that must be eased in underneath. Working with one half at a time, pin at the quarter point, then at the eighth point, until pins are easing in fullness at two-inch intervals.

As you sew, try not to make tucks. If they are unavoidable, make them at a point in the seam where they will be disguised, not where seams must meet and match a corresponding seam (Diagrams 82 through 90). Refer to "How to Machine-Piece," page 163.

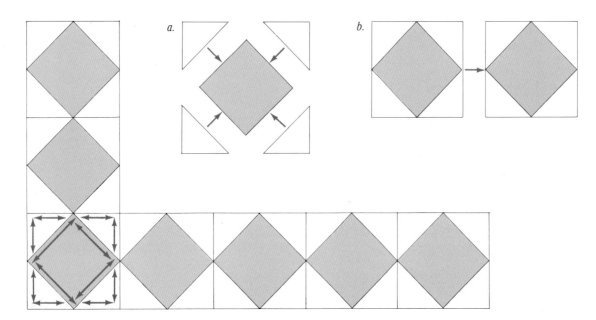

Diagram 82. Piecing sequence for single border unit.
The same unit links each corner.

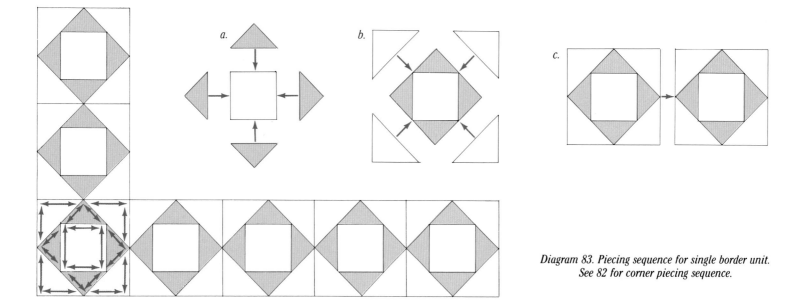

Diagram 83. Piecing sequence for single border unit. See 82 for corner piecing sequence.

Diagram 84. a and b represent the piecing sequence for single border unit. See 82 for corner piecing sequence.

Q·U·I·L·T·I·N·G T·O·G·E·T·H·E·R

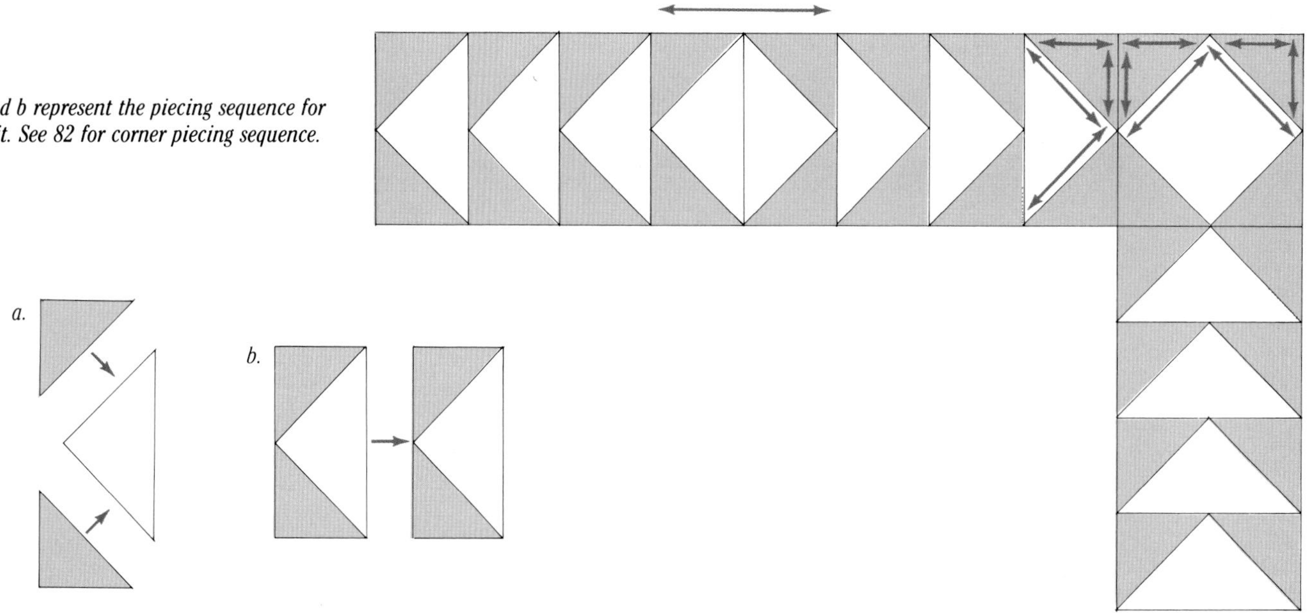

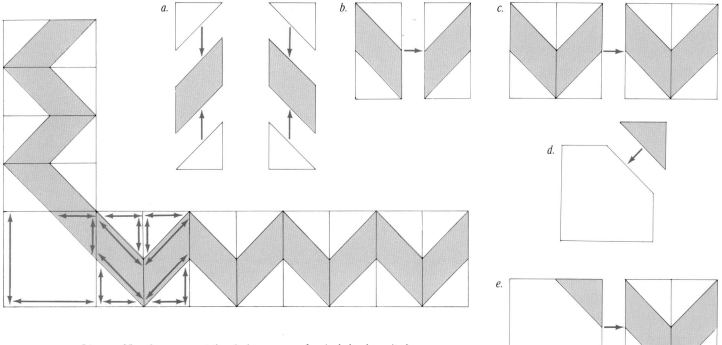

Diagram 85. a, b, c represent the piecing sequence for single border unit. d, e represent the piecing sequence for corner unit.

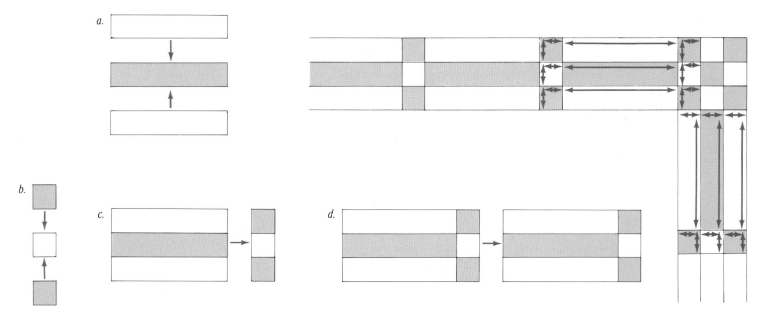

Diagram 86. a, b, c, d represent the piecing sequence for single border unit.

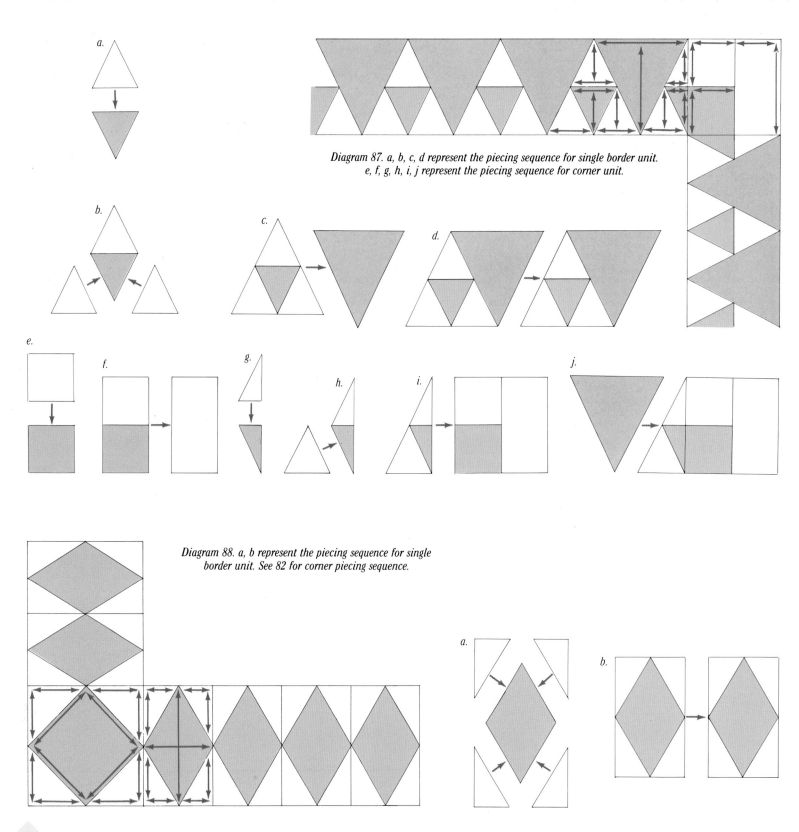

a.

Diagram 87. a, b, c, d represent the piecing sequence for single border unit.
e, f, g, h, i, j represent the piecing sequence for corner unit.

b.

c.

d.

e.

f.

g.

h.

i.

j.

Diagram 88. a, b represent the piecing sequence for single
border unit. See 82 for corner piecing sequence.

a.

b.

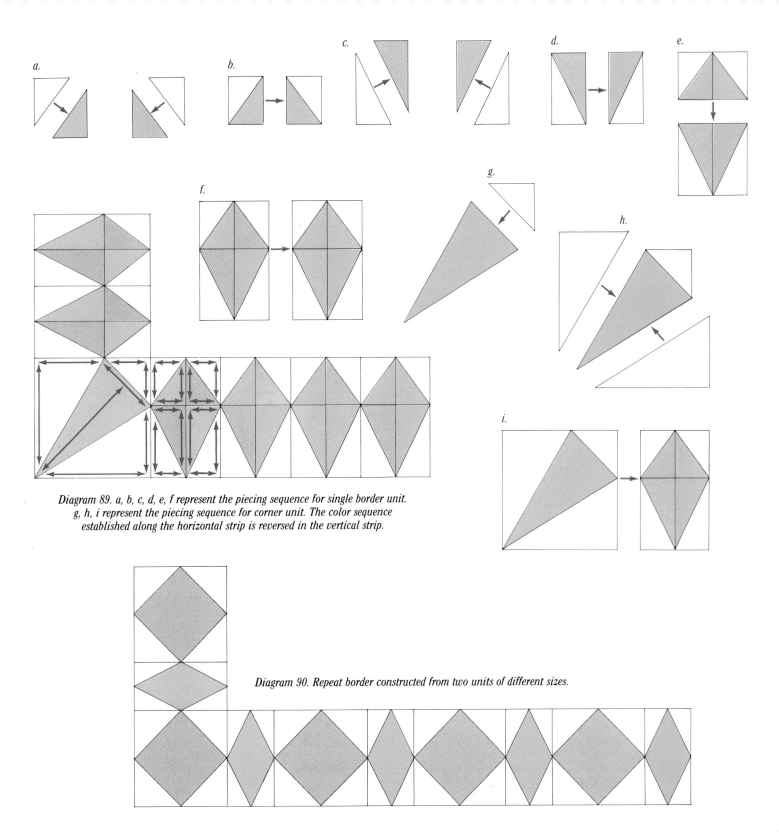

Diagram 89. a, b, c, d, e, f represent the piecing sequence for single border unit. g, h, i represent the piecing sequence for corner unit. The color sequence established along the horizontal strip is reversed in the vertical strip.

Diagram 90. Repeat border constructed from two units of different sizes.

Quilting, Binding, and Finishing the Group Quilt

QUILTING TOOLS

QUILTING THREAD

*Q*uilting thread, available in a variety of colors, is coated so that it slips easily through layers. If you need an odd-color quilting thread, regular cotton sewing thread can be transformed into quilting thread by coating it with beeswax.

If you plan to tie your quilt, use a fine washable three-ply yarn, such as baby or sport-weight yarn. Don't use embroidery floss; it will unravel, and maybe even untie the quilt.

QUILTING NEEDLES

Short stiff "betweens" are used for hand-quilting. The bigger the number, the shorter the needle. Buy a package of assorted sizes: begin learning with a #8 and work your way down. Throw out a needle that becomes sticky and won't pierce the fabrics smoothly. Some quilters sharpen dull needles with an emery board. Others prize their needles bent with use.

QUILTING PINS

Quilting pins are a special breed that hold the layers together before basting. They are long and thick with a small ball at the head.

THIMBLES

A thimble is imperative for quilting and must be strong enough to push a needle through the three layers. The thimble, worn on the middle finger of the sewing hand, should have grooves or a ridge on the top or sides rather than a rounded, smooth top. Some quilters wear a metal thimble or leather fingerguard on the index finger of the hand under the quilt.

QUILTING FRAMES

Traditional quilting frames are the stuff historical quilting bees are made of. The frame evokes images of womenfolk, gathered and gossiping as their needles punctuate in rhythm. Several people can crowd around them, providing instant camaraderie, and an instant conversation piece when not in use. ("Well, we can always play pool on it." "If you can't find your kids come bedtime, check under the frame.") Both frames and hoops eliminate a lot of handling of the quilt. Unfortunately, unless you can pulley yours up to the ceiling, these oversized embroidery hoops require their own semi-permanent room, so are fairly impractical for apartment dwellers—and they are expensive.

A quilt frame is made up of two sets of rails: the long frame rails, to which the quilt sandwich is attached and then rolled around, and the short end stretchers, which are usually adjustable. The stretchers determine how much surface is available for quilting at a time. The frame rail can't be any shorter than the width of your quilt. Historically, the frame was supported on the backrests of four ladder-back chairs—now coveted in the antiques world as Windsors, or fan-backs.

Here's a homemade frame recipe: Purchase four pieces of 2 × 2-inch or 2 × 1-inch lumber and four C-clamps. Cut two end rails at least the width of the quilt. Cut two three-foot stretchers. Sand them.

Cut a ten-inch piece of sturdy fabric the length of the end rail minus six inches. Use ticking, denim, or muslin. Fold it in half and staple it (using a staple gun) or tack it (using carpet tacks and a hammer) to each end rail. The quilt is basted or safety pinned every three inches to these strips.

Loop sturdy strips of fabric (3 × 12 inches) around the stretchers, and pin the sides of the quilt to them. Rest the end rails on four chairs or two sawhorses. Place the stretchers on top and C-clamps in the corners. Start quilting in the center. Roll each rail under until about two feet of the center is exposed.

QUILT HOOPS
♦

Like an embroidery hoop, a large, round wooden quilting hoop is portable. Quilting hoops are more solitary affairs than quilting frames. They can be worked on a lap, supported on a table or chair, or attached to a stand. You should be able to reach the center of the quilt easily. Use a hoop that's fourteen to eighteen inches across. Oval hoops do not maintain tension as evenly as round ones. Stitchers can't work on these mini-frames at the same time, but they can be shared as the quilt visits different homes. And they can be turned so a stitcher can sew comfortably in different directions.

BATTING
♦   ♦   ♦

Batting is the fluffy middle layer in the fabric sandwich that adds warmth and thickness to the quilt. Just as Nabisco now provides choices between regular or double-stuffed Oreos, the batting indus-

try provides stuffing choices to meet a quilter's every need. Your decision to go with a fat batt or a thin batt, a bonded or unbonded batt, will affect the quilt's overall appearance, texture, and durability.

Batting is available in fabric stores, quilt specialty shops, and from mail-order quilting suppliers. It's manufactured in sheet form and can be purchased precut and packaged by the manufacturer in dimensions that correspond to standard bed sizes or by the yard, at significantly lower prices. (Note: For the serious quilter, the manufacturers sell sample sizes of the varieties to experiment with.)

The most appropriate batting for group quilts, and the most accessible, is either cotton, polyester, or a blend of both.

Polyester batting stays flat when you wash it, so the lines of quilting stitches don't have to be so close together. That saves time and design problems. The linear relief designs created by the quilting stitches will look highly defined and textured on a polyester-stuffed quilt.

Cotton batting is generally for purists, not for first-timers. Very close quilting stitches are needed for a cotton-stuffed quilt because the batting tends to bunch, shift, and shrink when washed. Since it shrinks at the same rate as cotton fabrics, it should never be used to fill a quilt made of fabric blends. The loft is thin, providing little relief after quilting and a look similar in character to antique quilts.

Here's some help with the definitions:

Unbonded batt has fibers poking out of it and is responsible for a quilter's dreaded disease—"bearding," also known as "migration" by the industry. Bearding is when tiny unwanted batting fibers are pulled up onto the surface during the quilting process. Washing can also produce these uncouth results.

Bonded batt has a hard or soft finish depending on whether it's coated with resin or glue. Your bearding problems will be (almost) shaved away with bonded products. And they're easier to use, too.

(Note: Manufacturers sometimes confuse the issue by using terms like ultra-soft to mean unbonded, or extra-loft to mean bonded. Just when you've memorized the meaning of one set of advertising adjectives a new set is bound to pop up.)

Loft refers to the batt's thickness. Polyester batting can be anywhere from one-quarter to three inches thick. *Fat batts* are suitable for tying comforters, but not for large machine-quilted projects, because they get caught in the sewing machine's presser foot. *Thin batts* are easier to play with. Hand-quilting stitches can be much smaller and more evenly spaced, creating a sharply defined pattern. *Needle-punched batting* is a type of thin batt that has low relief and is good for small machine-quilted projects.

Quilting the Sandwich

Whether they create elaborate, sculpted surfaces, or simple, functional grids, quilting stitches are the thread that binds the top, middle, and back together. Without them, you have a coverlet, not a quilt. Historically, close quilting stitches were needed to keep the wadding from shifting. But now with newfangled, non-bunching polyester batting, people are free to choose quilting patterns for their aesthetic beauty, not for their anchoring potential. Hand-quilting is slow, but once you establish a stitching rhythm, it's very often soothing.

This is your last chance to trim and press the quilt top before getting down to the nitty-gritty quilting. The top can't be pressed after it's marked with quilting patterns—the marks might become permanently set. Clip away stray threads that could show through light-colored fabrics; trim bulky seams that will make quilting cumbersome.

CHOOSING A QUILTING PATTERN

Many considerations will affect your quilting pattern choice. Who's going to quilt it, and what are their skills? How thick are the appliqué designs? Do they need quilted outlines to help them stand out, or closely quilted lines to make them lie flat? Do you have only enough time to quilt around each block? Will it look funny if you don't treat each block the same? Will it be effective to quilt the blocks only where the ground fabric is revealed? Can you leave the blocks alone and concentrate on quilting the borders and sashing?

What kind of batt is concealed between the quilt layers? All cotton batts require stitches that are no more than two inches apart. Polyester bonded batting quilting lines can be as far apart as six to eight inches.

What is the quilt's intended function? A wall hanging may be better off looking puffy and lightly quilted, but a bed quilt needs lots of stitches to avoid everyday stress on each individual stitch.

In a group pictorial, there are two major arenas to quilt: the individual blocks and background, and the sashing and borders. Here is some general information about how quilting stitches and design work together.

Quilting patterns are made up of lines. Geometry books define a line as an infinite number of points, and sometimes, in the midst of a seemingly endless project, you're sure that you and your nimble thimble are just about to attain Guinness Book of Records status by reaching the limit of infinity. Lines have an inherent quality of movement. As the stitches carry the viewer's eye along their textured, indented path, they have the potential to convey moods and motion (see "Basic Elements of Design," page 132).

Closely quilted areas look highly *textured,* almost sculptured.

The stitched patterns create raised areas in relief, and contrasts and shadows between sparse and heavily quilted areas on the quilt. Diverse picture blocks often need the repetition of a *symmetrical* quilting pattern to unify them. *Solid fabrics* provide a showcase for your quilting designs. *Prints* tend to disguise the stitches.

The quilting motifs can be single or repeated, realistic or geometric. They can create recognizable designs, or echo shapes or themes from the quilt. The Yakima Valley Quilters planted quilted apples in each white square of their checkerboard (*Apple Box Labels,* page 80); the Boise Peace Group threaded banjos into a pieceful quilt for Pete Seeger. In *Sailors' Snug Harbor* (page 51), quilted stitches silhouette a phantom building, representing a house that was but is no more.

Here are some alternative routes for your quilting needle:

In the ditch means quilting along the seams. It's a particularly good technique for beginning machine-quilters because the seam provides a readymade guideline and the "ditch" camouflages stitches.

Outline quilting emphasizes the shape of each patchwork or appliqué piece. The stitches follow the contours one-quarter inch from seam line or edge of shape. I use it often for appliqué figures on the base block and for stitching inside the perimeter of each block (Diagrams 91a–d).

Echo quilting repeats the shapes of appliquéd pieces out into the background fabric using concentric lines spaced one-quarter to one-half inch apart. It "echoes" their contours, kind of like radio waves. The textured repetition creates visual rhythm (Diagram 92).

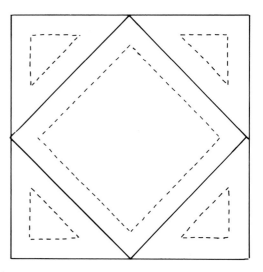

Diagram 91a. Simple outline.

Diagram 91b. Concentric outline.

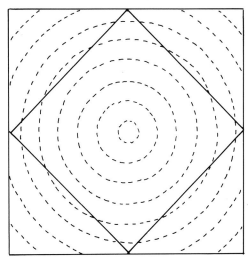

Diagram 91c. Concentric circles radiating from center.

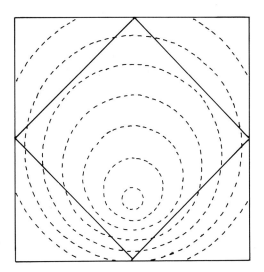

Diagram 91d. Concentric circles radiating from off-center.

Diagram 92. Echo quilting pattern.

Large areas of background can be quilted with *filler stitches.* These all-over patterns cover the background, providing a textured surface. Areas that are densely quilted with simple patterns will contrast with areas quilted in more elaborate designs (Diagram 93).

Thread color is traditionally white. But if you don't want your stitches to show, use a color that blends with the fabric you're quilting. Similar color quilting doesn't highlight a design, but it does create lovely textured hills and valleys on the surface. It's perfectly all right to use different colored quilting threads, but the stitches on the back won't develop a uniform pattern (Diagrams 94, 95, 96, and 97).

Diagram 93. Four filler quilting patterns.

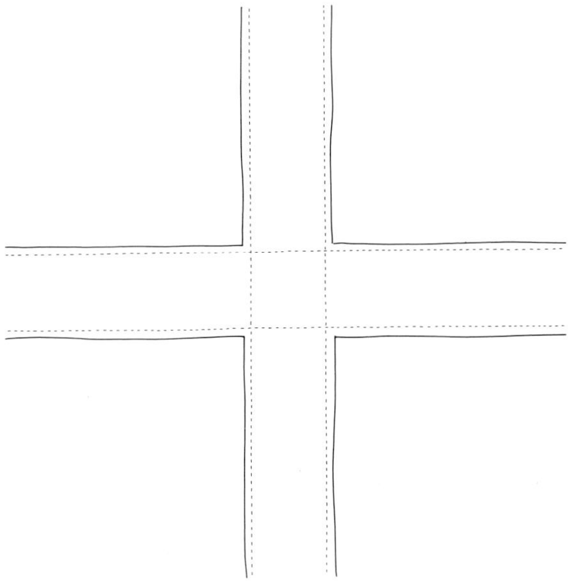

Diagram 94. Quilting pattern: one-quarter inch from edge. It meets in a square in each intersection.

Diagram 96. Quilting pattern: double chain overlaps in intersections.

Diagram 95. Quilting pattern: chain that meets in a diamond in intersections.

Diagram 97. Quilting heart pattern: each heart faces same direction and sits perfectly in each intersection.

MARKING QUILTING PATTERNS

•

Once the quilting design has been chosen, it must be transferred to the quilt top. You can either mark the entire pattern on the quilt before the layers are basted together, or mark as you quilt. Patterns with elaborate motifs are easier to transfer if you have a firm surface under the fabric. So mark them on the quilt top before the sandwich is assembled, in a way that will not disappear as the layers are being connected. An effective transferring method for elaborate patterns is a light box (or a glass table with a light under it). Of course, this must be done before the quilt is in the frame. Since I'm often eager to get started, my usual method is to mark in small areas while the quilt is stretched taut in the frame.

The patterns to be quilted can be traced directly (and lightly) onto the front side of the quilt top. Many of the simple classic shapes (hearts, parts of feathers, or cable patterns) can be purchased in cardboard or plastic template form. Or, you can make your own from any of the template materials suggested on page 155. Con-Tact paper can be used as an inventive quilt template material. Cut the shape out, peel away the backing paper, and the result will function like masking tape.

Straight lines can be marked along a ruler's edge. Some outline quilting can be done by eye without marking the quilt surface. You can also position a piece of one-quarter-inch masking tape along the edge of a seam or an appliqué motif, stitch beside the edge of the masking tape, and remove the tape. Don't leave sticky tape on your fabric for long periods of time.

There is much controversy about what utensil to mark with. Marked lines mustn't show after the project is finished. In other words, the line must not be permanent—it must either disappear, rub off, brush out, be washed out, or be erased by the time you declare your project a *fait accompli.* Test any marking technique first on a scrap of the same fabric that will be quilted to see how much handling it can take before disappearing. Also test to see how easily and completely the marks can be removed.

A well-sharpened #2 pencil can be used to mark a very, very light line on light fabrics. A light-colored pencil with erasable lead can be substituted for dark fabrics. Their lines, if light enough, will eventually be rubbed out by the time you're finished. If not, or if they smudge, they can be washed out or erased with an art-gum eraser. The lines of a dressmaker's pencil will brush off nicely, but it's so soft, that it needs to be sharpened frequently in order not to create a wide line. Other options are chalk, a sliver of white hard soap (an obviously clean, washable option) or a water-soluble or vanishing fabric marker. Don't mark the whole quilt top at once with a vanishing marker, unless you are Speedy Gonzales with the quilting needle.

An alternative method (that needs no removing) for marking small segments at a time is needle tracing. Place the template in the appropriate place and scratch around it with a needle. The scratched result will be visible enough to create a stitching line, but it will disappear fairly quickly. Dressmaker's carbon and ballpoint pens are not recommended. Their lines are too permanent. Refer to "How to Make Templates," page 156, "How to Mark and Cut Fabric," page 162, and "Tools of the Trade," page 153.

CONSTRUCTING THE
QUILT BACKING

•

Although you won't be binding the quilt's raw edges for a while, you should decide now what method to use. There are basically two binding choices: self-binding and separate binding (see "Binding," page 205). If you choose self-binding, which means bringing excess backing fabric to the front, include the additional fabric in the backing dimensions.

The backing fabric (also called the quilt lining) should be at least two inches bigger around than your quilt top. You can always trim away but it is much more difficult to add on. As mentioned previously, most fabric is available in forty-five-inch width, minus an inch of selvage. If the quilt top is bigger than this, the fabric must be pieced with a seam. The most desirable way is to sew together two pieces of fabric, of equal length and width, with a seam that runs vertically down the center. If you don't plan to enter your quilt in a show, however, you can obviously get by with a centered horizontal seam or with piecing the back in thirds (Diagrams 98a–d). For those of you who love the exception to every rule: this particular seam is pressed *open* to facilitate quilting.

CATERING THE AFFAIR:
THE QUILTED SANDWICH

•

Now it's time to make the sandwich. The quilt top and backing are the bread, the batting's the bologna. Select a batting that's at least two inches bigger around than your quilt top.

The first thing to do is find a clean, flat surface big enough to spread out the quilt. Vacuum your floor, visit a friend who has a large dining room table, or inquire at your local community centers or quilt shops about using their work areas. The most important thing is to center your layers, and to eliminate all wrinkles and bunches.

To find the center points on the backing and top, gently fold them into quarters. Safety pin the centers on the right side and on the outside edges of the quarter folds. Spread out the backing, wrong side up, and smooth out wrinkles. Gently unroll batting on top of backing, smoothing without stretching. Place quilt top over batting right side up. Match center and quarter marks. Pin the layers together with safety pins or extra large quilting pins, making sure you don't pin them to the carpet.

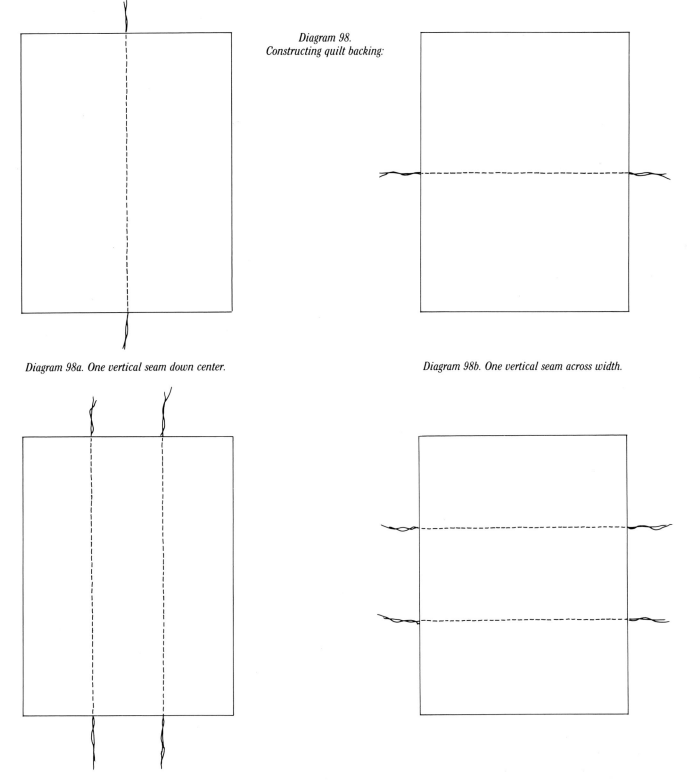

Diagram 98.
Constructing quilt backing:

Diagram 98a. One vertical seam down center.

Diagram 98b. One vertical seam across width.

Diagram 98c. Two vertical seams down center.

Diagram 98d. Two vertical seams across width.

Basting. The trick to basting is to keep the three layers from traveling around as you stitch. Concentrate on creating four square corners and straight lines in the sashing grid. This is fun to do with friends as you listen to your favorite music, stretching and contorting to reach the middle without messing things up. (Who said quilting was a sedentary sport?)

Use a large needle and a single, longish strand of white or light-colored regular thread—the dyes in dark-colored threads may discolor the top. Keep three or four more threaded needles within easy reach. Here's your chance to make big, rude, carefree stitches: approximately two inches long on top and one-half inch long on back. Don't baste directly on the quilting pattern, or else you might pull out the wrong stitches when you remove the basting. Begin with a big knot so you can see it when you need to remove it. End with a backstitch.

Baste with a running stitch in rows spaced four to six inches apart. You don't have to mark these lines—just measure with your eye. The traditional method calls for stitching from the center out to each corner, smoothing as you go, creating an X. Then work from the center to the middle of each side. Next, stitch concentric squares or rectangles that follow the shape of the quilt top, radiating from the center to the quilt's edges. End by basting around the perimeter (Diagram 99).

I find it really awkward to reach the center with this method, since I always work on my living room floor. Instead, I create a grid of basting stitches, smoothing as I go. Beginning one inch from the top or bottom edge, I stitch from left to right. (I'm a lefty, so reverse the order if you're not.) When I can't reach a new section comfortably, I roll the quilt top up to, but not including, the last line of basting. Then I shift my position, unroll the quilt, and repeat for the quilt's length (Diagram 100).

If the sandwich will be machine-quilted, or quilted on a hoop, it needs the extra security of double basting. Lay the batting down, lay the back face up over it, and baste these two layers together well. Then gently turn the two layers over so the back is on the bottom, place the quilt top face up, and baste all three.

Don't remove basting until the quilting is completed.

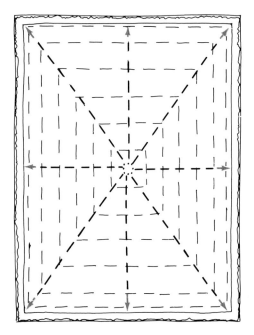

Diagram 99. Basting method for quilt sandwich.

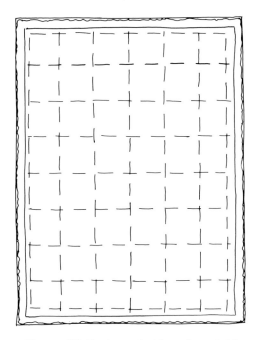

Diagram 100. Basting method for quilt sandwich.

ATTACHING QUILT TO
FRAME OR HOOP

◆

The job of securing the bulk of a quilt with tiny even-tempered stitches is best done when the three-layered affair is held prisoner, taut on a frame or hoop. The fabric is pulled, but not distorted. The frame helps the quilt remain wrinkle-free. Once the tension is released, the fabric between stitching lines puffs up.

A quilt in a hoop demands more extensive basting, because the weight of the excess quilt constantly shifts and tugs. For hoop quilting, fold and baste the extra backing over the batting to the front of the quilt. You may have to baste a temporary foot-wide border around your quilt, so the hoop can catch all the remote edges (Diagram 101). Don't leave your work in the hoop overnight—it can make a permanent groove in the quilt.

Refer to "Quilting Frames," page 194.

HOW TO QUILT

◆

Smooth and centered is the name of the framing game. Quilt from the center of the quilt top out to the edge in one direction; return to the center and quilt out again. Don't move all over the quilt, stitching one area here, another way over in the corner, skipping over large unquilted areas. This will make your quilt pucker. Since you smooth as you go, this method helps prevent wrinkles on the back. Once an area has been stitched, you can't readjust the front without creating ungodly bubbles. Lefties find it easier to quilt from left to right (righties like the reverse). Everyone seems to prefer to quilt toward his or her body, not away from it.

*H*and-Quilting Stitch. Don't expect to fall right into a natural stitching rhythm immediately—especially if you've never quilted before. The fabric before you is now static—you can't manipulate it freely as you did in your appliqué block. Don't give up. Practice, practice, practice. Do the best you can. Eventually a pleasant rhythm will be established.

Knots and threads should not be visible on the top or the back. Instead, they are popped into the batting layers and forever hidden. Don't be tempted to stab the needle straight through the layers, pulling the thread all the way through, and then pushing the needle straight up from the underside. This method may seem easier at first, but it's really much slower, and will create irregular, misguided stitches on the back, even though perfectly tiny stitches appear on the front. This "stab stitch" can be useful occasionally when you run into a thick seam.

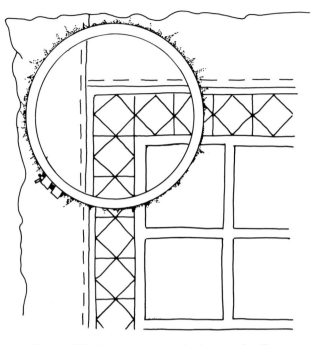

Diagram 101. Basting a temporary border around quilt to accommodate quilt hoop.

*H*ow to begin. A sewing thimble on the middle finger of the dominant hand is imperative. It's your choice whether to wear a metal thimble, a leather fingerguard, or nothing whatsoever on the index finger of the non-dominant hand under the quilt. Some say the index finger shoud be bare to feel the needle. If naked is your choice, expect a little blood on the back of the quilt before a callous can be formed. (To remove blood stains, dab with cold water or your own saliva, or apply cool water with a smidge of meat tenderizer dissolved in it.)

Make a small knot one inch from the end of an eighteen-inch single strand of quilting thread. If it's any longer, the thread will knot up and disintegrate. Working from the quilt's top, insert the needle about one inch from where you want to begin. Push the needle through the batting and up to the surface at the place you want to begin quilting. (Don't go all the way through to the back.) Pull the thread all the way through until the knot is resting on the quilt surface. Give a gentle tug on the thread, and the knot and its tail will be popped through the top to lodge in obscurity between the layers, happily ever after (Diagram 102a).

Diagram 102. Hand-quilting stitch.

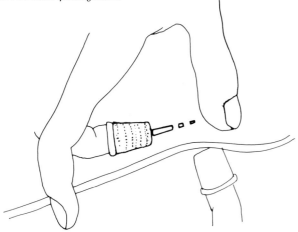

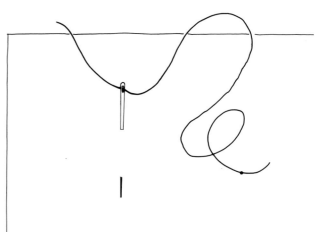

Diagram 102a. How to begin quilting stitch: pop knot between layers.

How to stitch. The hand-quilting stitch is a small, even running stitch through all three layers. Stitches should be the same size and evenly spaced on the front and back. If this is your quilting debut, concentrate on even, rather than small, stitches that reach the back. Work toward stitches that are about one-sixteenth inch apart. Some quilters are comfortable with the rhythm established by taking one stitch at a time. Others load the needle with three or four stitches. Either way is fine as long as the stitches are even.

Throughout the entire quilting sequence, the eye of the needle is held against the top or side of the sewing hand thimble. The top of the thimble guides the tip of the needle toward the index finger underneath, at a slight angle to the surface. (I use the index finger and thumb to help take the first stitch.) Use the thumb of the sewing hand to simultaneously press the quilt top down gently, just ahead of the needle's anticipated return. The underneath finger makes sure the needle takes a tiny stitch before deflecting the point back up through the layers so that just the tip of the point peeks out on the top surface. At this point you can pull the thread through to make a single stitch, or with the needle almost parallel to the quilt surface, tip the needle's point back into the sandwich and add another stitch (or two or three). Once it's loaded with stitches, use the top of the thimble to push the needle through, then pull the thread out firmly.

The goal is to repeat these motions in an established, almost unconscious rhythm, rocking the needle up and down through the layers. If the thread is pulled too tight, the fabric will pucker. If it's too lax, the thread will not create any relief. To test your thread tension, stick a pin under one stitch and pull up. If a lot of thread comes up with your pin, make your stitches a little tighter.

How to end. Make a small knot close to the surface of the quilt. Make the final stitch through the batting only. Then bring the thread back up to the top, about an inch away, and tug gently, so the knot pops into the batting. Carefully snip excess thread at the quilt surface so it will slip into the batting (Diagram 102).

MACHINE-QUILTING

•

Machine-quilting is, not surprisingly, faster. And if it's done correctly, it's even stronger. It produces a different effect than hand-stitching. Machine lines are more sharply defined and indented. It's more difficult to make intricate curves, so choose a quilting pattern based on straight lines. If you "stitch in the ditch" try to spread the seams open as much as possible, so the stitches will sink into the seams.

If you want a pucker-free quilt, take extra care and double-baste the layers (see "Basting," page 202). Be sure you quilt consistently from the center out. Don't move to a spot separated by an unquilted area.

Place your sewing machine on a large table so the quilt's weight doesn't hang over the edge. Smooth out the layers as they recede under the needle. To turn corners, lift the presser foot, leaving the needle in the fabric, then turn the quilt.

The quilt's fabrics will determine the needle and thread size. Some quilters advocate all-cotton quilt thread on top, and a matching cotton-covered polyester in the bobbin. Others suggest matching the thread to one fiber in the fabric. Generally, choose a needle one size larger than you would to machine-piece the same fabric—usually size 14. Begin sewing with a full bobbin.

Set your machine to twelve to fourteen stitches per inch. Don't back-tack the ends of the thread. Instead, draw the top thread to the backing. Knot each pair of threads, thread them on a sewing needle, and gently pull and pop the knot into the batting.

TYING

◆   ◆   ◆

Tying is, without a doubt, the easiest and fastest way to secure your quilt. It will look puffier, and possibly a little less finished than its finely quilted counterpart, but don't worry. It won't fall apart. And there is something to be said for getting it done. Tying is a great method for children to do by themselves. Kids may be suspicious of all the dangles in the back, but are quickly mollified when you remind them that the pioneers tied their quilts, too.

Use bonded or needle-punched polyester batting two inches bigger around than your quilt. Prepare the quilt sandwich as if you were quilting. Choose durable, washable, flexible yarn. It must hold a secure knot and be thin enough to make it through the layers. Use a wide-eyed needle, but not so big that it punches gigantic holes in the quilt.

Knots can be placed at six-inch intervals. On quilts with rows of blocks and sashing, you can place knots in the block's corners, and six inches in between along the block to sashing seam line. Ties can be made on the front or back; I prefer to dangle the ends on the back.

Thread your needle with two yards of yarn, doubled. Don't make a knot. If you want the ends to dangle on the back, pull them up from the back, leaving two inches of yarn dangling at the point you want to make a tie. Take a one-quarter-inch-long stitch, bring down the needle, tie a square knot, cut. Repeat at each point. If you want the ends to be tied on the quilt's top, you have to pull the yarn down from the top.

QUILT AS YOU GO

◆   ◆   ◆

With the quilt-as-you-go method, every contributor constructs a mini-quilt sandwich out of his or her block—little hors d'oeuvres that together will make up the final feast. Blockmakers piece sashing and borders to their picture, then batt, back, and quilt the miniature unit. Each segment is then sewn together to complete the quilt top. Analyze the entire layout graph to determine the most logical way of breaking it up into small units. This step-by-step method alleviates the need for mega-frames and mega-quilting sessions, but it must be carefully planned so all the pieces fit together, pucker-free.

PREPARATION FOR QUILTING

◆

Prepare each miniature quilt as you would one whole large quilt top. Mark quilting patterns; trim batting and backing fabric the same size as block; baste the little sandwich.

QUILTING THE BLOCK

◆

The block can be worked in the lap or stretched taut in a large embroidery hoop. You can buy special quilt-as-you-go frames, which serve the same function as hoops, or you can make one out of four strips of wood held together by bolts. Begin quilting from the center out.

JOINING THE BLOCKS

◆

Roll back the batting and backing and pin them out of way. Pin blocks right sides together, and stitch a quarter-inch seam.

On a flat surface, quilt top down, unpin the back and batting. Match the battings so the edges are "butted" together, making sure the junction is flat and the wadding is distributed evenly. If one piece overlaps another, shave some batting from each.

Overlap the backing of one block onto another. Turn under a one-quarter-inch hem of the overlapping backing. Hand-sew with matching thread to camouflage the stitches.

Continue piecing the smallest units together into rows; then join rows together using the same technique. Add binding.

BINDING

◆   ◆   ◆

Binding means finishing the quilt's raw edges. The edges of a quilt shouldn't be flat, so make sure the batting is evenly distributed out to the ends of the binding. If your quilt has a pieced border, the binding must be stitched or hemmed to it at exactly one-quarter inch, to meet points and corners precisely.

There are two basic methods to choose from: self-binding or separate binding.

Self-binding does not require cutting any extra fabric. It involves turning the quilt's back to the front and hemming it in place. So you must decide before you make the sandwich if you're going to use this method—you'll need enough extra fabric added to the quilt backing to bring to the reverse side, turn under, and hem (see "Constructing the Quilt Backing," page 200). In this case, the print and color of the backing fabric must be compatible with the fabrics in the quilt top. The width of the binding edge depends on the quilt's general mood. I usually opt for narrow bindings, one-quarter to one inch. To calculate how much fabric you'll need, add the width of the binding plus one-quarter- or one-half-inch seam allowance to each side.

Trim the batting to the finished quilt top's dimension. Roll the binding fabric onto the front, fold in the corners and seam allowance neatly, and hand-sew in place with invisible stitches (Diagrams 103, 104, and 105).

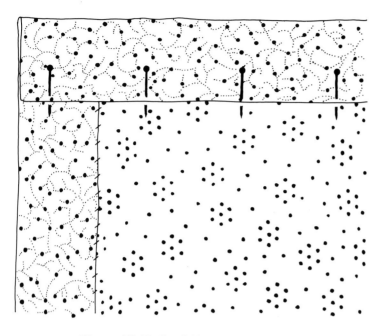

Diagram 103. Binding: fold corners and hem neatly.

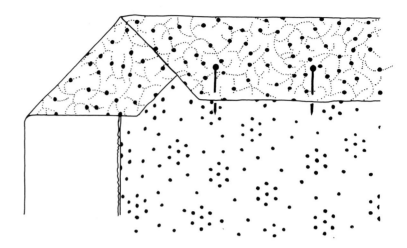

Diagram 104a. Turn binding over and hem neatly.

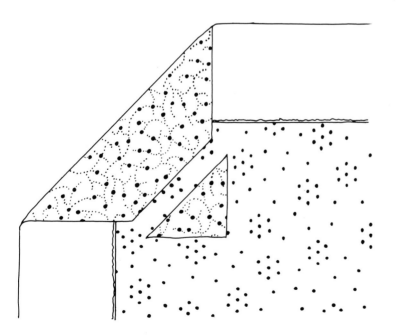

Diagram 104. Mitering the binding corners: fold down corner and trim off point.

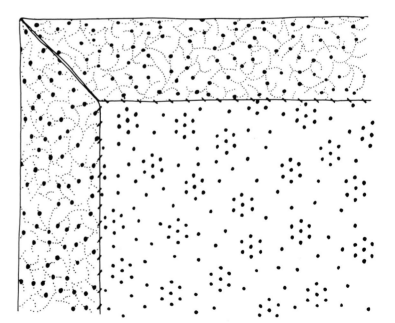

Diagram 105. Mitering binding corner: finished product.

Separate binding involves attaching a separate fabric strip cut from either the true bias or the straight grain (Diagram 106). This process is slightly more time-consuming, but provides a stronger edge and one that can be removed and replaced easily if it gets worn out.

Solid-color double-width bias tape can be purchased ready-made. If you want to match a print in your quilt, you must cut your own along the bias. There are two basic ways to make a bias binding.

The first way involves slicing up a sheet of fabric along the diagonal. To find the true bias, fold the fabric at a 45-degree angle from the straight grain (Diagram 107). Make the strips double the width of your finished binding choice plus seam allowance on both sides. From the fold, mark off the width of the bias on the wrong side of the fabric. Repeat by marking parallel lines (Diagram 108). Mark as many bias strips as you need to surround the entire perimeter of the quilt. The short ends of these strips will appear diagonal even though they are cut on the straight grain. Mark a seam line one-quarter inch from each of the short ends. With right sides together, match the *seam lines,* not the cut edges of these strips. Pin and stitch. Continue until the joined strips are the correct length. Press seams open (Diagram 109).

Diagram 107. Separate binding: to find true bias, fold fabric at 45-degree angle.

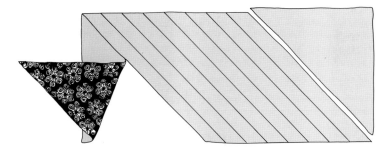

Diagram 108. Separate binding: mark off width of bias on wrong side of fabric. Repeat by marking parallel lines.

Diagram 106. Separate binding: fabric strips cut on straight grain.

Diagram 109. Separate binding: stitch at seam lines.

The second way involves making a tube of fabric—kind of like an unstuffed cannelloni—and cutting around and around, producing one long bias strip that needs no seaming. To do this, you need a large rectangular piece of fabric. Its dimensions should be the entire width of the fabric and at least one-half yard long. At one end, fold the fabric diagonally to find the true bias. Beginning at the fold, mark long diagonal lines for individual strips on the wrong side. Cut along the outermost marked lines only.

Join the shorter ends of this marked piece of fabric, right sides together. One strip width must extend beyond the edges at each side. Stitch ends together in a one-quarter-inch seam. Press seams open. The ends will appear diagonal, even though they are cut on the straight grain. Then begin cutting along the top line in a circular fashion, round and round.

Trim batting and backing equal with quilt top. With right sides together, pin the binding to the edge of the quilt backing, easing it around the corners. Machine-stitch in place. Now fold the binding over to the front, fold the corners neatly, and hand-sew, using an invisible hemstitch.

Signing and Dating

• • •

Quilts are made more for heritage these days than for cover. Chances are your fabric labors will outlive you. So take it from a Hancock (even though it's just a LynNell Hancock), a signature can make a significant difference. How many times have you seen antique quilts in books and galleries that say, "Maker unknown"? Even if your quilt isn't necessarily museum material, relatives and friends will still appreciate it if you add somewhere on their gift the quilt's date, its name, purpose, and contributors. A special poem or inscription of love will add immeasurable meaning to your stitchery efforts.

You can embroider, stencil, or indelibly ink your message right on the front of the quilt. Document it in a center patch, or on a label attached to the back—anywhere you can think of. Rowena Fisher made a pocket on the back of her *Beyond Friendship* quilt (page 15) that includes not only written documentation, but an extra basket patch for future repairs.

In the old days, one person schooled in fabric calligraphy signed everyone's block for them, for consistency's sake. If you've decided to let each blockmaker sign his or her own, you might want to give them instructions about color, size, placement, embroidery stitch, etc.

Writing on fabric is an art in itself. Sue Stein recommends using a Far Eastern pen—the Pigma Ball-03, from Sakura, Japan. It renders a very fine line and survives many launderings.

To embroider your inscriptions, use a small stitch—either chain, outline, backstitch, or even cross-stitch. If you're not comfort-able free-forming your signature, *Quilters' Newsletter Magazine* recommends writing it first on tracing paper, basting the paper to the quilt, and then embroidering it over the drawn line. Gently tear away the paper when you're finished. You can also mark the fabric first with a vanishing pen and embroider on top of it before it disappears.

Inscriptions can be worked right into the appliqué block. In *Lottie's Quilt* (page 62) I re-created a piece of work stationery topped with the occupational therapist insignia (Lottie was a successful therapist for thirty-two years). Embroidered in the lines of the mock-up memo pad are the following words:

> From: Friends and Family
> Date: June 26th, 1984
> We, whose lives you have touched, love you.

For the *Wedding Chupah* (page 66) the bride's sister, Myra Hirshberg, cross-stitched a panel that includes the couple's names, the wedding date, and the quilt contributors. The tiny block is stitched to the back corner of the quilt. Barbara Brackman embroidered her signature along the edge of Sue's beach towel on the *Ms. Sue: Alive and Liberated* quilt (page 82).

"Beyond Friendship"

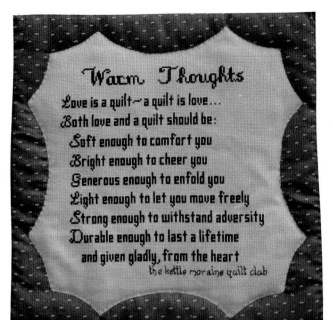

"Warm Thoughts"

"Ms. Sue at the Beach"

CARING FOR QUILTS
· · ·

When you give this kind of gift, expect the recipient to ask you how they should care for it. Be glad when they do. It means they appreciate your investment of time and love, and will handle the quilt with respect.

If they look stricken because their house collects more dust than Oklahoma in a drought, tell them they can gently vacuum their wall hanging a few times a year, so the dirt won't become imbedded in the fibers. If the quilt can be washed, suggest that they hand-wash it in lukewarm water with mild liquid detergent. Brands created specifically for quilts are available. Soak for a few minutes, and rinse well by gently squeezing. Don't ever wring a quilt. It ruins the quilting stitches and makes permanent wrinkles. (A quilt can never be ironed once it's quilted.) The damp quilt can be rolled in towels, then dried flat in the shade.

For a quilt that's meant to hang on a wall, hand-sew a sleeve or rod casing of double thickness all the way across the top of the back. This is better than loops attached to the top at intervals. Suggest that the recipient buy a café curtain rod or dowel to fit through it. This way, when the quilt is hung, its weight will be evenly distributed.

To make a casing, cut two strips equal in length to the quilt's top and as wide as you want the casing to be plus one-half inch. Right sides together, sew one-quarter-inch seams along one length, down the width, and back along the other length. Turn inside out. Turn under the raw edge on the open end by one-quarter inch and stitch closed. Hem it to the back without letting your stitches come to the front.

To keep the quilt from fading, recommend that the recipient keep it away from direct sunlight, spotlight, or intense, unfiltered fluorescent light. It should be stored in a cool, dry, place. Fabric needs to breathe. Plastic bags will eventually make it rot. Sew together a loose-fitting bag that will allow air to circulate, or inquire at the American Quilter's Society, or at your local quilt store or museum, about an acid-free, lignin-free box in which to store valuable quilts. Take the quilt out and refold it every few months to avoid permanent creases.

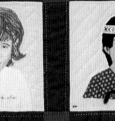

P·A·R·T

4

WORKING WITH THE GROUP

Background
•
THE JOINT SOVIET-AMERICAN
PEACE QUILT
•

How to Make the Group Work

*G*roups need a little loving custodial care if they are to operate efficiently. Coordinating them can be fun, it can be rewarding, or it can be that one commitment you wish you hadn't made. Assuming you're not in the communal quilt business to get bummed out, here are some helpful hints from both quilting and psycho-social experts on how to organize a collection of fabric-hungry humans.

There are basically two kinds of quilt groups: those that can meet, and those that can't. For the face-to-face kind, get-together time is important. After the first meeting where initial decisions are made, the curmudgeons among us can certainly stitch our masterpieces in the privacy of our bathrooms. But it's the *camaraderie,* the sharing of ideas, and the midnight sewing sessions that make the group effort so appealing. As group leader, you can help it happen.

WHAT THE LEADER NEEDS TO DO
◆　◆　◆

Plan a few in-progress sewing sessions, one big party on deadline day, and another celebration at the quilt top's unveiling. Don't make these moments mandatory. Camaraderie is not something you can dictate, nor is it just a frivolous romantic concept. At sewing klatches, stitchers share design ideas and materials, exchange pats on the back, and are made to feel like an integral part of the quilt's progress. Blocks by group-goers tend to look like they belong in the same family; hermit blocks are likely to look altogether apart.

THE FIRST MEETING
◆

Come equipped with a few suggested designs, this book for inspiration, and an idea about the kind of leader you need to be: autocrat, democrat, or advocate of laissez-faire. Experts tell us that the democratic style works best for cooperative projects where policies are determined through group decisions; a nice encouraging leader stands at the helm stimulating ideas, smoothing over problems, telling jokes. Laissez-faire (very little leader interference) works best when the group is already committed to a decision and has the resources to implement it—like a small group of friends planning a one-time-only baby quilt. And let us not slight benevolent autocrats; they too have their place in the quilting of things. If your chosen project demands precision, or you *want* to put it together all by yourself, or you have a collection of timid first-timers with ambitious plans—it may be time for your latent dictator instincts to come out.

EXPLAIN THE GOAL WELL

•

Don't scare off the skeptical by saying that your quilt will be double-king size and that you expect their work to put the Amish to shame. Emphasize that each stitcher makes only an itty-bitty section; that it's the layout committee's job to make sure everything works together. Take time to find out why certain people are saying no. Perhaps they feel uncomfortable making a free-form design. Ask someone else in the group to draw up a sketch for them. Perhaps they have a richly embroidered scheme in mind but feel totally unqualified with needle and floss. Find a needleworker who is willing to help. Offer your own time, resources, encouragement, and lots of food and refreshments to anyone who wants it.

MAINTAIN A SCHEDULE

•

Refer to "Organizing Your Time," page 123, for a detailed list of what you need to know.

COORDINATE MATERIALS
AND DESIGNS

•

After the color scheme is decided, either bring your own stash of materials to the second meeting or organize a trip to the fabric store.

PROVIDE INSTRUCTIONS
AND EXAMPLES

•

Prepare a letter with directions to go out with the base block fabric. Write what needs to be understood. If you've picked out sashing and border fabrics, include a swatch or two for color matching.

KEEP A PROGRESS REPORT
NOTEBOOK

•

List all participants. Jot down addresses and phone numbers—names of all the people you've contacted, including their answers. Keep track of how many potential blocks are happening. Note follow-up attempts; postcards, phone calls, or a newsletter letting everyone know what others are doing.

SAMPLE LETTER TO SOLICIT INTEREST
IN MAKING A FRIENDSHIP QUILT

• • •

Dear _____,

 I am planning a special friendship quilt for *Dick and Jane's wedding,* made up of original blocks appliquéd by friends and family. I hope you will be interested in participating.

 Here is what is involved: I will send you an *x*-inch fabric square on which you can appliqué any design you like and sign your name. When all the squares are returned to me, I will piece them together and quilt the finished product. If you are unable to make it to the wedding, I will provide a photograph of the entire quilt and a picture of the couple opening it up.

 Appliqué is quite simple. It involves cutting a design from one piece of fabric and sewing it to another. You don't have to have any sewing experience at all to do it. The appeal of this kind of quilt is in the sentiments expressed on the blocks, and the variety of designs, from the very, very simple to the relatively elaborate. I am encouraging everyone to contribute; women and men, old and young, sewers and non-sewers. It's my job to make all the blocks work together.

 Here are some possible ideas to incorporate into a design:

> • Something that reminds you of *Dick or Jane*
> • Something that will remind *Dick or Jane* of you
> • A symbol or image that represents a shared moment

I will be happy to provide ideas, trimmings, fabric, and sewing help whenever you need it. If you want to participate but can't be talked into sewing, feel free to contribute money to a quilt materials fund to help us defray costs.

 Please return the enclosed postcard with your decision by _____ so we can get started. If you know of anyone else I should ask, please let me know. I've printed a list of the names I have so far at the bottom of this letter.

 Thank you very much. And remember, this is a secret.

Sincerely,

_____

Your Name

Address

Phone Number

Names of potential participants

Include a self-addressed blank postcard

SAMPLE TECHNIQUES LETTER

• • •

Dear _____,

    Thank you for your interest in making a block for *Dick and Jane's wedding* quilt. I've included some helpful hints and instructions along with the enclosed *X*-inch square of background fabric marked with the seam allowance and the top and bottom alignment. Don't worry about pressing the block. I will do all of them at the end.

    Above all, have fun, and use your sense of humor and imagination. Feel free to call or write me. I will be happy to provide ideas, drawings, fabrics, trimmings, encouragement, expertise, etc. Please return the blocks to me by _____.

Yours in stitches,

_____

Sample Instructions

GATHER QUALITY MATERIALS

If you've never enjoyed sewing before, you have probably been using the wrong implements. Clean scissors make for clean, enjoyable cutting. Use dressmaker's shears to cut fabric, utility scissors for paper templates. An embroidery hoop holds the fabric still and keeps it from becoming warped. You'll also need graph paper, tracing paper, a #8 "sharp" or #10 "between" needle, a thimble, and fine pins. Extremely long, fine needles are available if you want to use beads with tiny holes. Match thread color to the appliqué patches, not to the background fabric. (When in doubt, go with the color that's slightly darker than the fabric.) Do not use fabric paints (yes/no).

Please don't mark any fabric with ballpoint pen or felt markers that might run. Use a pencil when you're absolutely certain it won't show. At a sewing or craft store you can buy fabric markers that make lines that either wash out with a drop of water or vanish all by themselves.

FABRICS AND TRIMMINGS

Test the fabrics to see if they are colorfast. It does/does not matter if the materials can be laundered. Use any fabrics you'd like: cotton, cotton-blends, furlike fabrics, silk, synthetic suede, felt (yes/no). Just make sure fabrics are colorfast, and that any raveling edges can be turned under and hemmed. Use any trimmings and doodads (beads, ribbons, lace) as long as they can be attached securely.

DRAW YOUR DESIGN ON GRAPH PAPER

Draw an *x*-inch square and add one inch for the seam allowance. When you plan the design, make sure some of the background fabric will end up showing, for consistency's sake. A centered design should take up most of the space, leaving just one inch of background all around it. You can trace from another source or have someone draw it for you. (Optional: Give directions for adjusting the size of the design.) IMPORTANT: If your design fills up the entire square, don't end it right at the seam allowance line. Otherwise, it won't look right when it's pieced to the next patch. Instead, extend the picture right into the seam allowance. Trimmings and fabric that begin or end in the seam allowance don't have to be hemmed.

TO PREPARE SHAPES FOR APPLIQUÉ

Make two maps of your design on tracing paper. Keep one intact for reference. Mark the other one with your sewing sequence (underneath layers are sewn first, and on up to the top). Cut apart the shapes for appliqué templates. Pin templates to the right side of the fabric you've chosen, and outline, very carefully. Add a one-quarter-inch seam allowance to each shape. So that the patch isn't enlarged, cut it just inside the marked line.

TO APPLIQUÉ

Use hand *or* machine appliqué exclusively. To find the center of the background block, fold it gently into quarters and mark a dot. Use any stitch you're comfortable with. To begin stitching, thread the needle with eighteen inches of thread cut diagonally and knotted.

Here's one way: come up from the back of the fabric, catching the folded edge of your appliqué shape, and pull the thread all the way through to the front. In one motion, put the point of the needle back into the ground fabric directly above its first entry, and then up from the wrong side to the front (no more than an eighth of an inch from the original stitch), pulling the thread all the way through. Repeat ad infinitum. To finish, make a few back stitches or knot on the wrong side.

The seam allowance of underlying pieces can be tucked under overlapping shapes; top-lying pieces must be turned under and hemmed. To turn under inside curves, make a few tiny clips in the seam allowance, up to but not through the sewing line. To remove fullness, clip outside curves with little Vs one-eighth inch from the raw edge. For shapes cut on the bias, stitch the inside curve first, then stretch and stitch the outside curve. To turn points, clip off some excess fabric at the tip. Don't worry what the back of your block looks like.

ADD PIZZAZZ

Feel free to play with combinations of embroidery stitches and colored threads. Couching (or tacking) is easy, and can be used for continuous lines, details, outlines, hairstyles. Use black silk thread for fine facial expressions.

Couching is done with two needles: one is threaded with yarn or embroidery floss, the second with a single strand of the same-colored floss or regular sewing thread. The thicker thread is laid on the surface of the fabric and tacked in place by the second more delicate thread. Both are knotted at the ends.

SAMPLE "HOW'S IT GOING" POSTCARD

· · ·

Dear Everybody,

I've received a lot of wonderful blocks already for Dick and Jane's wedding quilt. (Describe them.) I can't wait to see everyone else's. Remember, the deadline is very, very soon—*(date).* I need to know how many blocks are coming in before I can plan the layout and borders. Please call or write to let me know how things are going. Keep stitching! *Dick and Jane* are going to be so surprised!

Sincerely,

_____

Name

Address

Phone number

THIS IS YOUR LIFE PROJECTS

· · ·

Otherwise known as memory or presentation quilts, "This is Your Life" projects provide a particularly creative canvas for the group quilt. They take a little extra effort on the part of the organizer, but when you see the look on the recipient's face—whether it's your best friend, your retiring rabbi, your favorite teacher, your Aunt Lottie—you'll never regret a moment. It's the very personal touches on these quilts that bring tears to the eyes.

- Take the time to collect the most meaningful group to the recipient.

- Build in lots of schedule flexibility.

- Make it easy for anyone to participate. Gear your instructions to the person with no sewing experience.

- Accept any and all blocks, no matter how primitive, no matter how chartreuse.

- Make sure you have a camera ready and pointed when the quilt receiver opens the box.

Since this is the age of mobility, a group of old friends and relatives will probably be scattered coast to coast. If the quilt is supposed to be a surprise, finding these people will require some special spy skills and creative thinking. A good place to start amateur sleuthing is to contact a not disinterested third party, who knows addresses.

I decided to make a wedding quilt for my oldest friend, Cheryl. In order to contact her future husband's side of the family, I had to reach his brother—a carpenter. I obtained the necessary phone number by pretending to have a friend who needed cabinets—quick. Then I called Cheryl's workplace to contact a colleague she had mentioned in passing, wondering what I would say if Cheryl answered the phone.

After compiling the addresses of Cheryl and Dean's cast of important characters in their lives, I composed a scouting letter. To those who responded favorably, I then sent out precut, prewashed, light blue blocks marked with a fat seam allowance, and instructed stitchers to appliqué an image that expressed their connection to the couple. Knowing ahead of time that I wouldn't have time to quilt the project, I asked for contributions toward a quilt fund. In keeping with the impromptu nature of these kinds of quilts, just days before all the blocks were to be pieced together into an intricate layout I had sketched, a totally unexpected green Volkswagen block sputtered up to my doorstep. (Remember: be flexible!)

The blocks for *Cheryl and Dean's Wedding Quilt* gift (page 64) represent a true free-for-all spirit. On another marriage gift, a quilted chupah (the wedding canopy in a traditional Jewish ceremony), the mother of the bride had a more unified design in mind. I made up designs based on the images the family decided to portray on the quilted surface, and devised kits for everyone, which included a sketch, directions, embroidery threads, trimmings, and precut shapes glued to the ground fabric. Each block depicted something special in the couple's lives: The Bridge of Sighs in Venice is where the groom proposed. A cello laid on a sheet of real music represents the couple's mutual interest (see *Wedding Chupah,* page 66).

Here are some more general ideas for picture blocks on a life quilt:

Amusing incidents from the person's past. One square on *Lottie's Quilt* (page 62) shows two people climbing a mountain. One is waving triumphantly from the top, the other is schlumped in defeat halfway down. The lower figure is Lottie at fifty, totally outdone by her friend, Agnes, who was sixty-five years old at the time—a scene Lottie's friends still won't let her forget.

Hobbies. A Pez dispenser on a square for a baby pillow quilt represents the new parents' record-making Pez head collection.

Quirks. A "cookie monster" square on a quilt for a retiring college president hints at the man's insatiable appetite for chocolate chip bakery goods.

Significant events. One block on *Lottie's Quilt* illustrates the important voyage she took as a teenager: from a small village in Poland to her new bustling home—Manhattan's Lower East Side.

Images that connect the blockmaker to the receiver. On a wedding quilt for a sanctuary refugee worker, one Texas first grade teacher created a "Sanctuary Sí!" lunch box and a "Casa Romero" thermos on his square. The teacher is famous for his extensive lunchbox collection (in the hundreds!). Casa Romero is the name of the refugee center where he met the quilt's owner.

Special roles played by the individual. Rabbi Wolf's retirement quilt has a hiking boot, for his role as camp director, and a Torah to signify his spiritual duties.

Special inscriptions: Using either embroidery thread or an indelible fine-point pen, sign your block, or inscribe a poem (see "Signing and Dating Your Quilt," page 208). The center square of *The Rose Quilt* (page 34) is a poem, "Warm Thoughts," which Rose herself had shared at an initial guild meeting. On *Debby's Quilt* (page 72) scripture verses reflect the sister's interest in Quakerism.

Miscellaneous. A block of books on a shelf can incorporate a miscellany of images that remind you of the quilt's intended. For instance, on *Cheryl and Dean's Wedding Quilt,* I added eight ideas on one square using book titles. "The Art of Roller Skating" refers to

the time Cheryl rolled a few feet and then broke both of her wrists. "The Joy of Greek Cooking" refers to Dean's native culinary skills. "Casey at the Bat" refers to Cheryl's tendency as a teenager to launch into a recitation of this entire epic poem, verse by verse, beginning to end, at inopportune moments. I must admit, at age fifteen we friends were completely unimpressed.

With a little ingenuity, This is Your Life quilts can be made in patterns that remind you of the person: a sampler of roses for your friend Rose, a monkey wrench signature album for that special custodian in your life.

"Lunch Box and Thermos"

"Boot and Torah"

Once you give the quilt away, it is no longer yours. But a part of you and all the contributors will always linger in the sashing, under the appliqué, between the stitches. So this final piece of advice should not be forgotten: Include instructions on how to care for quilts within the gift box (see "Caring for Quilts," page 209). Explain to the recipient that quilt preservation doesn't necessarily mean putting it away in a closet. If the quilt will be hung, add a rod casing and instructions for where and how to display it. Sew a storage bag yourself, or package the quilt in a sturdy box. You can even purchase special acid-free boxes made specifically for valuable quilts.

Write little thank-you notes to those members who couldn't be there for the presentation. Of course, the person who receives the gift should also thank them, but since you are the connection, be their eyes and let them know that your combined efforts made Aunt Mary cry like a baby. You may be calling on them again for another project. They spent some part of their lives investing time at your request. They deserve a reward.

GUILDS AND FRIENDSHIP CLUBS

◆　◆　◆

More than seven hundred quilt guilds boasting close to seventy thousand members have evolved worldwide in the last couple of decades. No matter how huge or how intimate, all of them seem to generate at least one group quilt per year, for many reasons: to teach beginners, to raise money, or simply to have an excuse to pull out the needles and get down to doing what they do best.

Many guilds have condensed the communal quilting art into a science, and any collection of would-be fabric fanciers can learn from their methods. Guilds have one foot in the group quilt door from the beginning; they don't have to drum up participants. Eager stitchers already attend monthly meetings and communicate through regular newsletters. Their group projects are generally organized around one of three approaches: *personal pattern, take your chances,* or *raffle winner takes all.* A single factor unifies them: a hat. (A hat?) The only difference is where the hat lies in the scheme of things: at the beginning of the project, or at the end. (Two more innovative options —*duplicate your design* and *pen pal quilts*—are usually chosen by smaller friendship groups.)

The *personal pattern* is a clever labor-saving method that promises a quilt for everyone, eventually, if your name is ever picked from . . . the hat. It works like this: one member's name is drawn at the beginning of a meeting. She chooses a pattern she's always yearned for, such as a basket, a schoolhouse, a butterfly, Sunbonnet Sue set in Drunkard's Path. Members will make blocks according to her specifications. When the blocks come back, she is on her own. She arranges them, assembles the sandwich, provides the quilting, and becomes the proud owner of the final result.

The hat person has total control over the shape of the quilt to

come. If she had a highly unified look in mind, she may also provide kits with background fabric, precut shapes, intricate instructions, and maybe even matching threads, so that all the blocks look as identical as possible. If the similar-yet-different look is OK by her, she may just distribute background fabric, templates, and color instructions: "blues and greens" or "happy colors." And finally, the let-it-all-hang-out option: any colors and fabrics you want. Sharon Flueckinger's *Butterflies* (page 19) is an example of a free-for-all composition that works beautifully.

"Butterflies"

Other guilds either choose the owner at the end or hand over the final fund-raising quilt to the lucky raffle winner. In both these methods, all the design decisions and all the quilt's stages are group efforts, directed by one or two people. The owner is determined when the finished quilt is unveiled, often at some big wingding, when the lucky winner's name (be she quilt worker, be she raffle winner) is drawn from . . . the hat.

Close to one hundred members in the Quilters' Guild of Tucson, Arizona, have evolved a Mother Bee-like system for their annual show projects (see *Southwestern Medallion,* page 27). They give themselves nine months ("a sort of pregnancy") from start to finish. The member with the design idea usually volunteers to be "mother" of the project. She and her assistants make drawings on graph paper, create accurate templates, decide on color schemes, buy supplies, prewash and iron fabrics. The "mother" plays queen to the quilt's drones, who gather to assemble kits of fabric, drawings, and directions for the group at large. Member Kittie Spence writes, "If we execute two challenging quilts in a row, we have to ask: How can we top the last one? What will we challenge ourselves with next?"

For more cozy-sized guilds, the *duplicate your design* option produces innovative results. Say you have a group of twelve members. Each member chooses one design and makes it twelve times. At a given date, the blocks are exchanged, and presto-chango! Suddenly parts for a dozen quilts exist where there were none before. Everyone gathers up her booty and goes home to set it, border it, and quilt it to her heart's desire.

Obviously some consistent element must be determined. Base block size and base block fabric should probably be identical. Theme and colors can provide automatic unifiers. For *Baltimore Friendship Album* (page 36), a group of nine Baltimore citizens agreed to make miniature classic albums in the spirit of their ancestors. Each stitcher chose a different pattern (a pineapple, a basket, a cornucopia) and duplicated it in the same reds, greens and blues nine different times. The nine settings, borders, and quilting patterns are all slightly different.

You can see why you wouldn't want to attempt this method with a cast of thousands. The Fiber Fanciers of Sunnyvale, California, got around the tedium factor by duplicating its designs in different colors. (See four of their quilts pictured on pages 30–33) The group, an offshoot of the Peninsula Stitchery Guild, organized a Christmas quilt exchange through the mail. Members were instructed to design their own block and to re-create it in the color preferences of the other eight members (blue-greens, brown-blue-rust, etc.). The inventive (and in one case, desperate) layouts of each of the quilts

show how flexible this approach can be. One fiber artist found it painful to work her block in colors she didn't like, but was pleased to see how compatible it looked in the final quilt.

Pen pal quilts pool needlework talents across the miles. One person sparks the design idea and recruits stitchers through the mail to help her realize it in fabric. A little more time and several more letters are necessary to make it work. Scout out interested parties with a general letter explaining the project (page 212). If speed is of the essence, include self-addressed postcards with your letter. They work magic—they get returned. Once your core group is established, send a more detailed letter with enough instructions and/or fabric to get them going (pages 213–214). If it's a long, drawn-out project, you may want to communicate with occasional newsletters to keep quilters informed and stitching.

For *Ms. Sue: Alive and Liberated* (page 82), Odette Teel invited friends and well-known quilt artists to make satirical Sue blocks. Miss Sue—a faceless little girl in silhouette, capped forever with the proverbial pioneer bonnet—is a traditional American pattern. She's usually engaged in one ladylike activity or another—sewing, gardening, cooking, etc. Odette's quilt is the feminist answer to the feminine image. She sent out muslin squares, green sashing strips for color matching, and instructions encouraging participants to have fun; "just make sure Sue's sunbonnet appears somewhere in the design, hung on the wall, under her foot, whatever . . . " Odette bordered her letter in tracings of Miss Sue and Overall Bill from other sources.

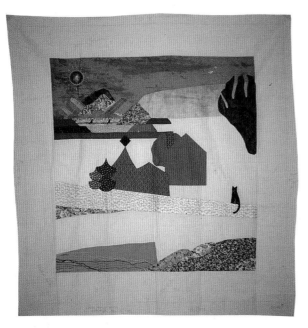

"Progressive Pictorial I"

"Progressive Pictorial II"

CHAIN-LETTER QUILT

◆

Caron Mosey, of Flushing, Michigan, author of *America's Pictorial Quilts*, invented a chain-letter project that operates much like the telephone game we all played as kids. Armed with a list of fifty names and addresses of all the quilters who were featured in her book, Caron cut a forty-two-inch-square piece of muslin, outlined a simple house on it, and sent it on its way. This animated lakeside scene, which she calls *Progressive Pictorial* (pages 116–118), evolved piecework by piecework. Each quilter was asked to add anything she wanted to the emerging picture, sign the border in pencil and send it to the next person on the list within five days. Caron instructed contributors to use only washable materials, and not to use fabric paint. Every fifth stitcher was asked to send Caron a postcard so she'd know where it was along the line; every tenth was asked to send the work-in-progress back so she could document it with her camera and embroider over the signatures.

"It's been a lot of fun seeing the quilt take shape," Caron says. "One of the first gals I sent it to added a church, because she says she always puts something religious in her quilts, and a later person added a star on the steeple. Then, after a few more stitchers, it got turned into a barn!"

"Progressive Pictorial III"

FUND-RAISERS

◆　◆　◆

Quilts are excellent money-makers for nonprofit organizations. They make unusual first-prize gifts for raffle tickets, and they cost relatively little to put together. Sometimes you can reduce the costs to almost nothing by soliciting material donations from fabric shops or manufacturers.

The work on fund-raisers has only just begun when the last quilting stitch is secured. Form special committees early on to take charge of the money-raising end of things. Put the artist in charge of the quilt, the writer in charge of publicity, the salesperson in charge of printing and selling raffles, the numbers whiz in charge of bookkeeping. The more members who participate in decision making, the more responsible they will be for making those decisions work. Time constraints are usually more harried for fund-raisers than for your average friendship quilt. We recommend the following:

- Make a twin-sized quilt.

- Choose one organizer to oversee the whole project and to crack the deadline whip more often than not.

- Plan to finish the quilt two months before the main raffle event (festival, banquet, etc.). The more time you have to sell raffles, the more money you'll raise.

- Organize publicity, raffle selling, and bookkeeping committees before it's quilted.

SIZE

◆

A quilt for a fund-raising event should always be at least *twin-sized*, for advertising reasons. When approached by enthusiastic raffle sellers on the street, the average Joe will not automatically respond to the inherent charm of a group-made quilt. He sees "Top Prize: Quilt" and thinks "blanket." Could be he needs a blanket. You can be sure he doesn't think he needs an arty wall hanging. So, until "group quilt" is a household word in America connoting "priceless folk art," raffle sellers will need to emphasize function over beauty.

PUBLICITY IDEAS

◆

If all your hard work is to be worthwhile, make sure you have plenty of time in your schedule to publicize your beautiful quilt, and sell as many raffles as possible.

Plan to have at least the quilt top finished way before your final raffle date so that a good *photograph* can be taken. Take color pictures for all the raffle sellers to carry with them. Take black and white glossies to send to the local newspapers.

Write your own *press release* or feature article to send along with the photo for the local newspaper. Include the quilt's purpose, a lively description, quotes from people who worked on it, and details about where raffles can be bought. Include anecdotes that provide either human interest stories or news pegs. For instance, newspaper readers from Newton, Massachusetts, were interested to note that the blocks for the town's special quilt were stored in a bank vault before assembly, and that the mayor sat at the quilting frame and added his own two stitches to the work in progress. (The stitches were later removed.) Small papers with limited staff are much more likely to run your well-written article than send their own reporter and photographer to the scene of the quilt.

RAFFLE SELLING

The most effective salesperson is the quilt itself. Display it in a public place—the local library, museum, bank, school, craft fairs, churches, etc.—and station a raffle seller next to it whenever possible. When raffle sellers hit the streets for our very first Amalgamated Nursery School quilt, sans photo, they had a hard time convincing potential contributors how special this quilt was. But when a group of parents took the finished quilt to a hospital cafeteria, they sold more than two hundred tickets in one afternoon.

If you can't have the quilt, use the next best thing—a picture of it. Make sure all the raffle sellers have a color photo to show. If you have the resources, make postcards, or even color posters.

Constance Bastille of the Monadnock (New Hampshire) Quilters Guild devised a display board to be used outside stores and other areas where the quilt couldn't be hung. The large photo of the finished quilt behind the plastic was framed by swatches of fabric used in the quilt.

The Monadnock guild managed to raise $4,500 for the New England Quilters Guild Museum, so we think its selling techniques may be useful to others. Constance's favorite place to sell tickets was at the liquor store, "since those people were usually in a good frame of mind." The newsstand on Sunday was another prime spot, "since folks had generally been to church and were feeling charitable." She doesn't recommend grocery stores, because "people were thinking how much their food was costing so didn't feel as generous."

Professionally printed raffle tickets can be expensive. If you have no freebie connections, mimeographed raffles are the cheapest way to go. Try to add one or two other donated items to your list of prizes (for instance, the quilt or $100 in cash), in case you run into that one Scrooge who couldn't be bothered with a quilt.

Add incentives for your raffle sellers by offering them prizes for the most tickets sold: a free book of raffles, cold cash, a hot-tub-for-two gift certificate. Try to keep your bookkeeping personnel down to one or two people so you won't have receipts floating all over.

OTHER FUND-RAISING GIMMICKS

Raffling isn't the only method. Some groups sell signature space on the quilts. You can either offer space in the lattice for people to set their signatures for all eternity, or you can sell whole blocks to organizations or families for a set fee. If you choose the block method, you may want to plan a quilt with small blocks. The benefit of signature-selling is that you have the option of keeping the quilt in the end (if you've raised enough money), offering it to a community institution that will display it, or doubling your returns by raffling it again.

QUILTING WITH CHILDREN

Children, like adults, respond to more than a quilt's warmth. They love the story of the quilt, the design, the sewing, the opportunity to be creative, and they love to dive into anything new—including ironing—with enthusiastic abandon. Quiltmaking provides the perfect opportunity to teach a little history, some design and color theory, a few work-sharing techniques, and even a touch of math. Obviously children need a lot of direction and hands-on help, but the end result makes them, and their adult compatriots, beam with shared accomplishment.

GROUPS

Schools, preschool on up, are obvious places to attempt a project. They provide good resources for grants, artist-in-residence programs, materials, womanpower, and, of course, endless supplies of eager children.

Families are the other natural groups that are ready-made for children's quiltmaking projects. One mother and daughter team (Anne MacDermott and Kristine, eleven) came up with an unusual idea: *European Memories*. A wonderful answer to "what did you do on your vacation?" this quilt is made up of fabric crayon blocks drawn by children the two encountered on their travels from Austria to Sweden. One student, who shared a compartment with them on a Swedish train, drew the Sphinx, the sight that had impressed him most on his backpacking journeys. Another son of a quilter in Germany drew his mother—he saw her as a "patchwork."

KID DESIGNS AND MATERIALS

If you're orchestrating a group, it's important to gear your design to the skill level of the children. Don't plan something so difficult you'll have to do most of the work yourself—the kids will become bored. Don't plan something too simple for their age, or too outrageous to their special aesthetic sensibilities—the children won't feel proud of the final result.

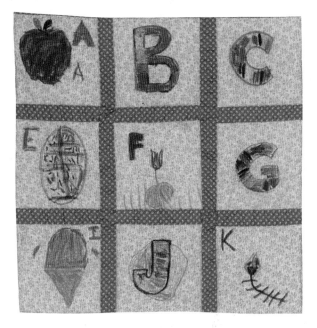

"Alphabet Quilt"

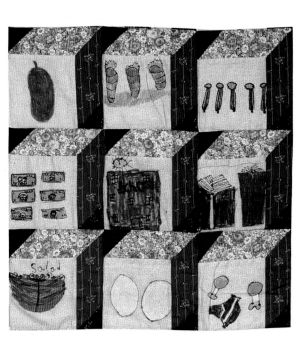

"Ethiopia Quilt"

For the total child-made quilt, adjust your materials, your instructions, and your expectations to the age group. Fabric crayons can replace appliqué, felt can replace cottons, fabric glue can replace basting, yarn can replace thread, and tying can replace quilting. Older children may be happier using tracings for designs or doing pieced projects that give them a chance to use the sewing machine.

Children's drawings translated into fabric by adults require much less kid input. Laura Ashley's *Through Children's Eyes* (page 100) is an example of a quasi-children's quilt.

FABRIC CRAYONS

◆

Fabric crayon drawings are most successful for children from pre-school age to about second grade. After that, youngsters are a lot like adults; unless they have a special artistic gift, they often expect too much from their own drawings and are not always satisfied with them. Most fabric crayons are heat fusible. Some are drawn right on the fabric, others are drawn on paper, which is then transferred to fabric, creating a mirror image. Read the directions on the box, and experiment at home before you try them on your audience.

Little ones need a lot of guidance and explicit instructions before they put crayon to fabric. Kids are very often so anxious to start that they begin to draw with reckless abandon, forgetting to follow directions. To avoid bringing on heartbreaking tears of frustration (both yours and theirs), work closely with small groups of

children. Talk about the theme of their drawing: a gift they want to give their teacher, a scene from their vacation, a CARE package to the children in Ethiopia. Make sure they know what they want to draw before they draw it.

School-age kids should start with a sketch on scratch paper. I explain to them that this is my method when I make a quilt. I don't expect my designs to be perfect the first time: I make mistakes, I make changes. Bring plenty of extra fabric squares for the bloopers. Show the class the stack of finished pictures. If you don't have weeks and weeks to work with the children, the easiest thing for you to do next is to take the blocks home, arrange them yourself in a simple layout, and bring the final result back for the children to admire. This is what New York's P.S. 195 did to produce *Ethiopia Quilt* (page 108) and *Alphabet Quilt* (page 105).

Janet Springfield, a nursery school teacher, diverges from the block-block-block layout by substituting children's drawings for certain elements of a traditional pattern in *Barbara's Bowen Nursery School Quilt* (page 114). The artwork is arranged in a Barn Raising pattern. Other patterns she suggests are the classic Log Cabin, Double Irish Chain, Ohio Star, Churn Dash, or Nine Patch. For toddlers (three and under) who are great scribblers but can't yet make representational pictures, Janet decided to have mothers embroider the children's hand outlines on blocks for *Billie's Bowen Nursery School Quilt* (page 115).

THREE HAND-APPLIQUÉ APPROACHES

◆

Hand-appliqué with children is probably best not attempted with teeny ones. Third grade may be the ideal starting point. There are three successful appliqué projects in this book, each one slightly different in approach.

*O*ne Square Per Child. Each child can be given a pattern or a block and fabric crayons. *P.S. 217—Our Heritage Quilt* (page 107) is an example of the total one-block-per-child quilt.

*O*ne Square Per Class. When an entire class collaborates on one square, a lot more cooperative planning is involved. *We're All Equal—Let's Go For It!* (page 111) is a successful example of an entire school-made quilt, with each class picking a topic and executing it in appliqué.

*O*ne Square Made in Shifts. Jean Linden, a dedicated librarian in a Queens elementary school that has since closed, coordinated twenty quilt projects before she retired, all designed to encourage children to read. The final quilt would hang in the library as an enticement for others to read. See *International Year of the Child* on page 110 for an example of Jean's work.

"Our quiltmaking is a cooperative effort," Jean explains. "We avoid the 'That's my block' approach. The children who are working that day continue on whichever block needs finishing. The best tracer does most of the tracing, the best cutter does all the cutting of small details. I have found that the quilting frame is hard for the children to use. Quilting a single block is easier for them to manage, and they can check the back to find mistakes."

"Our Heritage"

"We're All Equal"

"International Year of the Child"

"Puzzle Quilt"

PIECED PROJECTS

•

I was asked to make a quilt with a fourth grade class at P.S. 95 in the Bronx, as part of my community's artist-in-residence program. Among other things, I wanted to introduce the children to color theory, so I decided to attempt a Puzzle Sampler Quilt in solid colors. (It was easy for me to rule out appliqué—I couldn't envision how one adult could keep thirty-two needles threaded all at once!)

In the initial sessions, I introduced them to quilt history, and hence American history, by showing slides of old quilts and teaching them traditional patterns with catchy names like Snail's Trail, Boy's Nonsense, Monkey Wrench, Log Cabin. We talked about what a P.S. 95 pattern might look like.

To spark their interest in color, I showed the class two crayoned facsimiles of patchwork blocks and asked them to applaud their favorite. These two blocks were actually the identical pattern in completely different color combinations. When I superimposed a clear plastic sheet with the pattern outlined in black over both blocks, the children "oohed" and "aahed"; they saw the underlying design immediately. Now they were eager to experiment with the color wheel and with their own color combinations on prepared sheets of patchwork patterns.

Working in pairs, the fourth graders chose a pattern and colors from a palette of fourteen Amish solids. I provided templates, and the children cut, marked, basted, and ironed their own fabric. A sewing machine and iron were temporarily installed in the assistant principal's office, where I worked with small groups to piece their blocks.

After I attached black lattice at home, the class basted and tied the sandwich. At first the children were surprised to see the strings hanging down on the back of the quilt. They expected a more finished look. But when I explained that the pioneers used to tie their quilts the same way, in order to secure their paper- and corncob-stuffed covers, the children were appeased. When asked later what they enjoyed most about the project, the boys piped up with "ironing" and "sewing," while the girls seemed to prefer playing with the designs and colors.

Quiltmaking is a wonderful medium for enticing children to play with shapes, fabrics, and endless color possibilities. Children, who are chronologically closer than we adults to the infant age of cuddly blanket dependency, seem automatically to appreciate the functional role of the quilt. By creating a soft fabric cover with splashes of their own imagination, children learn through doing about one rich facet of the American folk art tradition, and about the timeless value of cooperation.

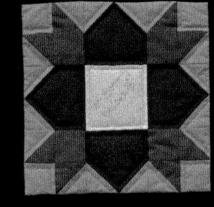

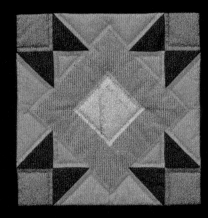

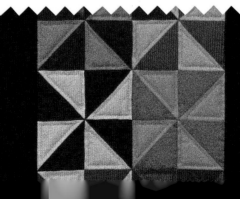

P·A·R·T

5

A FEW
SCRAPS
MORE

Background
·
AMISH FRIENDSHIP QUILT
·

Appliqué To appliqué is to sew smaller fabric shapes onto larger ones to create a design. It's the common technique used in pictorial quilts.

Base Block The unit of background fabric, usually square, on which fabric shapes are sewn. Finished base blocks are assembled into quilt top.

Borders The fabric frame that completes the quilt; often a change of pattern or color around the edges. It can be appliquéd, a strip of whole cloth, or a series of pieced units.

Layout or Set The arrangement of blocks in the quilt top.

Medallion Quilt A quilt design beginning with a central motif or medallion that is surrounded by a series of concentric borders.

Pictorial Quilt A quilt that depicts one picture or a series of pictures. It can be appliqué, pieced, or both.

Piecework A pattern created by sewing two or more shapes together at the seams to make a larger piece of fabric.

Quilt A bed cover with three layers—the top, the filling, the back—held together with quilting stitches. The top is either appliquéd, pieced, or a combination of both. The top is made first.

Quilt Top The top layer of the quilt sandwich.

Quilting The small, even-spaced running stitches used to connect the quilt top, batting, and back.

Repeat Pattern Quilt One block pattern (either appliqué or pieced) is chosen for each base block. It can be repeated in exactly the same colors or in different colors.

Sampler Quilt Each of the base blocks represents a different design. The design can be either pieced or appliquéd from identical colors or a variety of colors.

Sashing or Lattice The strips of fabric pieced between the base blocks.

Signature Quilt A quilt in which each block is signed, usually by the maker. Poems are often inscribed on signature quilts.

American Quilters' Society
P.O. Box 3290
Paducah, KY 42001
•
Boise Peace Project
1820 N. 7 Street
Boise, ID 83702
(Publishes newsletter linking
peace quilt projects)
•
Cross Country Art Center
152 MacQuesten Parkway South
Mount Vernon, NY 10550
(For art supply mail-order catalog)
•

Dover Publications, Inc.
Clip-Art Series
31 East 2 Street
Mineola, NY 11501
(Copyright-free design ideas and
sources of inspiration)
•
Quilters' Newsletter Magazine
P.O. Box 394
Wheatridge, CO 80033
•

Quilts in Women's Lives
16mm color film, 1980
Distributor: New Day Films, Box 315
Franklin Lakes, NJ 07417
•
Reva
389 Fifth Avenue
New York, NY 10016
(For Ultrasuede scraps)
•
Pat Yamin
Come Quilt With Me
P.O. Box 1063
Cadman Plaza Station
Brooklyn, NY 11202
•

QUILT-MAKING SKILLS
◆ ◆ ◆

Fanning, Robbie, and Tony Fanning. *The Complete Book of Machine Quilting.* Radnor, PA: Chilton Book Co., 1980.

Hassel, Carla J. *Super Quilter II.* Des Moines, IA: Wallace-Homestead Book Co., 1982.

James, Michael. *The Quiltmaker's Handbook* and *The Second Quiltmaker's Handbook.* Englewood Cliffs, NJ: Prentice-Hall, 1978 and 1981.

Leone, Diana. *Fine Hand Quilting.* Los Altos, CA: Leone Publications, 1986.

COLOR AND FABRIC DESIGN
◆ ◆ ◆

Beyer, Jinny. *The Scrap Look.* McClean, VA: EPM Publications, 1982.

Itten, Johannes. *The Elements of Color.* New York: Van Nostrand Reinhold Co., 1970.

Martin, Judy. *The Patchworkbook.* New York: Charles Scribner's Sons, 1983.

ELEMENTS OF DESIGN
◆ ◆ ◆

Lauer, David A. *Design Basics.* New York: CBS College Publishing, 1985.

Beyer, Jinny. *The Quilter's Album of Blocks and Borders.* McClean, VA: EPM Publishers, 1980.

Walker, Michele. *The Complete Book of Quiltmaking.* New York: Alfred A. Knopf, 1986.

DESIGNING BORDERS
◆ ◆ ◆

Beyer, Jinny. *The Art and Technique of Creating Medallion Quilts.* McClean, VA: EPM Publications, 1982.

Beyer, Jinny. *The Quilter's Album of Blocks and Borders.* McClean, VA: EPM Publications, 1980.

HISTORY OF GROUP QUILTS
◆ ◆ ◆

Bacon, Lenice Ingram. *American Patchwork Quilts.* New York: William Morrow & Co., 1973.

Denton, William Rush, Jr. *Old Quilts.* Catonsville, MD: published by author, 1946.

Finley, Ruth E. *Old Patchwork Quilts and the Women Who Made Them.* Newton Center, MA: Charles T. Branford Co., 1929.

Gutcheon, Beth. *The Perfect Patchwork Primer.* New York: Penguin Books, 1974, 1976, 1977, 1978.

Hall, Carrie A. *The Romance of the Patchwork Quilt in America.* Caldwell, ID: The Caxton Printers, Ltd., 1935.

Ickis, Marguerite. *The Standard Book of Quiltmaking and Collecting.* New York: The Greystone Press, 1949.

Kolter, Jane Bentley. *Forget Me Not: A Gallery of Friendship and Album Quilts.* Pittstown, NJ: The Main Street Press, 1985.

Safford, Carleton L. and Robert Bishop. *America's Quilts and Coverlets.* New York: E.P. Dutton, 1972.

Webster, Marie D. *Quilts: Their Story and How to Make Them,* New York: Tudor Publishing Co., 1915.

Wilson, Erica. *Erica Wilson's Quilts of America.* Birmingham, AL: Oxmoor House, Inc., 1979.

*T*his book could not have been written without the scores of women quiltmakers from around the nation who answered our ads, sent us slides of their projects, filled out our endless questionnaires, and basically supported us sight unseen. We can only single out a few: Rowena Fisher, Anita Murphy, Susan Frye, Odette Tell, Madeline Guyon of J.C. Penney, the *Scrappy Quilters* of Santa Monica, California, and the *Boise Peace Quilters* of Boise, Idaho. Many thanks to Roberta Horton for graciously allowing us to print her no-math method for enlarging designs and to the *Yakima Valley Museum Quilters Guild* for their last-minute contribution. We also want to acknowledge all the unknown quilters who we know must have contributed hours of piecing and stitching to the masterpieces pictured in this book, but whose names were not furnished for us.

Special thanks to Teri Cohen Meskin for reading the manuscript and offering valuable opinions, to Elizabeth McNamara for her expert advice, and to Judith Werner for helping us to sew the first seed. Much appreciation to our friend, Bobby Hansson, for entertaining us while taking excellent photographs and to V.I.P. Fabrics for donating Museum Classic prints for *The Crown Quilt.*

The people who became our friends at Crown are so terrific they deserve their own paragraph. Thanks to Gail Kinn for introducing us, to Amy Boorstein for her patient production editorial skills, and to Nancy Kenmore for her classic and classy design. Thanks also to Milt Wackerow, Ken Sansone, and Peggy Goddard. We want our editors, Pam Thomas and Erica Marcus, to know that we are grateful for their joint genius and for the respect they gave to our ideas.

Thanks to our solid core of neighborhood friends who gave us endless encouragement and poured their time and talents into five nursery quilts. We give a special tribute to Rosie Steinberg who patiently boosted our egos and praised our efforts. Thanks to both our families for their support: to our parents, Clara and Ralph Lyman and Marna and Eugene Hancock, for being so proud of us; to our in-laws, Eva and Mark Nadelstern, for their delicious CARE packages, and Ota and Charlotte Bondy, baby-sitters par excellence. And thanks to all our children: Ariel Nadelstern and Stefan and Halley Hancock Bondy for keeping us in stitches and for giving us uncontested dibs on the family computers.

And now for the husbands: Eric Nadelstern and Filip Bondy—you're welcome.

A·C·K·N·O·W·L·E·D·G·M·E·N·T·S

The following is a partial list of blockmakers who worked on the quilts pictured in this book. Unless otherwise indicated with an asterisk, the blocks are listed top to bottom, left to right, with the creator's name corresponding to each block in order.

FRIENDSHIP CACTUS BASKETS
♦ ♦ ♦

Rosanna Blumenberg • Marjorie Newland • Susan Milstein • Joan Rudman • Loann Haegele • Jean Cogley • Kim Richards • Barbara Gillette • Danita Rafalovich-Smith • Kathryn Pellman • Linda Graham • Barbara Spielberg • Kit Gustke.

BEYOND FRIENDSHIP
♦ ♦ ♦

Lenore Chused • Nola Colbert • Ruth Edwards • Julie Gonzalez • Louise Horgan • Sheila McIntyre • Brenda Matthews • Janet Springfield • Christine Wellman • Beth Wipperman.

BASKET OF FLOWERS
♦ ♦ ♦

Eleanor Kapfenstein • Marie Andrew • Mari Etta Fowler • Carol Merchen • Jan Kelly • Charlie Swan • Barbara Brennan • Carol Doyle • Sharon Flueckinger • Beverly Maines • Delores Kelly • Jo Graham • Orleen Peterson • Mary Wilson • Evelyn Rose • Kate Bradley • Dortha Hester • Gerry Good • Julie Lantis • Dorothy Borelson • Jennie Swinehart • Jane Quinn • Diane LeClair • Marian Filibeck • Lucille Freeman • Doris Maslack • Beckie Langsdorf • Tanya Kelly • Nancy Werner • Donna Gardner.

CANADA GOOSE IN THE MEADOW AT SUNSET
♦ ♦ ♦

Jane Stickney • Carol Crova • Gerry Sjue • Madelyn Horvath • Brenda Davie • Nyla Gorham • Elaine Holditch • Christine Bolitho • NG • Ann Degan, Connee Morris • Deanna Juergens.

BUTTERFLIES
♦ ♦ ♦

Kate Bradley • Evelyn Rose • Marian Filibeck • Beverly Maines • no name • Carol Doyle • Marie Andrew • Mary Wilson • Beckie Langsdorf • no name • Donna Gardner • Carol Merchen • Dortha Hestin • Dorothy Borelson • Charlie Swan • Barbara Brennan • MariEtta Fowler • Diane LeClair • Jane Quinn • Gerry Good • Julie Lantis • Jennie Swinehart • Mildred Ferren • Jo Graham • Orleen Peterson.

MONKEY WRENCH
♦ ♦ ♦

Kimie Kurahara • Modesta Laforte • Shirley Jones • Marilyn Johnson • Midge Kraetzer • Linda Perkins • Jody Bush • Michael Storwick • Pat Bell • Jim Cara • Cheryl Palmer • Evelyn Gahtan • Regina Minudri • Richard Brown • Diane Davenport • Coleen Fawley • Joyce Baird • Nayiri Bouboussis • Sharon Frey • June Nash • James and Sylvia Nomura • Heo Park • Marty Powers • Janet Sutterley • Mitsie Yatabe • Mae Britain • Martha Shogren • Bob Derbin • Janet Turman • Elaine Buckingham • Dagny Bills • Anne-Marie Miller • Sandra Balderrama-Escobar • Dory Ehrlich • Norine Gerber • Earl Drumm • Francisca Schneider • Mary Boyd • Connie Tresser • Beth Benjamine • John Rockelman • Karin Soe-Lai • Betty Hall • Sayre Van Young • Carol Naito •

Kathy Churchill • Marcus Siu • Johnnie C. Batchan • Sydney Isobe • Mary Shea • Barbara Alesandrini • Anita Ingram • Amy Kuo • James Jacobs • Margaret Kirihara • Guen Logan • Pat Nagamoto • Lynn Wold • Lillian Lee • Jean Leiby • Dolores Wright • Mary Schrader • Betty Anger • Charles Chou • Clover Scott-Jackson • Nita Allen • Carol Madore • Madeline Gong • Margot Lucoff • Nadine Goode • John Mathews • Carol Aird • Claudia Berger • Larry Johnson • Jean Haseltine • C. Horbs Span • Helen Harris • Cecillia Shearron-Hawkins • Michael Duffy • Harold Brunson • Barba Sargent • Betty Hall • Pete and Donna McElligott • Liz Tynan • David Hoffman • Martha Swartz • Michael Eichenholtz • Pat Mullan • Jane Scantlebury • Uma Paul • Ruth Beloof • Yvette Pleasent • Connie Reyes • Pat Ritchie • Candace Marshall • Phyllis Partridge • Tim Brown • Warren Middleton • Starr and John LaTronica • Leo Benjamine • Susan Annette Peterson • Helen Anderson • Nichole Barrett • David Uyeno • Gwen Jones • Carole Leita • Joan MacBeth • Paul Miller.

GRANDMOTHER'S FAN*
♦ ♦ ♦

Pat Bell • Claudia Berger • Starr LaTronica • Mitzie Yatabe • Phyllis Partridge.

LAUREL CROSS*
♦ ♦ ♦

Dortha Asher • Annie Bacon • Nancy Bierbaum • Gertrude and Miles Bloomfield • Bernice Busch • Eleanor Cole • Gladys Fish • Ollie Grewell • Dawn Hatley • Virginia Hegland • Jean Holmes • Blanche King • Lucy Kittrick • Kathleen Roger • Muriel Lamb • Pat Magaret • Maggie McGreevy • Therese Parry • Annette Patterson • Betty Robocker • Allie Secor • Donna Slusser, Karyl Street • Daleah Thiessen • Sharon Wiser.

STAR OF PALOUSE
♦ ♦ ♦

Pat Magaret • Lucy Kittrick • Donna Slusser • Ollie Grewell • Allie Secor • Daleah Thiessen • Dorothy Waelti • Alice Martin • Eleanor Cole • Gladys Fish • Kathleen Koger • Dortha Asher • Annie Bacon • Virginia Hegland • Nancy Bierbaum • Gertrude Bloomfield • Sharon Wiser • Karyl Street • Shirley Perryman • Charlotte Ostrom • Muriel Lamb • Dawn Hatley • Bernice Busch.

THE GILBERT HOUSE
♦ ♦ ♦

Design Committee: Marie Mather • Terri Schaake • Lois Downey • Barbara Beck • Khay Norris • Felicia Holtzinger • Patty McCartney • Quilters: Ruth Scheinost • Eula Bustetter • Helen Sutton • Edith Bartz • Marcella Martin • Jane Hutchins • Bertha Shumacher • Belle Gekler • Minnie Canon • Peggy Anderson • Barbara Beck • Martha Glasscock • Marge Schmitt • Helen Davis • Mildred Van Amburg.

MONADNOCK SAMPLER QUILT
♦ ♦ ♦

Corner and center blocks: Constance Bastille • Clockwise: Hoszkiewicz (Lady's Slippers) • Pat Hansen (Country Roads) • Misty Gray (Purple Finch) • Diane Basanen (Purple Lilacs) • Dorothy Lang (Steps to the Alter) • Avis Power (Covered Bridge) • CB (Foothills of Monadnock) • Lillian Power (Birds in the Nest) • CB (New Hampshire's Granite Hills) • Diane Rasanen and Linda Blair (Quilter's Mountain) • Lisa Bean (New Hampshire!) • Pat Hansen (Pine Tree) • Elizabeth Fowle (Berry Basket) • CB (Weathervane).

PALOUSE HILLS QUILT*

Vickie Purviance • Monica MacFarland • Shirley Nilsson • Alice Maki • Lillian Green • JoAnn Thompson • Maybelle Carson • Becky Behre • Elna Barton • Pat Hungerford • Polly Cline • Barbara Wenders • Irene Williams • Irene Furniss • Judy Ferguson • Ann Jensen • Tricia Horn • Barbara Stellmon • Donna DeWitt • Terry Huhte.

JULIA'S FRIENDSHIP QUILT

Judy Fox • Sharon Metzler • Wilma Wool • Julia Borne • Leanne Untulis • Ellen McHenry • Nancy Armstrong • Ellen Furman • Julia Borne.

NANCY'S FRIENDSHIP QUILT

Nancy Ellen Armstrong • Ellen Furman • Leanne Untulis • Sharon Metzler • Judy Fox • Ellen McHenry • Willie Wool • Julia Borne.

WILLIE'S FRIENDSHIP QUILT

Sharon Metzler • Marcia Curran (Card Trick) • Leanne Untulis, Julia Borne (Sun Print) • Judy Fox • Willie Wool • Nancy Armstrong • Ellen McHenry • Ellen Furman.

CONSENSUS: WITH A LITTLE HELP FROM MY FRIENDS

Julia Borne • Ellen Furman • Nancy Armstrong • Wilma Wool • Ellen McHenry • Sharon Metzler • Leanne Untulis • Judy Kellar Fox.

THE ROSE QUILT

Lavern Doll • Bonnie Oppermann and Marge Lynn • Dorothy Arndt • Carolyn Schulz • Kate Miller • Rosy Rahoy • Barb Hinz • Colleen Lepper • Ginny Dunn • Kathy Doman • Helen Liepert • Judi Mezcra • Carol Clingan • Carol Butzke • CB • Donna Shaw • Sherry Reischel • Ruth Wolf • Norma Herrmann • Margaret Gawlik • Jeanette Steger • Betty Ludwig • Marian Clarke • Jeanette DeBano • Leigh Pollpeter • Lavern Werner • Maxine Frank • Barbara Brenker • Anita Roemer • Vivian Walden • Erna Peters • Julie Dedrick • Helen Clarke • Phyllis Wilson • Sue Peters • Bette Williams • Rose Berchem • Sue Laubenstein • Ceil Knoll • Ann Olson • RB • Gail Ziegler.

LOURETTE QUILT

Mabel Shepard (1967) • MS • E. Renaud (1941) • Esther Higgins • Florence Lourette • Marie Stubbs (1941) • Margaret Robison • Jennie Bannister • Elsie L. Arnold (1942) • Katherine Farmen • Eunice Weidmann (1966) • Bessie Page • Annie Foos (1966) • Freda Shubmehl (1946) • Ada I. Landon • Mamie Schied • Margaret Topham (1949) • Georgia Feasel (1967) • Emily A. Emery (1941) • Lulu Wing (1964) • Olive E. Redfern (1945) • Beth Shubmehl (1950) • HS (1967) • Rose McManus (1941) • Frances Hill • Minnie O. Farrell • Minnie DeBliek • Maude MacBride (1948) • Philota M. Brydges • Lorena Dennington • Helen Stubbs • Nellie Hynes (1940–41) • Mrs. E. Lenhard (1941) • Charlotte King Zipfel • Ella Schnorr (1941) • Ada Akeley • Nelly Post • Adelaide Trompeter (1966) • Sylvia Dineen (1966) • Sophie P. Paul (1951) • Mrs. Miller.

BALTIMORE FRIENDSHIP ALBUM

Norma Campbell (Wreath of Hearts) • Laurie Scott (Urn of Flowers) • Margaret Ward (Strawberry Wreath) • Barbara Schafer (Bird Wreath) • Dawn Schaefer (Hospitality Pineapples) • Evelyn Buck (Bow Wreath) • Dallas Clautice (Rose Wreath) • Mimi Dietrich (Basket) • Dorothy Hunt (Lyre Wreath).

CHRISTMAS FRIENDSHIP

Linda Morrissey • Joyce Murrin • Joan Enright • Shirley Etkin • Missy Mulligan • Mary Kennedy • Boots Breden • Rose Laitman • Elizabeth Goroshko • Elise Butterfield • Margaret MacNichol • Marie Raish • Marian Piehler • Claire Kammer • Marian Piehler • Vivian Rothermal • Margie Weiner • Shirley Dolan • Kathy Kennedy • Jean Jenkins • Cathy Heslin • Marie Ruggiero • MaryAnn Luccketti • Wilda Lagrosa • Edna Pedersen • Marjorie Puzziferri • Judy Kittine • Dorothy Cromarty • CK • Mary Boyes.

SAMPLER BABY QUILT

Kim Richards • Kit Gustke • Linda Graham • Joan Rudman • Danita Rafalovich • Barbara Spielberg • Barbara Gillette • Loann Haegele • Marjorie Newland • Kathryn Pellman • Susan Milstein • Jean Cogley.

SPIKE THE RAT BABY PILLOW QUILT

Patti Oji • Susan Holland • Nan Sykes • Gwen Kaplan • Susan Britton • Kim Buck • Jill Russell • Leila Page and Florence Norris • Bonnie Allen • Carolyn Buck • Julie Page • Ellen Alderette.

PEZ PILLOW QUILT

Claudia Page • Chris Haupt • Laverne Davey • Julie Leavens • Margot Gerson • Lucretia Lee • Lesley Kasavan • Bonnie Allen • Chris Allen • Nancy Russell and Lucy Nelson • Andy Russell • Teri Shagouny • Pat Steinert • Debby Brewer • Cathy Aydelott • Denise Balma.

ARGYLE AND AMISH SCHOOLDAYS

Kit Gustke • Susan Milstein • Rosanna Blumenberg • Kathryn Pellman • Barbara Gillette • Jean Cogley • Danita Rafalovich • Kim Richards • Orlene Neal • Joan Rudman • Barbara Spielberg • Loann Haegele • Danita Rafalovich • Linda Graham • Marjorie Newland.

MORNING, NOON, AND NIGHT*

Dorothy Stone • Jane Patterson • Jean Beard • Ruth Beverly • Helen Brake • Karen Browning • Emma Brugh • Mary De Municas • Carolyn Dillow • Agnes Edmiston • Ruth Edwards • Betty Fagan • Valena Hager • Margaret Hartsock • Naomi Himmelwright • Darlene Kirk • Virginia Moran • Judy Niner • Jane Peterson • Helen Price • Dorothy Radcliffe • Caro Roach • Barbara Seymour • Julia Sheehe • Grace Stark • Janet Williams • Linda Williams • Sue Young.

PATCHWORK ACRES
◆ ◆ ◆

Kathy Dolan • Marilyn Bisk • Loretta Krieger • Pauline Mayer • Margot Cohen • Catherine Zegers • Eleanor Steinle • Sunny Margolis • Grete Weidman • Nancy Cohen • Dorothy Gedat • Loris Tuttle • Tom Cohen • Louise Miller • Gilda Hecht • Pat Seligman • Barbara Sklar • Blossom Berman • Buddy Gottlieb • Merle Darensbourg.

TARBELL HOUSE
◆ ◆ ◆

Carol Kessler (Her Apartment Building) • Kathleen Henson (Pigeons) • Amy Berry (Reupholstered Chair) • Rhonda Keels (Brenda's Sister Catching Keys to Apartment) • Sandy Burrows (Her Apartment Building) • Rebekka Siegel (Her Home in Rural Kentucky) • Deborah Pyle (Laundry Hanging Out to Dry) • Mary Provosty (Old Schoolhouse) • Shirley Osterbrock (Street Scene) • Brenda Tarbell (Her Home) • DP (Her Home) • Carolyn Jones (Brenda's Potter's Wheel and Kiln Gathering Dust) • CJ (Her Home) • KH (Street Scene) • Brenda Tarbell (Her Apartment Window) • Sandy Burrows (A View From Her Window) • Anna Marie Borich (Her Home and Pups on the Front Porch) • DP (Arnold's Restaurant) • Linda Massey (Her Home and Buildings) • KH (Her Home).

A HOUSE FOR ALL SEASONS*
◆ ◆ ◆

Top and bottom panels by Paula Nadelstern. • Nancy Mann • Esther Sas • Paula Nadelstern • Lorraine Butler • Shelley Spiegel and Annmarie Pitta-LaScala • Minia Sas • Irene Klaw • Minia Sas • Lorraine Butler • Ronnie Ranere • Susan Hickey • Pam Padernacht • Janet Riordan • Judy Kurzawa • Teri Cohen Meskin • Mindy Walters.

OUR NURSERY NEIGHBORHOOD
◆ ◆ ◆

Paula Nadelstern (Top Panel) • Anne Simon Lugo and Dee Gomez (Playground) • Paula Siegel-Miranda (Nursery School) • Carolyn Rudeck (Train Park) • Sandy Gold-Medina (Volkswagen) • Minnie Mortillo (Water Sprinklers) • Ellen Mui (Sleigh-riding) • Pam Padernacht (Jewish Center) • Wendy Holtzman (Pizza Italia) • Leona Blum and Julie Goldman (Kazan Plaza) • Minia Sas (Joint Community Activities Committee) • Isabel Suss (Credit Union) • Ariya Blitz (Feeding the Pigeons) • Sylvia Phillip (Jogger) • P.N., Kathleen Lefkowitz and Annmarie Pitta-LaScala (Arch) • Johanna Sparks (Theater).

HOUSE ON THE HILL
◆ ◆ ◆

Susan Frye • Rita Gray • Susan Dooley • Janine Jones • Kathy Galvez • Marjorie Waxman • Cynthia Herbert • Bertha Francis • Illona Thomas • Martha Galvert • Liz Goldfarb • Barbara Kavannagh.

SAILORS' SNUG HARBOR*
◆ ◆ ◆

Susan Frye • Susan Dooley • Sally Jones • Cynthia Herbert • Marjorie Waxman.

CARBONDALE COMMUNITY HISTORICAL QUILT
◆ ◆ ◆

Mary Alice Kimmel and Mary Brown (Rapp House) • Vera Grosowsky (John A. Logan) • Carolyn DeHoff (Old Main Fire, 1969) • Jean Foley (Foley Home) • Millie Dunkel (First Train into Carbondale) • Vivian Marks and Margaret Vallo (Interurban) • Jody Moeglin (Robert's Hotel) • Claribel McDaniel (Old Train Station) • Susan Perry (Training School) • Bonnie Moreno (Hundley House) • Marilyn Boysen (Daniel Brush) • Donna Hertter (Opera House) • Jewell Vieceli (West Side School) • Doris Dale (Paul and Virginia Fountain) • Ann Gardner (Harker-Mitchell Home) • Bonnie Miller (Original City Plat) • Ellen Hall (Woodlawn Cemetery) • Myers and Francis Walker (Dr. Lewis First Airport) • Bette Deniston (Squirrel Tale) • Kathy Sanjabi (Dr. Allen Home) • Kara Nasca (Halloween) • Libby Moore (Methodist Church) • Alma Taylor (The College) • Rene Potter (Daniel Brush Declaiming for the Union).

SUTTON BICENTENNIAL QUILT
◆ ◆ ◆

Betty Wells (Schoolhouse) • Jean Bennett (Huntoon House) • Audrey Snitko (Muster Day) • Rena Robinson (Grange Hall) • Genevieve Abbott (Central School) • Priscilla Foster (Soldier's Monument) • Barbara Burns (Firehouse) • Janet Ballard (Hearse) • Dorothy Wright (Pillsbury Memorial Hall) • Diane O'Neil (Sugaring) • Ellie Almstrom (Library) • Dawna Davis (Wadleigh State Park) • Wendy Wadman (Follansbee Inn) • Marion Devir (King's Ridge) • Robin Kelley (Church) • Betty Whittemore (Town Seal) • Irene Davis (Church) • Carol Curliss (Maple Leaf Golf Course) • Martha Wells (Pillsbury Homestead) • AS (Harvey Homestead) • Dr. Anne Wasson (Country Doctor) • Wendy Wadman (Smiley Grove) • Priscilla Foster (Church) • AS (Snow Roller) • Billie Tyler (Old Store Museum) • Sally Biewener (Primeval Pines) • Harriet Martin (Camp Penacook) • Betty Palmer (Town Pound) • Phyllis Shultz (Blaisdell Lake) • SB (Map of Sutton) • Norma Burns (Sawmill) • Barbara Allen (Penacook Indians) • Jean Gerhard (Kearsarge Mountain).

HASTINGS PAST AND PRESENT
◆ ◆ ◆

Gino Gualandi (Farragut School, 1902) • Debbie Gaynes (HCAC Symbol) • Leslie English (view of Palisades) • DG (HCAC Symbol) • Marina Rauh (Municipal Bldg, 1929) • Mary Gualandi (Warburton Ave. 1930) • Betty Tootle (Long-vue) • Elizabeth Keith (Sloop on Hudson) • Dorma Barker (Grace Church, 1867) • Theresa Welch (Bridge Over Aqueduct) • Evelyn Drewes (Uniontown Hose Co. 1899) • Jan Young (The "Mary Powell") • Arlene Sklar-Weinstein (Lipchitz statue and library, 1967) • Pat Coploff (Schooner on Hudson) • Patty Mitzman (V.F.W.) • Sue Bates (Draper House, 1848) • Jean Mendelsohn (Hirsch House, 1852) • Jeane McDonagh (Cropsey House) • SB and Marina Rauh (Mt. Hope Cemetery, 1886) • Ann Marie Ellis (The "Buccaneer") • Ruth Cadwell (Wateringg Trough, 1930) • Harriet Holdsworth (Stone Cottage) • Marylin Eager (Dock Street) • Susan Dzubak (Tower Ridge Yacht Club, 1891–1895) • Edna May Young (Dyckman House) • DG (Warburton Ave., 1982) • Helen Cornwall (Young Whaley Rogers House) • Hope Eagle (Phillips House) • Edna Brereton ("Food for Thought") • Genie Lehr (Copper Beech) • Susan Dzubak (Katterhorn House, 1850) • Carole Krack (Krack House, 1859).

HERITAGE WALL QUILT
♦   ♦   ♦

Irene Veuleman (Junior Forum House) • Mary Peddycord (Tyrell Library) • Denise Nevills (Alice Keith Park Gazebo) • Easter Rouen (St. Anthony's Cathedral) • Helen Cox (French Trading Post) • Vivian Godkin (Rice fields) • Anita Murphy (Port of Beaumont) • Beth Johnson and Anna Oddo (Lucas Gusher Spindletop oil well, Lamar University) • Cecelia Ewald (farm lands) • Lou Sander (Jefferson Theatre) • Margaret Chenella (O'Brien Oak) • Louise Luebstorff (Babe Zaharias Memorial).

THE NEW YORK LIBRARY CLUB CENTENNIAL QUILT
♦   ♦   ♦

Leslie Levison (Library Lion) • Karen Berkenfeld (Logo) • Diane Rode Schneck (42nd St. Library) • Liz Curtain (Melvil Dewey) • Jackie Berg (Computer Chip) • Alice Rothman (Telephone Reference Librarian) • Judy Klein (Bookshelf) • Myra Rubin (Columbia) • Taffy Knauer (Anthiphonal Music) • Louise Sherlock (City Skyline) • Jean Capalbo (Newspaper Rack) • TK (Manuscript Page) • Dee Danley Brown (Staten Island Ferry) • Lise Kristianson (Brooklyn Bridge) • Helen Castellano (Queens) • Susan Faeder (Audio Visuals) • Mercedes Sorrentino (Card File) • Carol Turchan (Tools of the Bronx Book Preservation Center) • DRS (Jefferson Market Library).

NEWTON COMMEMORATIVE QUILT
♦   ♦   ♦

Beth Wipperman (Thomsonville Farm) • Nola Colbert • Victoria Marston (Jackson Homestead) • NC • Kate Ruth • Christine Wellman (Allen Homestead) • NC • Julie Gonzalez • Kate Ruth (Gothic House) • Mark Dooling • Brenda Matthews (Strong Block) • Elean Coen • Mark Dooling • Louise Horgan • Sharon Kleitman (Newton Free Library) • Shelly Leahy • Gerry Goolkasian (Transportation) • Emily Little • Jessica Mosher • Harriet Solit (Original High School) • LH • William Horgan • Sharon Kleitman (Bigelow House) • NC • Brenda Matthews • William Roesner • Gloria Weller (Marathon) • Craig Chandler • BW (Brick Grist Mill) • Janet Springfield • Sharyl Benovitz • Ruth Edwards • Ruth Matthews • Mary Troyan (City Hall and Grounds) • Robbie O'Rourke (House of Worship) • Craig Chandler • Sharon Kleitman • Karen Levine (Silver Lake Cordage Co.) • Brenda Matthews • Rosalind Smith • Gloria Weller • Doris Wells (Chief Waban with John Eliot) • Lenore Chused • Rowena Fisher • Sophie Harrison (Horse Trough) • Eleanor Apholt • MD (Richardson R.R. Station) • Judy Green • Laurie Green • Gerry Goolkasian (Inns and Hotels) • Dora Bard • Mark Dowling (Stone Barn) • Ruth Lazarus • Marcia Schenk • Mary Troyan (Nonantum Clock) • Charlotte Feldman • Shiela McIntyre • Sharon Kleitman • Marge Schwartz (Crystal Lake) • NC (Baury House), MD • KR • Judy Santos (Echo Bridge) • NC (Hammond House) • Brenda Matthews • Mary Troyan (Norumbega Park). • Calligraphy, Mildred Bloom • Embroidery for titles, Beth Cohen • Ruth Krinsky.

RABBI ALFRED WOLF'S QUILT
♦   ♦   ♦

Lane Magnin (Two Wolves) • Jenny Spitzer (Wilshire Boulevard Temple's Stained Glass Windows) • Doris Engelman (The Rabbi's Hiking Boot) • Bobbie Finkle ("Boggle") • Alice Raskoff (Clock Collection set at 3 and 6 for 36th anniversary) • Blanche Diamond (Camp Jacket) • Rev Melczer (Family Tree) • Paula Hoffman (Camp Load) • Esther Lewis (Star of David) • Vera Traub (Wilshire Boulevard Temple) • Elsie Harris (Covered Wagon) • Lois Cameron (Torah Scroll) • Greta Solomon (Shofar) • Justine Mandelbaum (Camp Menorah) • Deanne Kass (Dome of Wilshire Boulevard Temple) • Estelle Schwartz (Havdalah Candle) • Joyce Rosen (Wine Cup) • Bunny Wasserman (The Ten Commandments) • Suzanne Weinstein (Interfaith Group Work) • Helen Rogaway (License Plate).

FESTIVAL OF A LIFE
♦   ♦   ♦

M. Skiles and S. Bird • Pat and Roger McQuire (Cookie Monster) • Matey and Dick Rice (A Lifetime Festival) • Matey and Dick Rice (A Festival of a Lifetime) • Phyllis Holt (Godspell) • Karen Cruiser (College Mace) (Remember Brigadoon) • Gayle Childress (Yale Logo) • Beth Hitterick Berry (Blue Ridge Mountains) • Margaret and Harold Johnson (Alma Mater) • Elspeth Clarke (Bit of a Persian Shawl) • Sally Bierhaus (Holden Dogs) • Betty Heald (church banner) • Kathe Masher (Renaissance Festival King) • Jean Thune (throne) and (Church Banner) • Lisa Ohler (Court Jester) • Billy Edd Wheeler (Country Musician) • Graham (Students Come First) • Terri Godfrey (Brigadoon) • Don and Margaret Hart (Shalom) • Joe Fox (Wiseman) • Phyllis Holt (Church Banner) • Catherine Showalter (Graduation) • Jean Abernathy (Rotary banner) • Arlene (Swannanoa Chamber Music) • Kay Smith (Church Banner) • Beverly Ohler (Happy Birthday Pooh Bear) • Matey Rice (Thanksgiving at Chapel) • Chrissanne Ohler (Labor of Love) • Ginny Calloway (Appalachian Music Program) • Martha Hanson (Owl and the Spade Weathervane) • Beverly Ohler (The Man Who Is Loved by Children) • Lola McMillan (To the Piggery, Warren Wilson Farm) • Pat Laursen (Farm) • Dick and Matey Rice (Save the Whales) • Mary Jean Herzog (Moon over the Mountain) • Evelyn Jones (Old College Logo) • Dinny Roth (Trash Collector) • Ed and Mary Torrence (W.W. II flying over the hump) • Polly Fitton (Warren Willson 90th Anniversary) • signatures on patchwork.

LOTTIE'S QUILT
♦   ♦   ♦

Ariel Nadelstern, five years old (Lottie's Husband Fishing) • Amy Taubin (Handmade Silver Jewelry) • Kay Lascelle (Mountain Climbing) • Paula Nadelstern (Lobster Feast) • Eric and Paula Nadelstern (OT Memo) • PN (Sewing Niche) • PN (Polish girl) • Jocelyn Barth (Female family portrait) • Ruth Perlstein (Chai and Dove) • Alexis Barth (Lottie at the Beach with a Crazy Hat) • Clara Lyman (important Buildings in Lottie's Life) • Kay Lascelle (Lottie's House on Long Island) • Amy Taubin (Yard Sale) • Abby Taubin (Voyage from Poland to New York) • PN (Bookshelf Reflecting Lottie's Interests in Jung, Feminism, Aging, Oriental Rugs, Weaving, and Anatomy).

CHERYL AND DEAN'S WEDDING QUILT
♦   ♦   ♦

Hank Albert • Louis and Yael King • Roann Barris • Sue Levinstein • Vivian Silver • Diane King • Miryam Gerson • Anita and Elliot King • Paula Nadelstern • Suzanne White • Milton Hadiks • Anna Kurz.

WEDDING CHUPAH*
♦   ♦   ♦

Paula Nadelstern • Sonya Hirshberg • Anne Kleinfeld • Phyllis Hollander • Rorri Feinstein • Myra Hirschberg • Adele Kampf • Pearl Sasonow • Claire Darrow • Mary Feinstein • Toby Deutsch • Allison Deutsch.

THE FRIESEN WEDDING QUILT

◆　　◆　　◆

Paula Massey (Psalm 37) • Sue Youngquist ("Lift up Your Voice") • Sue Argubright ("Be Filled with the Spirit") • Rich Iverson ("Two Are Better than One") • Margaret Gale (Fall Leaves) • Mary Ann Berry (Poppies) • Penny Lukens (Scripture from Wedding Ceremony) • Virginia Brown (Igolochkoy Butterflies) • Nina Frantz (Tree) • Mary Anderson ("Love Is Eternal") • Mary Ann Childs (Wheat) • Vicki Lichti (Basket and House) • Bev Fleming and Elsie Mast (Farm) • Cindy Warner (Scripture) • Ann Belser (Toads) • Minna Regier and Jeanne Howe (Reading to Her Son) • Ann Kingsley and Carolyn Ruth (Bird and Birdhouse) • Charlotte Oda ("May Your Joy Be Complete") • Judy Belser (Butterflies and Flowers) • Judy Kalina ("Great Is Thy Faithfulness") • Joanna Lehman (Cheese and Apples) • Martha Reed and Lois Engleman (Butterflies) • Carol Steiner (Rings and Cross) • Peggy Belser (Flower) • Maureen Chesley ("Marriage Takes Work") • Suzanne Coalson ("Jesus Loves You Warts and All").

MERKT-BLATZ WEDDING QUILT

◆　　◆　　◆

Sheila Kelly • Richard and Ruth Ann Friesen • Lisa Brodyaga • Ann Cass • Sr. Charles Miriam Strassel • Bishop John Fitzpatrick • Laura Sanchez • Rose Cozine (Stacey's grandma) • Diane Elder • Kelly Josh • Julie and Gregg Merkt • Walter Blatz (John's dad) • Sr. Ann Darlene • Marie Nord • Mary Lynn Stephen and Emmy • Pate and Gale McCarty • Mary Ellen O'Brien • Peter Sprunger-Froese • Donna Johnson • Anita Cain • Julie and Gregg Merkt • Debbie and Andy Glatz • Weil family • Betty Blatz (John's mom) • Fran Ferrara • Jack Elder • Margaret Safranek • Mary Sprunger-Froese • Linda Romey • Lenny de Pasquale • Bindy • Sr. Marion Strohmeyer • Sheryl Opgaard • Claire Greg and Sarah Blatz • Hesed family • Cindy Drennan • Blake Gentry • Laura LaBree • Sue Byler • Clare Dione • Valerie Ramirez • Jeff Larsen • Geoff • Merkt family • Elaine Burns • Rosemary Smith.

RHODES'S FIFTIETH ANNIVERSARY QUILT

◆　　◆　　◆

Donna Lawler • Ella Hostetler • Katie Frey • Alta Marner • Dorothy Rhodes • Wanda Miller • Esther Marner • Walter Marner.

THE CROWN QUILT

◆　　◆　　◆

Ann Meador (The Hitchhiker's Guide to the Galaxy) • Florence Porrino (Nat's Desk) • Sandra Still (Lee Bailey's Country Weekends) • Pam Thomas (The Rising of the Moon) • Jan Melchior (Ophelia) • Gael Towey (Caribbean Style) • Pam Thomas (The Joy of Sex) • Norma Leong (The Saga of Baby Divine) • Pam Krauss (101 Uses for a Dead Cat) • Bobby Mirken (The Kovels) • Kate Burleson (Be Here Now) • Erica Marcus (Willie Mosconi on Pocket Billiards) • Diane Cerafici (The Nutcracker) • Linda Torraco (Pies and Tarts) • Paula Breen (A Treasury of African Folklore) • Michelle Sidrane (Princess Daisy) • Beth Hovanec (Angelina Ballerina) • Hilda Pasco (American Country) • Sarah Wright (Clan of the Cave Bear) • Rita Blau (I'll Take Manhattan).

DOLLS

◆　　◆　　◆

Joan Hamiel • Dorothy Borelson • Sharon Flueckinger • Beverly Maines • Gerry Good • Marie Andrew • Lucille Freeman • Julie Lantis • Mary Wilson • Orleen Peterson • Jane Quinn • Jo Graham • Carol Doyle • Marian Filibeck • Diane LeClair • Jennie Swinehart • Doris Maslack • Dortha Hester • Eleanor Kapfenstein • Barbara Brennan • Evelyn Rose • Pat Havelaor • MariEtta Fowler • Carol Merchen • MA.

APPLE BOX LABELS

◆　　◆　　◆

Jane Freitag • Diana Schmidt • Mildred Rogers • Karen Cameron • Marybeth Dart • Malinda McCoy • Lois Wedge • Pat Sundquist • Marcella Martin • Delores Berg • Cari Morgan • Karen Kerns • Belle Gekler • Marna Parkhurst • Eula Bustetter • Jean Smith • Betty Jo Dowd • Velma Baylor • Jane Hutchins • Mary Ann Kershaw • Janice Newbill • Ruth Scheinost • Marg Fisher • Dorothy Smoot • Kiane Kokenge • Dorothy Monney • Gen Rennie • Betty Strand • Betty Wight • Peggy Smith • Margaret Strausz • Felicia Holtzinger • Bess Haynes • Barbara Schultz • Erma Nelson • Virginia Cooper • Barbara Beck • Sherry Udell • Dorothy Smoot • Anne Marie Van Luenen • Helen Hansen • Mary Nebeker • Helen Johnson • Mary Freihauf • Rosaline Wakin • Mildred Van Amburg • Judie King • Lucille Rosenau • Jackie Snyder • Lilli Ann Pollock.

MS. SUE: ALIVE AND LIBERATED

◆　　◆　　◆

Judy Robbins (Nude Sue) • Audrey Magie (Travelin' Sue) • Jean Cuddy (Telephone Worker Sue) • Jackie Dodson (Candidate Sue) • Elaine Hotra (Virginia Slims Sue) • Sheila Groman (Farmer Sue) • Amy Mesnier (Reporter Sue) • Odette Teel (Hang Glider Sue) • Julie Draska (Marathon Sue) • Mary Ann Spencer (Painless Sue, D.D.S) • Lila Bridgers (Rocketship Sue) • Wyn Reddall (ERA worker Sue) • Ruth Reunig (Preacher Sue) • Judy Mathieson (World Traveler Sue) • Odette Teel (two logos and mottos) • Elaine Miles (Dragon Slayer Sue) • Pam Smith (Preacher Sue) • Nancy Halpern (Woodcutter Sue) • Jean Johnson (Candidate Sue) • Mildred Morgon (Bra Burner Sue) • Norma Locke (Racecar Driver Sue) • Josie Carraher (Protester Sue) • Jean Ray Laury (Out of the Closet Sue) Margaret Wetherson (Orchestra Conductor Sue), • Blanche Young (Olympic Champ Sue) • Nancy Crawford (Graduate Sue) • Sydne Yanko-Jongbloed (Windsurfer Sue) • Sally Firth (Firefighter Sue) • Hazel Hynds (Policewoman Sue) • Bernice Sherman (Ms. Sue) • Charlene Anderson-Shea (Briefcase Sue) • Bev Kniss (Cowgirl Sue) • Jane Irwin (Dr. Sue) • Barbara Brackman (Beachcomber Sue) • Betty Hagerman (Speechmaker Sue) • Gen Guracar (Cartoonist Sue) • Mary Harvey (Mountain Climber Sue) • Dotty Zagar (Judge Sue) • Helen Kelley (Weight Lifter Sue) • Karen Drellich (Dreamer Sue) • Gretchen Thomas (Bumper Sticker Sue).

A FRIENDSHIP QUILT OF CELEBRATION*

◆　　◆　　◆

Gertrude Lynn • Mildred von Drehle • Paula Brenner • Dorothy Morley • Glenna Dean • Ruth Phillips • Ruth Ostrow • Theresa Murphy • Josephine Gullo • Agnes Tuitt • Kathleen Huertas • Lucy Toomey • Marguerite Hatfield • Naomi Concepcion • Francis Fixler • Gertrude Blaut • Ruby Stevenson • Clair Schlesinger.

ME AND MY PIANO

◆　　◆　　◆

Sheila Garland • Janet M. Miller • Joanne Edwards • Carol Cleary • Kim Masopust • Wilda LaGrosa • Kim Masopust • Florence Scott • Carol Cleary.

SCENES OF CHILDHOOD

❖ ❖ ❖

Shelley Spiegel (Balloon) • Paula Nadelstern (Ferris Wheel) • Chris Marcell (Sailboat) • Vicky Marone (Turkey) • Joan Fersonbaum (Parrot) • Shelley Speigel (Whale) • Karen Khan (Baby) • Riva Danzig (Animals) • Molly O'Brien (Miss Sue), Paula Nadelstern (Jack in the Beanstalk) • Karen Khan (Girl) • Minia Sas (Carousel) • Diane Wolfthal (Clothesline) • Paula Nadelstern (Gingerbread House) • Eva Nadelstern (Little Miss Muffet) • Paula Nadelstern (Russian Nesting Dolls) • Paula Nadelstern (Teddy Bear) • Ronnie Ranere (Mother Goose) • Mintzie Kaminsky (Sheep) • Joan Shapiro (Ice-Cream Cone) • Molly O'Brien (Train) • Nancy Mann (Beach) • Beverly Falk (Flower) • Shelley Spiegel (Snowman).

FANTASIES

❖ ❖ ❖

Wendy Bass (The Streets Are Paved with Gold) • Annmarie Pitta-LaScala (Outer Space) • Ceil Hartstein (Man in the Moon) • Toby Butler (Pot of Gold) • Beverly Falk (Pegasus) • Wendy Bass (Treasure Chest) • Shelley Spiegel (Balloons) • Anne Lugo-Simon (Cow Jumped Over the Moon) • Myra Sternheim (Shoe House) • Karen Khan (Wizard) • Paula Nadelstern (Dragon) • Minia Sas (Flying Carpet) • Mindy Walters (Children) • Ann Aylman (Mermaid) • Riva Danzig (Deserted Island) • Ronnie Ranere (Unicorn) • Buffy Callaghan (Valentine) • Irene Klaw (Elves) • Lynn Silver (Where the Wild Things Are) • Chris Marcell (Lace Window) • Joan Shapiro (Dinosaur) • Adrienne Bornstein (Gingerbread House) • Rose Klaw (Presents) • Carole Foresta (Fantasy Beast).

UNDER THE BIG TOP

❖ ❖ ❖

Johanna Sparks (Four Flying Feigenbergs) • Carolyn Rudeck (Clown) • Mindy Walters (Girl with Rope) • Sylvia Phillips (Cannon Man) • Ethel Wickham (Poodle) • Laura Ford (Monkey) • Teri Meskin (Clown with Sequins) • Sandy Gold (Seal) • Minnie Mortillo (Cannon) • Wendy Holtzman (Clown in Car) • Dee Gomez (Lion) • Carol Jaslowitz (Tiger) • Diane Dowling (Bear on Skates) • Judy Kurzawa (Elephant) • Ronnie Ranere (Bear on Ball) • MW (Ringmaster) • Kathleen Lefkowitz (Horse) • Paula Nadelstern, Minia Sas, and Nancy Mann (Audience).

MOTHERING AMERICA

❖ ❖ ❖

Karin Lanzoni (Pregnant Belly with Hand) • Valerie Bolling (Abstract) • Michael Weinberg (X-ed out Pinup Girl) • Alan Moskowitz (Scene from The Color Purple) • Karen Johns (Her Mother and Two Daughters) • Cynthia Thompson (Mother and Child) • Elizabeth Ammons (Scene from My Old Sweetheart) • Susan Pratt (Gifts from Women in Her Family) • (Pants Celie Makes in The Color Purple) • Lara Sanders (Women Writers) • Mary Reichelt (Supermom) • Suzanne Shavelson (Symbols) • Frank Connelly (Landscape from The Color Purple) • Gina Nortrom (Birth Scene) • Ann Wooster (Twentieth-century Sampler) • Sonja Rudder (Women and Flowers) • Sara Frost (Sign Posted by Tufts Professor).

J.C. PENNEY EASTERN REGION

❖ ❖ ❖

Assembled by Martha Washington Quilters Guild, Pennsylvania: Joanna Pasvolsky • Mary L. Bowman • Jennifer Bailey • Judith A. Golas • Rose Fritsch • Katherine Inman • Jean A. Talafous • Ruth Manz • David J. Addis • Kathleen L. Daniels • Linda Snyder • Elaine G. Kirby • Anna Pac • Miriam F. High • Rudee Ann Rudd-Rodriguez • Karen Kay Buckley.

J.C. PENNEY SOUTHEASTERN REGION

❖ ❖ ❖

Assembled by Gwinnett Quilters, Georgia: Susan M. Riger • Anna Bell Imbert • Lucy E. LeGrow • Kathryn L. Schultz-Kemmerling • Leanne R. Roos • Kit D. Carpenter • Naomi A. Royer • Sylvia Pickell • Evelyn S. King • Carole R. Humphreys • Sally Smith • Patricia Phillips • Colleen Shoemaker • Sharon Kaye Carter • Lucille E. Maier • Marilyn S. Kelley.

J.C. PENNEY SOUTHWESTERN REGION

❖ ❖ ❖

Assembled by The Quilters' Guild of Dallas: Mrs. John Wolf • Sharon Gagnon • Loretta B. Kelley • Michelle Mitchell • Linda Lancaster • Judith B. Fischer • Gina Redding • Carolyn Peterson • Mary Lou Griswald • Beverly Goebel • Glenna Jones • Carol Crabb • Janelle Jones Knox • Terry Christian • Sylvia Dresser • Melanie Cash.

J.C. PENNEY WESTERN REGION

❖ ❖ ❖

Assembled by The Friendship Quilt of Whittier, California: Ann M. Albers • Anne H. Brasher • Pam Roche • Carol Richards • Lenore M. Messenger • Patricia Gourley • Vicki Reichow • Toni Maloon • Mrs. Nyla J. Dominguez • Tanna L. Bay • Patricia Faver • Anna Ashford • Gina F. Casey • Debby Hartel • Carol Manning • Suzanne Reichardt

THROUGH CHILDREN'S EYES*

❖ ❖ ❖

Quilters: Susan Frye • Marge Parks • Kathy Fuchs • Jackie Pentony • Dorothy Capelli • Dolores Bray • Minnie Connor • Children: Marcia Lin • Paul Robert Kenny • Marco Scardigno • Gabrille Mitchell • Moish Aronow • Jacqueline Anne Bormann • Matthew Mandell • Melissa Diamond • Marcie Gorsline • Kathy Ryn • Beth Suzanne Waxgiser • Eric Korsh • Katie O'Leary • Melissa Brevin Horne • Leonor Daza • Michael O'Leary.

QNM: FIFTEENTH-ANNIVERSARY FRIENDSHIP SAMPLER

❖ ❖ ❖

Jackie Paton (Fifteen Years of Inflation) • Elaine Sparlin (Show and Tell) • Helen F. Anderton (QN15) • Helen R. Scott (Stitch by Stitch, Hour by Hour) • Diana Van Wagoner Speer (Fifteen Fingers) • Louisa A.F. D'Addario (Finish the Blooming Block) • Janelle Jones Knox (Yesterday Reconsidered) • Anne Peterson (Colonial Heritage).

LIBERTY WINNERS

◆ ◆ ◆

Signatures: *Moneca Calvert • Charlotte Warr-Andersen • Helen Cargo • Judy Hopkins • Marla M. Hattabaugh • Judy Tipton • A. Diann Logan • Pat Karambay • Iran Lawrence • Marilyn Dorwart • Barbara Thurman Butler • Helen Mary Friend • Joyce Stewart • Sidney Allee Miller • Mary Kay Horn • Marianne Fons • Suzanne Warren Brown • Rebekka Siegel • Deborah Sims • Hilary A. Ervin • Yvonne M. Khin • Carol Anne Grotrian • Isolde Sarnecki-de Vries • Carol Wagner • Sally Smith • Lea Hillis • Shirley Barrett • Paulette Peters • Julia S. French • Beth J. Ide • Judy B. Dales • Carol Meyer • Paula Nadelstern • Jeanne Champion Nowakowski • Lillian A. Twamley • Julia K. Swan • Mary Kay Boswell • Victoria T. Crawford • Donna Barnett-Albert • Barbara Barber • Sandra Kuss • Dawn E. Amos • Rosemary Wade • Anita Murphy • Ione Bissonnette • Violet S. Larsen • Ruth Carol Coombe • Hazel B. Reed Ferrell • Carol Butzke • Donna Schneider • Cathy Patton.*

PUZZLE QUILT

◆ ◆ ◆

Alex • Jason • Joel • Jamel • Luba • Beth • Mariza • Adram • Tracey • Keitra • Karen • Caryn • Aisha • Tracey M. • Denise • Veronica • Susan • Makunda • Ahmad • Jami Varra • Daniel S. • Antonio M. • Eric M. • Daniel P. • Luis • Tarun • Janet • Josh • Eva • Rachel • Terrile • Christopher.

P.S. 217: OUR HERITAGE QUILT

◆ ◆ ◆

Tanya Garcia • Rebecca Ment • Jimmy McCormack • Elie Ghaleb • Jennifer Peng • Paul Thiem • Cindy Tse • Tanya Regis • Bicky Wong • Laura Cole • Patricia McCormack • Osiris Torres • Annie Li • Tomen Tse • Nicole D'Orazio • Michael Warner.

BILLIE'S BOWEN NURSERY SCHOOL QUILT *

◆ ◆ ◆

Children's hands: Anna Ashkouri • Beth Baratz • Tony DiCarlo • Robbie Dolezal • Anthony Freniere • Kim Gentile • Kristen Lovett • Lindsay Lowe • Michael Maddens • Jesse Mehrbach • Caitlin Schlauch • Anne Springfield.

BARBARA'S BOWEN NURSERY SCHOOL QUILT

◆ ◆ ◆

Children's drawings: Rachel Rubinow • Tarin McCarthy • Benjamin Schmidt • Kenny Liebensperger • Rachael Omansky • Cleo Buster • Alex Weiss • Kate Springfield • John Goodson • Jared Miller • Chip Wyman • Zachary Kolpan • Rebecca Lay • Michael Freedman • Chace Estes • Shaun DeWeese.

I·N·D·E·X